News at Work

News at Work

*Imitation in an Age of
Information Abundance*

PABLO J. BOCZKOWSKI

The University of Chicago Press   Chicago and London

PABLO J. BOCZKOWSKI is a professor in the Department of
Communication Studies at Northwestern University. He is the author
of *Digitizing the News: Innovation in Online Newspapers*.

The University of Chicago Press, Chicago 60637
The University of Chicago Press, Ltd., London
© 2010 by The University of Chicago
All rights reserved. Published 2010
Printed in the United States of America

20 19 18 17 16 15 14 13 12 11 10   1 2 3 4 5

ISBN-13: 978-0-226-06279-2 (cloth)
ISBN-10: 0-226-06279-1 (cloth)
ISBN-13: 978-0-226-06280-8 (paper)
ISBN-10: 0-226-06280-5 (paper)

Library of Congress Cataloging-in-Publication Data
Boczkowski, Pablo J.
    News at work: imitation in an age of information abundance /
    Pablo J. Boczkowski.
        p. cm.
    Includes bibliographical references and index.
    ISBN-13: 978-0-226-06279-2 (cloth: alk. paper)
    ISBN-10: 0-226-06279-1 (cloth: alk. paper)
    ISBN-13: 978-0-226-06280-8 (pbk.: alk. paper)
    ISBN-10: 0-226-06280-5 (pbk.: alk. paper) 1. Online journalism—
Argentina. 2. News audiences—Argentina. I. Title.
    PN4784.O62B63 2010
    079'.82—dc22   2009051785

♾ The paper used in this publication meets the minimum requirements
of the American National Standard for Information Sciences—
Permanence of Paper for Printed Library Materials, ANSI Z39.48-1992.

Para el pibe de las frutillas con crema . . .

Contents

Figures

Tables

Preface

I finished writing my first book, *Digitizing the News: Innovation in Online Newspapers,* in 2003. The book was published in 2004 by the MIT Press. MIT was then also my home institution, so when I was invited to talk at the Authors @ MIT series, it felt like the official launch of the book. The presentation took place on March 30, 2004. At the end of the evening, as I crossed the Longfellow Bridge back to my apartment in Boston, I thought about what I would tell my parents, who had followed the progress of my book with great interest from their home in Buenos Aires, Argentina. The phone rang as I was opening the door of the apartment, and I rushed to pick it up. I heard my mother's voice. She said that my father had died unexpectedly an hour earlier.

My family and I flew to Buenos Aires the next day. Guillermo Culell, then director of Clarín.com—Argentina's largest news site and the online counterpart of *Clarín,* the country's leading print newspaper—called to offer his sympathies. He also asked whether I would be interested in meeting to talk about some new initiatives he had in mind. At that meeting, Culell told me that he and his colleagues had discovered that most users accessed the news site at work, that is, between nine and six o'clock, Monday to Friday. He added that Clarín.com was planning a major increase in the volume and frequency of news published on the site to satisfy a constant demand for new stories by people at work. I was intrigued, because the news in traditional media was consumed primarily during nonworking hours and outside the workplace. After days of mourning, my mind shifted into research mode and back to the world of news. The conversation with Culell became the genesis of this book.

Over time I realized that the passing of my father also symbolized the fading of the cultural formations that are at the heart of this book. He woke up each day at dawn and spent a couple of hours consuming the news. He began by listening to radio news while taking a shower and shaving. Then he read two or three newspapers at the breakfast table while sipping his *mate;* reading a single paper would make him miss important stories. These twentieth-century habits of consuming the news are becoming relics in the twenty-first century. The movement from print and broadcast to digital media has been tied to consuming the news at the time and place of work. Many online news consumers still access multiple news sources, and there are many more sources today than previously. But the consumers do not assume that the main stories of the day are very different across the sources. They are correct; the content of the news has become increasingly similar due to the increase in imitation in editorial work, which is tied to the rise in the speed and volume of production. The news industry has shifted from a situation of a low number of stories in each media outlet but a high level of diversity among the media outlets in the stories covered to one of a greater number of stories but a lower level of content diversity. This book unpacks this fundamental transition in the logics of producing and consuming the news and assesses its social and political consequences.

The contributions of research participants and collaborators made this book possible. Guillermo Culell and Marcelo Franco at Clarín.com, Ricardo Kirschbaum and Miguel Wiñazki at *Clarín*, Gastón Roitberg at Lanacion.com, and Fernán Saguier at *La Nación* generously helped with logistical issues associated with fieldwork. Sixty-seven journalists at these four newsrooms and sixty-three online news consumers kindly agreed to be interviewed and/or observed. These journalists and consumers are the lifeblood of the ethnography reported in the book. There are too many to thank individually, but this does not diminish my gratitude to each of them for allowing my collaborators and me to enter their worlds. I hope the account offered in the pages that follow does justice to the experiences they shared with us.

Every ethnographer is aware of the difference that key informants make in the quality of the research enterprise. The studies of news production would not have been the same without the participation of Omar Lavieri, a seasoned journalist and dear friend since the days of *la cena de los jueves* (Thursdays' dinner). Omar helped me navigate the choppy waters of Argentine journalism and answered an unimaginably wide array of questions. *Gracias por todo, Gordo!*

This book was also made possible (and a lot more fun!) through the collaboration of an outstanding group of students in Argentina and the United States. My Buenos Aires–based team—Romina Frazzetta, Diego López, Victoria Mansur, and Martín Walter (all at Universidad de San Andrés)—undertook data collection and analysis tasks with intelligence, creativity, and responsibility. Romina and Victoria worked for the duration of this project. Romina also read preliminary versions of each chapter and improved them with her unparalleled attention to detail. In addition, Andrés Mendoza Pena at MIT undertook industry research; Martín de Santos at Yale University and Gabriela Cantarero and Marie Silver at Northwestern University helped with content analyses of homogeneity in the news; Nicolás Trachter at the University of Chicago and Juan Passadore at Universidad Torcuato Di Tella assisted with quantitative data analysis; and Eugenia Mitchelstein at Northwestern University performed additional data analyses and provided thoughtful feedback on an earlier version of the book.

A project of this kind is the product of many conversations. Several led to decisive contributions. In chronological order, I thank Guillermo Culell for the encounter that started it all; Marcelo Franco for opening up *"el cerebro corporativo"* (the corporate brain); Shane Greenstein for the idea to include a longitudinal dimension to the studies of homogenization of print news; Dan O'Keefe for helping integrate the logics of qualitative and quantitative inquiry; Jean-François Fogel for a memorable lunch in which we brainstormed about *"el cierre de la tienda"* (the closing of the shop) and the end of the news; Geof Bowker for insisting that I account for the focus on imitation by digging not only into the data but also into how this topic fits with my (intellectual) identity; Karin Knorr-Cetina for encouraging me to submit the manuscript to the University of Chicago Press and referring the project to Doug Mitchell; Woody Powell for helping me think about how different publishing options are tied to the development of scholarly trajectories; and Trevor Pinch for sage advice that was essential to bringing the publishing process to a successful completion.

In addition to these key conversations, the book greatly benefited from discussions with many people, including Jaafar Aksikas, Ken Alder, Diane Bailey, François Bar, Steve Barley, Lance Bennett, Amahl Bishara, Matt Bothner, Dominic Boyer, Michael Delli Carpini, Manuel Castells, Jess Cattelino, Guillermo Culell, Mark Deuze, Susan Douglas, Wendy Espeland, Jim Ettema, Roberto Fernandez, Daniel Fernández Canedo,

Jean-François Fogel, Marcos Foglia, Marcelo Franco, Janet Fulk, Hernán Galperin, Gerry Garbulsky, Tom Gieryn, Tarleton Gillespie, Ted Glasser, Shane Greenstein, Dan Gruber, Hugh Gusterson, Tom Haigh, Jay Hamilton, Keith Hampton, Eszter Hargittai, Bob Hariman, Paul Hirsch, Henry Jenkins, Steve Kahl, Paul Karoff, Elihu Katz, Jorge Katz, Ricardo Kirschbaum, Ron Kline, Karin Knorr-Cetina, John Lavine, Bruce Lewenstein, Mike Lynch, Peter Monge, Diana Mutz, Russ Neuman, David Nord, Willie Ocasio, Chris Ogan, Dan O'Keefe, Wanda Orlikowski, Limor Peer, Chick Perrow, Damon Philips, Trevor Pinch, Francis Pisani, Woody Powell, Linda Putnam, Gastón Roitberg, Fernán Saguier, Harmeet Sawhney, Ernesto Schargrodsky, Michael Schudson, Dan Sherman, Susan Silbey, Mike Smith, Leigh Star, David Stark, Ithai Stern, Federico Sturzenegger, Kathie Sutcliffe, John Thompson, David Thorburn, Fred Turner, Joe Turow, Nikki Usher, Derek Vaillant, Eliseo Verón, Jorge Walter, Klaus Weber, Jim Webster, Karl Weick, Barry Wellman, Chuck Whitney, Miguel Wiñazki, Noah Zatz, Barbie Zelizer, Viviana Zelizer, and Ezra Zuckerman Sivan.

The ideas in this book were also shaped by comments received during seminars at Northwestern University, MIT, the University of Chicago, Cornell University, Stanford University, the University of Pennsylvania, the University of Southern California, the University of Wisconsin, Indiana University, the University of Texas, Columbia College Chicago, Universidad de San Andrés, and the Boston Consulting Group. I benefited, too, from feedback during talks at the annual meetings of the International Communication Association, the American Sociological Association, the Society for Social Studies of Science, and the Academy of Management and at the 2006 Spanish Conference on Digital Journalism and the Tenth Anniversary of Clarín.com.

Northwestern University was a very conducive environment for the interdisciplinary work represented in this book. Dean Barbara O'Keefe provided ample time and financial resources, gave content and publishing advice, and encouraged the pursuit of this project. My department chairs, Bob Hariman and Peter Miller, supported this research; Jane Rankin and Sheri Carsello helped with funding issues; and Sharron Shepard and Sonia Watters provided administrative assistance. Part of the research reported in chapter 4 was supported by funds from the University Research Grants Committee and the School of Communication Innovations Fund. The second study included in appendix B was supported by the Robert and Kaye Hiatt Fund for Research on Media, Technology, and Society.

Working with the University of Chicago Press was an outstanding experience. I thank Doug Mitchell for his depth of knowledge, insightful take on the book's main arguments, and unfailing support of the project.

I am also grateful to Tim McGovern and Erin Dewitt for able editorial assistance. Two reviewers greatly improved the manuscript with helpful suggestions and exacting requests. Eric Klinenberg revealed his identity at the end of the review process and kindly agreed to meet and discuss his recommendations. Kay Mansfield and Pam Bruton did wonders to streamline the text. The early stages of the writing process also benefited from feedback from Margy Avery and Trevor Pinch at the MIT Press, Lew Bateman, Lance Bennett, and Bob Entman at Cambridge University Press, and the anonymous reviewers commissioned by these publishing houses.

Friends and family provided much appreciated encouragement and support. They are too numerous to name individually, but my heartfelt appreciation goes to all. A handful of them deserve special thanks. Gabo Charrúa, Gerry Garbulsky, and Omar Lavieri made my visits to Buenos Aires especially rewarding. My mother, Aída Schwartz, followed the whole enterprise with loving support. Jorge Boczkowski, my brother, was always present with his caring and reassuring persona. My daughters, Sofía and Emma, filled the interstices of research and writing with pure joy and selfless love. Their sheer presence energized my work by reminding me how blessed I am to have them around. Irina Konstantinovsky, my life companion for nearly a quarter century, did so much for this project that I dare not even begin to characterize her contributions. Above all, and paraphrasing one of her favorite songs, when I was lost, I knew I could look and would find her, "time after time." My deepest gratitude goes to my late father, Abraham "Zito" Boczkowski. As a young boy, I learned that the news was something special by watching him consume it so passionately. Many of our shared moments during my subsequent, formative years revolved around the news—from listening to *Magdalena* on the radio on the way to school to discussions about politics and society that marked my adolescence. It has been a privilege to spend the past five years remembering and celebrating him by working on a book about a subject that united us in such a mundane yet profound fashion. *Adiós, Viejo.*

An earlier version of some parts of chapter 2 appeared in Pablo Boczkowski, "Rethinking Hard and Soft News Production: From Common Ground to Divergent Paths," *Journal of Communication* 59 (2009): 98–116; reprinted with permission from the International Communication Association and Blackwell Publishing. An earlier version of some parts of chapter 3 was published in Pablo Boczkowski, "Technology, Monitoring and Imitation in Contemporary News Work," *Communication, Culture &*

Critique 2 (2009): 39–59; reprinted with permission from the International Communication Association and Blackwell Publishing. Some fragments of chapter 3 also appeared in Pablo Boczkowski, "Materiality and Mimicry in the Journalistic Field," in *The Changing Faces of Journalism*, edited by B. Zelizer (New York: Routledge, 2009), pp. 56–67; reprinted with permission from Routledge. Finally, some of the content included in chapter 4 had previously been published in Pablo Boczkowski and Martín de Santos, "When More Media Equals Less News: Patterns of Content Homogenization in Argentina's Leading Print and Online Newspapers," *Political Communication* 24 (2007): 167–90; reprinted with permission from Taylor & Francis.

Introduction: When More Becomes Less

On a rainy morning in July 2005, in an auditorium in downtown Buenos Aires, Guillermo Culell was speaking at a workshop about the policy and management of information technologies. Since its launch in March 1996, Culell had been in charge of Clarín.com, Argentina's most popular online news site and the Internet presence of *Clarín*, the country's highest-circulation daily.[1] Ten minutes into his presentation, Culell showed a slide with a figure with a semi-circular shape in the middle that flattened toward the edges. He polled people in the audience about what they thought it was. One attendee shouted, "A hat!" Another said, "A bell curve." A third declared that it was the well-known image of the boa that ate the elephant, from *The Little Prince*. Culell nodded and showed a slide with the illustration from that book. He paused, and a smile momentarily lit up his face. Within a presentation about the online news operation of an established newspaper, perhaps he smiled because of the connotation of the small devouring the big. But no doubt it was also because he knew that the audience would react with bewilderment when he told them that the illustration from *The Little Prince* also represented fairly accurately the temporal pattern of online news consumption at Clarín. com during the workweek. He illustrated his claim by showing the slide reproduced in figure I.1. He then asked, "What do most people do from nine in the morning until six in the afternoon, Monday to Friday? They are at work. Our public is people who get the news at the time and place of work."[2]

Prime Time
(L a V)

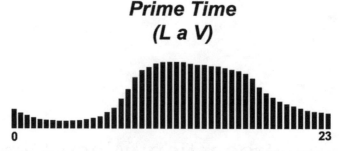

I.1   Illustration of the news-at-work pattern used by Guillermo Culell in his July 2005 presentation. ("L a V" stands for *lunes a viernes*, or Monday to Friday. The numbers 0 and 23 represent the hours of the day, starting at midnight.) © Guillermo Culell.

In the world of print and broadcast media, the news is largely conceived as a good that is consumed primarily before and after work and outside the workplace. Culell's claim signified the emergence of a novel temporal and spatial pattern of news consumption for the general public.[3]

I empathized with the workshop attendees because I had experienced both intrigue and excitement when Culell had told me of this "news-at-work" phenomenon more than a year earlier. We had met in the summer of 1996, shortly after I had begun to conduct research on online news, and had kept in touch over the years. In April 2004, while I was in Buenos Aires, he wanted my opinion about a new development on which he had been working. During that conversation he shared with me the news-at-work phenomenon that he and his colleagues at Clarín .com had discovered. He added that it had inspired a transformation of the editorial offerings, organizational structure, and graphic design of the site. An analysis of patterns of site usage led Culell and his colleagues to conclude that people who accessed online news at work would best be served by many, constantly updated, breaking, and developing stories (to keep them coming back to the site numerous times during the day), mixed with a handful of attention-grabbing features (to entertain them during more extended breaks from work tasks). Based on this conclusion, they planned to increase the frequency and volume of news publication during the day and the number of more elaborated feature stories. They planned also to restructure the newsroom into two units—one devoted to the production of breaking and developing news and the other to features. In addition, they would divide the homepage into two parts—one for news and the other for features.

Culell showed me the prototype for the new site, and we discussed the implications of the changes that were about to take place. As the conversation unfolded, I realized the potential significance of these changes in news production and in the consumption behavior that had motivated them. Newspapers have often been read at the breakfast table or in transit to and from work. Television news has commonly been watched in the evening. During the second half of the twentieth century, media organizations aligned their editorial strategies, work processes, and production and distribution technologies to cater to this dominant temporal and spatial patterning of news consumption. Thus, the emergence of the news-at-work phenomenon could trigger transformations in core work, editorial, and technological dynamics of the journalistic enterprise. But did that happen? If it did, what kinds of transformations took place?

The research journey began in April 2005, when, aided by a team of research assistants, I launched an ethnographic study of editorial work at Clarín.com. By then, its main rival, Lanacion.com, and a new but aggressive competitor, Infobae.com, had also moved into a regime of constant publication of breaking and developing news during the day. Shortly after starting the research, it was clear that the above-mentioned editorial, organizational, and design changes implemented almost a year earlier at Clarín.com had evolved into a stark division at the site between the production of news and other kinds of content. As will be shown in chapter 2, the two divergent modes of journalism coexisted within one news organization, but with little in common other than a shared brand and office space.

Another issue rapidly caught the attention of the research team. The changes at Clarín.com, implemented to satisfy perceived alterations in the nature of demand, had had an unintended and unanticipated consequence in the production sphere. They triggered a qualitative leap in journalists' knowledge of stories deemed newsworthy by their colleagues. Although monitoring and imitation have long been staples of editorial work, it became apparent that staffers devoted to the production of breaking and developing news took advantage of this leap to incessantly monitor coverage at competitors' sites. Moreover, learning about a story published by another organization dramatically increased the likelihood of its publication by Clarín.com. That is, journalists reacted to the discovery of the news-at-work experience by increasing the number of stories made available to consumers, but the intensification of monitoring and imitation also caused the diversity of the stories' content to decrease. As will be analyzed in chapter 3, this intensification applied to the construction of news but not the production of features. Moreover, interviews conducted in 2006 and 2007 with journalists who worked in other online and print newsrooms revealed that these monitoring and imitation practices varied little by medium and organization. The rise in imitation appeared to be widespread across the journalistic field.

Did these production practices have any systematic effects on the resulting editorial products? To answer this question, I conducted a content analysis of news stories that examined patterns in the selection, presentation, and narrative construction of the top stories published by Clarín. com, Lanacion.com, and Infobae.com during the autumn of 2005. The analysis also looked at similar issues about the front-page stories published by *Clarín* and *La Nación*, Argentina's second-largest newspaper and the print counterpart of Lanacion.com, at four points in time between 1995 and 2005. (Since the launch of the online sites and throughout this ten-year period, the respective online and print newsrooms had operated in a relatively autonomous fashion at both *Clarín* and *La Nación*.) The analysis, presented in chapter 4, shows an increase in the similarity of the print newspapers' stories that coincided with the timing of the growth in the volume and frequency of online news publishing. It also shows a high level of homogenization in the stories published by both print and online outlets in the contemporary setting. Last but not least, these patterns apply to news stories but not to other types of content, such as features or opinion pieces.

Many of my informants were well aware of these transformations in news production and products. But they often exhibited a sense of unease talking about them, to the point of preferring to say almost nothing at all. On one of my research trips to Buenos Aires, Ricardo Kirschbaum, managing editor of *Clarín,* asked to discuss my research progress. As I prepared my presentation for him on the morning of July 27, 2006, I compared the front pages of *Clarín* and *La Nación* on that day (figure I.2). The papers had a striking similarity in story selection, placement, and headline construction: the dotted arrow marks the top national story of the day in both papers; the dashed one, the top foreign story; the dotted and dashed one, the top metro story; and the long-dashed one, the top health story. A few days later, I showed Kirschbaum a series of charts with quantitative findings and then illustrated them with a slide with these two front pages. He said little, but his facial expression and body language conveyed a sense of discomfort yet lack of surprise, a reaction that I encountered often during the fieldwork process. Another common reaction from journalists about this pattern of similarity is captured in the phrase *"todos tienen lo mismo"* (everybody has the same). The phrase was often followed by brief comments about a dislike for this state of affairs—people do not become journalists to imitate competitors' work—

I.2   Front pages of *Clarín* and *La Nación*, July 27, 2006. © *Clarín* and *La Nación*.

and belief that one could do little to change it because it had become a part of "how things are now."

These transformations began as a reaction to changes in consumption. But what were the actual routines of consuming news at work, and what did the homogenization of news mean to consumers? To answer these questions, two studies were conducted in 2006 and 2007. The first study consisted of a content analysis of the most-clicked stories on Clarín.com, Lanacion.com, and Infobae.com, as an expression of actual consumer behavior. The second was an ethnography of news consumption to understand the interpretation, affect, and experience associated with appropriating online news. (The main findings from both studies are the subjects of chapters 5 and 6.) The results from the content analysis show a much lower level of homogenization in the stories that consumers read more frequently than in the stories that journalists consider most newsworthy. These results also indicate the existence of divergent thematic distribution in the selection patterns of journalists and consumers: the choices of the former are concentrated on national, business, economic, and international topics (or "public affairs" news), and those of the latter on sports, entertainment, and crime subjects (or "non–public affairs" news). Thus, changes in imitation were triggered by the discovery of the news-at-work phenomenon, but the magnitude and thematic composition of the changes emerged from unintended consequences of transformations in work and organization. Otherwise, imitation would have been less common and the resulting stories less similar and focused on different subject matters. The ethnography of consumption underscores this by showing that a mix of dislike, resignation, and powerlessness also marked people's experience of reduced diversity in the news. In the words of Lorena, a twenty-nine-year-old teacher of Spanish as a second language, "The market is like this. And newspapers are part of the market, so they're all going to go in the same direction. Do I like it? Of course not. Do I know of any solution? To be honest, no" (personal communication, March 2, 2007).

The rise of homogenization in the news has led to a state of affairs that neither journalists nor consumers like but feel powerless to alter. This spiral of sameness and powerlessness has important cultural and political implications. The analysis presented in chapter 7 argues that it might be tied to a rise in the prevalence of generic news content and the importance of the wire services providing it. It may also be related to a decrease in the watchdog role traditionally played by news organizations and the concomitant alterations in the balance of power in society. The analysis also highlights the inability of consumer-driven alternatives to reach large segments of the population with a wider and more diverse set of stories. Because this book sheds light on broader trends in the media industry, appendix B also includes findings of a study of news homogenization among the leading online media of the United States during the 2008 presidential election. The preliminary analysis shows that the diversity in what is reported is quite low, even during a period of major historical significance when resource constraints are relaxed and public interest in the news is higher than usual. In an age of information plenty, what most consumers get is more of the same.

The dynamics of increased imitation come full circle, from the process of production, to the resulting news products, to the experience of their consumption, to the cultural and political implications. It is this circle—in the context of a new time and place of online news consumption—that this book aims to understand. More precisely, what follows is a tale of two distinct phenomena and the paradox that binds them. The two phenomena are the emergence of the workplace as a key temporal and spatial locus of online news consumption and the intensification of imitation in news production on the Web and in print. The paradox is the remarkable increase in the amount of news available and a perplexing decrease in the diversity of its content. This paradox has become a defining element of the contemporary media landscape. The 2006 edition of the authoritative *State of the News Media* report sums it up as "the new paradox of journalism is more outlets covering fewer stories" (Journalism.org, 2006). Thus, making sense of the paradox is critical to understanding a current dynamics of a central social institution. In addition, accounting for how and why this paradox came to be affords a privileged opportunity to undertake much-needed theoretical and methodological innovations in the study of imitation. Realizing the potential of these innovations enables this account to offer novel ways of studying and explaining the common processes whereby the power of imitation turns more (knowledge of a given social world) into less (diversity of options pursued by the actors). These innovations are succinctly introduced next and described in detail in chapter 1.

Theoretical and Methodological Underpinnings

The conceptual goal of this book is to offer an examination of the dynamics and consequences of imitation in work, organizational, and economic processes. In addition, it focuses on the media industry and pays special attention to the role of technology in these processes. To this end, it relies on an interdisciplinary framework that draws from scholarship on imitation in each of these areas and from technology research. From the communication and media studies field, the book builds on accounts of the practice dynamics involved in imitation during everyday editorial work, often under the guise of "pack journalism," and the attention to the situational forces that affect these dynamics. It also draws on the growing concern expressed by academics in this field about the homogenization of news content. From relevant research in sociology and economics, it builds on analyses of the outcomes of imitative action in interorganizational mimicry and herd behavior, respectively. It supplements the efforts to understand the structural factors that shape these outcomes. From technology scholarship, the book adopts the view that social processes are often intertwined with material formations. Thus, any explanations of variance in social life must, in principle, take into account the possible role played by technological infrastructures, actions, and knowledge.

In addition to bringing together domains of inquiry that are often kept separate, this framework contributes to solving three important limitations that cut across this scholarship. The first limitation arises from the complementary foci of the imitation analyses typically offered by the scholarship in communication, sociology, and economics. These analyses usually split production practices (the preferred focus of work in communication and media studies) from product outcomes (the dominant focus of inquiries in sociology and economics). They look at either practices or outcomes but not both. For instance, on the one hand, communication scholars examine how journalists from different organizations who share the same beat often focus on similar topics and disregard alternative angles, but these scholars do not systematically analyze the effects on the resulting stories. On the other hand, economic sociologists study how membership in interlocking boards of directors is frequently tied to shared organizational structures, but they only infer the existence of imitation from these outcomes. Splitting production practices from product outcomes complicates theory development efforts by making it difficult to establish clear connections between a particular practice pattern and specific changes in the resulting products. For instance, an increase in the similarity of news stories or organizational structures can be caused by changes in practices other than imitation. The customary separation between production and products, in turn, diminishes the ability to shed light on the specific practice mechanisms that generate these outcomes and to adjudicate between competing explanations.

The second limitation of relevant existing scholarship is that the role of technology has been overlooked. Not paying attention to technology is potentially a serious flaw because of the many ways in which artifacts are central across the domains of media and economic action. It is also problematic in light of recent research that provides examples of technology and imitation that resonate with phenomena examined in this book. For instance, in their analysis of the development of electoral campaigning on the Web in the United States, Foot and Schneider include dialogues with Web masters about their common monitoring and imitation patterns that differ little from what I heard in the newsrooms of Argentine media. One Web master commented, "We want to be able to match what other campaigns are doing, so we consistently monitor their Web sites" (2006, p. 179), and another visited opponents' sites "all the time" to "see what kind of content they have, whether there are some ideas they have, or features they have that we should be having. I think we all have just about the same" (p. 180). Without access to certain Web technologies, these actors could not have monitored their competitors and imitated some of their actions and products in the way they did. Thus, an account of their practices that rests solely on social forces and mechanisms would be critically incomplete. This does not mean that technology always matters, but that it can. Therefore, a determination of the actual role of technology should be an essential part of the research process.

The third shortcoming is a disregard for the consumption stage of the imitation life cycle. That is, the dominant focus on production practices and product outcomes seems to have been at the expense of attending to how end users incorporate these products into their everyday lives. Two problems arise from this neglect of consumption. First, it assumes that consumer behavior has no bearing on the practices of producers, and therefore imitation can always be satisfactorily explained by resorting only to production dynamics. This might be adequate in many cases but should be an outcome of the inquiry rather than one of its premises. Second, studies that adopt a normative view of the socially deleterious effects of a homogenized news supply fail to anchor it in an understanding of how people appropriate and make sense of such news. This, in turn, diminishes the ability of the analysis to yield a realistic assessment of the prospects for social reform.

Building on the valuable insights of existing scholarship, yet aiming to overcome some of these limitations, this book develops the following framework. First, it bridges the production-product divide. Thus, it looks at how journalists from one organization monitor and imitate the work of their colleagues in other organizations, and it systematically analyzes the effects of these practices on the resulting stories. Second, it conceives imitation as emerging at the intersection of situational and contextual factors. In other words, it pays attention to the workplace dynamics and the patterns of the larger organizational field that shape the intensity and direction of imitative activity. Third, it directly examines the role played by technological infrastructures, actions, and knowledge. That is, it inquires into whether changes in the availability and use of technical resources have any links to transformations in imitation. Fourth, it accounts for the consumption of imitated products. Thus, it analyzes how consumers appropriate an increasingly homogenized news supply within their everyday routines and the cultural and political consequences that various modes of appropriation have.

To demonstrate the heuristic power of the four elements of this framework, this book relies on a research design that combines ethnographic and content-analytic studies of the production practices of journalists, the resulting news stories, and how consumers appropriate these stories. Unlike most existing scholarship on imitation, this design overcomes the production-product divide that has dominated the literature. It also extends the empirical gaze by including data on the consumption of the products of imitative activity.

More generally, this framework presents an alternative to the common stance of most social studies of media, technology, and economic processes, which focus on either production or consumption. That is, media studies either examine the making of news and entertainment content or look at their effects on or reception by consumers. Similarly, technology accounts either inquire into the construction of artifacts or analyze their appropriation and consequences. V. Zelizer argues that a parallel trend characterizes the divide between scholarship in economic sociology, on the one hand, and sociological studies of consumption, on the other: "Economic sociologists examine production and distribution with no more than occasional gestures toward consumption, while specialists in culture, gender, family, inequality, and other fields lavish attention on consumption almost without regard to the questions—or answers—posed by economic sociologists" (2005a, p. 332). A handful of recent studies examine both production and consumption matters in these various fields.[4] They show the power of illuminating processes that are far more interconnected in society than in scholarly accounts. Thus, and to continue with the case of economic sociology, it is not surprising that Fligstein and Dauter label studies that bridge production and consumption a "frontier" in scholarship on markets (2007, p. 119). Therefore, in addition to its methodological contributions to the study of imitation, this book adds to an emerging movement that offers integrated accounts of production and consumption.

Temporal and Spatial Context

Like the news-at-work phenomenon, the account offered in this book is marked by a particular time and place. Thus, it is worthwhile to reflect briefly on some key aspects of the temporal and spatial contexts that frame the book. The time is the recent period from 2005 to 2007, with the analysis of news products going back to 1995 for added longitudinal perspective, and the place is Argentina. (A more detailed examination of these contextual matters is offered in chapter 1.)

The inquiry that resulted in this book was conducted during a recent period of rapid, momentous, and ongoing (at the time of this writing) transformations in the world of news. The contemporary, fast-paced, and evolving character of these phenomena presented challenges, because it is usually easier to study phenomena that happened in a more distant past and whose contours have long been settled. The upside of confronting these challenges is that the findings can potentially inform public discussion about the future evolution of the phenomena. The downside is the risk that the evidence will become dated in the short term. However, the main contributions of this book are not about the print and online operations of the two leading news organizations of Argentina or the practices and experiences of the consumers of their products at a particular point in time. Rather, the critical contributions of the book are (*a*) its illumination of the underlying dynamics of imitation that depend on basic sociomaterial processes that are shared across many social worlds; (*b*) its demonstration of the value of an innovative research design that can capture multiple dimensions of these dynamics; and (*c*) its formulation of a theoretical framework to explain how and why these dynamics unfold as they do. Thus, these analytical contributions are somewhat decoupled from the timing of the data collection efforts.

One recent transformation in the media industry that is of relevance for this book is the rise and growth of a number of alternative platforms for news production and distribution on the Web, such as blogs and citizen media sites. Considerable optimism about a more diverse news landscape often accompanies academic and popular discourse about these platforms. Therefore, one may wonder how much an account of a decrease in news diversity among leading, mainstream media companies matters in a period marked by an explosion in consumer choices for accessing information? The answer is that it matters even more than when a handful of print and broadcast media dominated the journalism field. Research summarized in chapter 6 shows that the content of news blogs is highly dependent on stories produced by the media. Blogs commonly comment on stories generated by traditional and online media but very seldom break new stories. Furthermore, in Argentina and other parts of the world, the development of these alternative platforms has accompanied an increase in the relative market power of the leading news organizations on the Web. Nearly all of these organizations are tied to mainstream journalism companies. This is not surprising since, as Hindman argues, "In a host of areas, from political news to blogging to issue advocacy . . . online speech follows winner-take-all patterns" (2009, p. 4). Thus, a decrease in the diversity of news content among the larger players is likely to reverberate strongly across the media landscape.

That rapid speed also characterizes recent transformations in the media is shown by the fact that potentially relevant changes in structure and leadership at the main organizations included in the ethnography of news production have already taken place since most of the research for this book was conducted. A critical structural transformation was the merger, following a global trend in the industry, of the print and online newsrooms at *Clarín* and *La Nación,* respectively. This process began at both organizations in the spring of 2008. A major leadership change occurred with the departure of Clarín.com's longtime, founding editorial director to head all the Internet operations of Grupo El Comercio, Peru's leading media conglomerate, and his replacement by a newcomer. Do these changes alter the analytical argument presented in this book? A study undertaken in the summer of 2008 with a doctoral student included interviews with editors at Clarín.com and Lanacion.com and at four other sites in Argentina. These interviews featured discussions about issues directly related to the ones examined in this book. This additional evidence, reported in appendix B, suggests that the recent organizational transformations in these two newspapers have not altered the underlying dynamics of imitation that are the focus of this book.

Why is Argentina a suitable choice to explore the issues at the heart of this book? As noted above, the genesis of the project was largely opportunistic and triggered what was then conceived as a stand-alone study of editorial work at Clarín.com. The decision to turn this study into the first empirical building block of a much larger project was made after realizing that the Argentine setting is an asset for the goals of this book in terms of what it shares with other settings and also its unique features.

The Argentine news industry and its counterparts around the world have much in common. The country has a modern media system, and new technologies such as cable, mobile telephony, and the Internet have diffused rapidly in recent years. The leading players, such as the organizations studied in the ethnography of news production, are well networked. The top editors and executives regularly exchange information with peers through participation in forums organized by the World Association of Newspapers and the Inter American Press Association, and journalists routinely receive training overseas. In collaboration with local universities, *Clarín* and *La Nación* offer graduate programs in journalism that incorporate modules on recent developments in the field and are often attended by their respective reporters. These programs are supported by exchange agreements with Columbia University in the United States and Bologna University in Italy (*Clarín*) and with *Diario El País* and the Autonomous University of Madrid in Spain (*La Nación*). In addition, the online news consumers interviewed for this book are similar to their counterparts in other countries in terms of age, educational attainment, and occupational profile. Several even work in local branches of leading multinational corporations, where they are in daily contact with colleagues in offices located in other nations and regions of the world.

Four distinct elements of the Argentine context also make this location advantageous for the analytical objectives of this book. First, the Argentine newspaper industry is mostly national, highly concentrated, and privately held. This makes certain factors that affect imitation easier to identify than in countries such as the United States, where the industry has a more complex geographic configuration, is less concentrated, and is more open to the influence of capital markets. Second, the print and online newsrooms in each of the two newspaper companies examined for this book operated in an autonomous fashion throughout the period of the study. This allowed a better analysis of intermedia influences than if they had been organizationally integrated. Third, a special labor relations agreement contributed to much higher levels of personnel stability in the print newsrooms studied than in those of many other countries. This, in turn, moderates the role of fluctuations in resource allocation, a central aspect in political-economy explanations of imitation, and makes the effect of alternative or concurrent factors more visible than would be possible in other contexts. Fourth, the recent history of institutional instability in Argentina has made the average news consumer a savvier interpreter of journalistic texts, in particular those that deal with public affairs subjects, than in countries where people take for granted that political and social institutions in their everyday lives function adequately. When the institutional context is uncertain, citizens constantly look for news that can help them anticipate events and navigate difficult times. This, in turn, provides particularly fertile ground for inquiring about people's perceptions, interpretations, emotions, and experiences as consumers of news content. Mindful of the existence of these and other, perhaps less central, idiosyncratic traits of the Argentine location, I address different aspects of what might be locally unique and what might be shared across national settings in the chapters in which they are directly relevant. Chapter 7 assesses these various aspects of the findings from a comparative perspective.

The Argentine location is an asset for yet another reason. The vast majority of scholarship on online news, in particular, and the social, political, and cultural implications of digital media, in general, relies primarily on data from the United States and, to a lesser extent, other industrialized nations. But the emergence and evolution of digital media are not only global but also globalizing phenomena that deepen information flows across often very distant and quite different locales. Therefore, it is essential to expand the geographic gaze of the research enterprise to reach a more global understanding of digital media and their consequences. Locating the inquiry in Argentina furthers this goal as well.

The evidence available in scholarly articles and technical reports that is summarized in chapter 1 suggests that online news consumption at the time and place of work, the expansion of imitation practices in news production, and the homogenization of the resulting news stories are not unique to the contemporary Argentine media scene. This is further underscored by additional findings about news homogenization during the U.S. 2008 election cycle that are included in appendix B. Thus, it is reasonable to believe that the location chosen for this book is a useful mirror to reflect news phenomena and imitation dynamics that are taking place in other locations. It is certainly not a perfect mirror and perhaps is better understood as a fun house mirror or a broken mirror. But like the absurd stories of Miguel de Unamuno or the cubist paintings of Pablo Picasso, the exaggeration and reconfiguration of critical elements of the object of inquiry might teach aspects of social life that are more difficult to understand from the location choices that dominate studies of digital-media phenomena and imitation processes in a number of disciplines.

In sum, this book offers an account of three separate but interrelated elements that are central to contemporary journalism and its publics: the emergence of the time and place of work as key parameters for the consumption of online news, the substantive rise of imitation in news production, and the unforeseen paradox of a greater volume of news but a less diverse content. It presents a theoretical analysis that encompasses the multiple stages in the life cycle of imitation—from production and products to consumption and cultural and political consequences—and how they affect each other. The book also fosters theory development by taking into account the role of technology and the causal force of situational and broader contextual factors. It makes these theoretical contributions by combining qualitative and quantitative methods in a research design conceived to overcome the divides between studies of production, product, and consumption that dominate relevant scholarship on imitation, in particular, and general tendencies in studies of media, work, and technology. Finally, this book makes these descriptive, theoretical, and methodological contributions through a history of the present undertaken in a well-suited, yet unusual, setting. This setting helps to deepen a global outlook in the understanding of developments at the intersection of digital technology, organizational action, and cultural formations.

The next chapter discusses in depth the theoretical, methodological, and contextual aspects of this book that are summarized in this introductory chapter. Readers who wish to move directly into the empirical analysis might want skip to chapter 2. For others, what follows is a more extensive account of how I studied imitation in the South.

ONE

Studying Imitation in the South

The arguments made in this book are intellectually animated by a particular set of theoretical concerns made empirically possible by resorting to specific methodological strategies. The arguments are both enabled and constrained by features of the temporal and spatial context in which the inquiry was conducted. This chapter offers further elaboration of the theoretical, methodological, and contextual issues that were succinctly addressed in the introductory chapter.

Theorizing Imitation

Imitation not only is a common feature of social life but has also been one of the most fruitful concepts across the biological, behavioral, and social sciences and the humanities. As such, it has garnered the attention of scholars in fields as varied as neurobiology, animal behavior, developmental psychology, social stratification, public opinion research, international relations, and cultural and business history (Baller & Richardson, 2002; Goldsmith, 2005; Hurley & Chater, 2005a, 2005b; Noelle-Neumann, 1993; Orvell, 1989; Westney, 1987). In light of the diversity of goals for which imitation has been studied and the wide array of how it has been understood, it is essential to delineate what it means in the context of this book, in the fields that are most directly engaged in the analysis, and for the theoretical contributions this study aims to make.

The canonical source on imitation in classical social theory is the work of Gabriel Tarde, in particular *The Laws of Imitation* (1903 [1890]). Tarde's work has experienced a recent revival in studies of media (Katz, 2006), science and technology (Latour, 2002, 2005), and economic action (Barry & Thrift, 2007). Tarde proposed a highly inclusive conception of imitation that is captured in the idea that "all resemblances of *social origin* in society are the direct or indirect fruit of the various forms of imitation" (Tarde, 1903 [1890], p. 14, emphasis in original). Recent work based on this idea often treats imitation as shorthand for different forms of relational influence. I adopt a more restricted notion of imitation that is conceptualized as the act that occurs when one actor, based on knowledge of another actor's behavior or output, decides to completely or partially reproduce this behavior or output instead of pursuing a different course of action.

As stated in the previous chapter, I look at imitation in work, organizational, and economic activities, with a focus on the media industry and mindful of the potential role of technology. In light of these foci, I do not address two cognate traditions of inquiry that concentrate on what could be broadly construed as the representational dimension of imitation. The first consists of humanities scholarship on the notion of mimesis in literary criticism (Auerbach, 2003 [1953]; Gebauer & Wulf, 1995; Girard, 1966), the theory of aesthetics (Halliwell, 2002; Lacoue-Labarthe, 1989), and cultural studies (Jenson, 2001; Taussig, 1993) that looks at how symbolic works mirror or construct reality. Because I examine imitation in the production of symbolic works and *not* in terms of these works' "world-simulating" or "world-creating" (Halliwell, 2002, p. 23) character, this valuable tradition of inquiry in the humanities is not of direct relevance to the present inquiry. The second stream is represented by social-scientific research in psychology, communication, and epidemiology that analyzes whether consumers imitate violent (Bandura, Ross, & Ross, 1963; Gerbner, Gross, Morgan, & Signorielli, 1994; Huesmann, Moise-Titus, Podolski, & Eron, 2003; Paik & Comstock, 1994) and suicidal (P. Jamieson, Jamieson, & Romer, 2003; Pirkis, Burgess, Francis, Blood, & Jolley, 2006; Stack, 2000; Weimann & Fishman, 1995) content provided by the media. Because I am concerned with how people consume increasingly similar news content rather than whether their actions imitate this content, this important stream of social-scientific research is not directly relevant either.

I develop an interdisciplinary framework on imitation that builds on communication studies of pack journalism and the homogenization of news, sociological accounts of interorganizational mimicry, and economic analyses of herd behavior. Despite the divergent intellectual character of scholarship about these fields, or perhaps precisely because of this divergence, their respective analyses of imitation have complementary strengths and shared limitations. In the remainder of this section, I elaborate on the key ideas that each of these fields brings to the analysis and their common blind spots. On the basis of this elaboration, I present the main elements of the framework advanced in this book and outline how the book contributes to scholarship on imitation.

Communication studies have long analyzed imitation in journalism (Graber, 1971; Halloran, Elliot, & Murdock, 1970; Noelle-Neumann & Mathes, 1987; Shoemaker & Reese, 1996). In his dissertation research on social control in the newsroom, conducted more than fifty years ago, Breed already noted "the tendency of many papers to feature the same stories atop their front pages, to the exclusion of others" (1955, p. 277). Two decades later, Crouse published *The Boys on the Bus,* an account of news making on the campaign trail during the 1972 presidential elections that has since become the *locus classicus* on imitation processes in news production. Crouse offered a detailed portrait of "the notorious phenomenon of 'pack journalism,'" in which "a group of reporters were assigned to follow a single candidate for weeks or months at a time, like a pack of hounds sicked on a fox" (2003 [1972], p. 7).

A separate line of research on the media asserts that the news is strongly homogenized (Bennett, Lawrence, & Livingston, 2007; Bourdieu, 1998; Cook, 1998; Gans, 1980; Glasser, 1992; Hamilton, 2004).[1] Moreover, a number of scholars argue that it has become even less diverse in the past couple of decades (Gans, 2003; García Aviles & Leon, 2004; Klinenberg, 2002, 2005; Norris, 2000; Rosenstiel, 2005; Schudson, 2003). However, there is often a disjunction between these assertions about the homogenization of news products and the accounts of imitation in journalistic practice. In addition, only a few studies provide systematic evidence about the degree and kind of similarity in the content of news products.[2] Reflecting on this matter, Cook recently concluded: "I fear the homogeneity hypothesis is too often treated as a matter of faith rather than a starting point for empirical analysis" (2006, p. 164).[3] Moreover, the available empirical analyses focus on "a single medium at a single point in time" (Boczkowski & de Santos, 2007, p. 169), thus limiting their value in shedding light on evolutionary dynamics across media. In sum, communication and media scholarship has focused on the practices whereby journalists imitate their peers—often providing an engaging depiction of the situational factors that shape these practices—and called attention to the homogeneity of news content. However, it has often not integrated studies of imitation practices with those on the homogeneity in news products and failed to furnish systematic evidence of the concerns regarding these product effects.

Sociological studies have increasingly underscored the pervasiveness of imitation in organizational life (Abrahamson, 1991; Conell & Cohn, 1995; DiMaggio & Powell, 1983; Greve, 1996; Strang & Macy, 2001). Rivkin maintains, "The profound influence of imitation on industrial dynamics is, by now, well established" (2000, p. 824). Perhaps the most developed research area on this phenomenon has been the study of interorganizational mimicry. Inspired by DiMaggio and Powell's (1983) seminal work on "mimetic isomorphism," scholars have theorized how factors such as uncertainty, status, legitimacy, social networks, and ecological processes lead a firm to imitate others in its organizational field or market (Davis & Greve, 1997; Galaskiewicz & Wasserman, 1989; Haunschild, 1993; Haunschild & Miner, 1997; Haveman, 1993).

Economics also examines imitation dynamics, in part in recognition of its ubiquity in social life (Bernhardt, Hughson, & Kutsoati, 2006; Chamley, 2004; Choi, 1997; W. Cohen, Nelson, & Walsh, 2000; Levin, Klevorick, Nelson, & Winter, 1987). Bikhchandani, Hirshleifer, and Welch write, "One of the most striking regularities of human society is *localized conformity*" (1992, p. 992, emphasis in original). Perhaps nowhere has imitation been studied more within economics than in finance, where the analysis of "herd behavior" has blossomed (Avery & Zemsky, 1998; Bikhchandani & Sharma, 2001; Trueman, 1994; Welch, 1992; Wermers, 1999). To Devenow and Welch, this is due to the "belief, not only among practitioners but also among financial economists—when asked in conversation—that investors are influenced by the decisions of other investors and that this influence is a first-order effect" (1996, p. 603). Research on herd behavior conceptualizes the information, reputation, and compensation forces that make it rational for an actor to mimic other market players instead of deviating from the perceived consensus (Banerjee, 1992; Bikhchandani, Hirshleifer, & Welch, 1992, 1998; Drehmann, Oechssler, & Roider, 2005; Scharfstein & Stein, 1990).

Despite their differences, the studies in sociology and economics converge in furnishing the opposite view of those in communication. On the one hand, they infer the existence of imitation from systematic analyses of the outcomes of mimicry and theorize the role played by an array of structural factors in shaping those outcomes. On the other hand, they feature a disregard for the practices that generate those outcomes and the situational factors that might affect these practices. For instance, Barreto and Baden-Fuller note that "most research on interorganizational imitation has tended to adopt indirect measures of the existence of mimetic behaviour" (2006, p. 1566). Moreover, for Cipriani and Guarino, "the problem for the empirical research on herd behavior is that there are no data on the private information available to the traders and, therefore, it is difficult to understand whether traders decide to disregard their own information and imitate" (2005, p. 1428).

Together, the analyses in communication, sociology, and economics provide major insights about the situational shaping of imitation practices and the structural factors that affect the resulting product outcomes. However, these analyses usually split production practices from product outcomes and look at only one side of the imitation coin. Even the examination of news homogeneity in communication scholarship enacts this production-product divide: news production scholars concentrate on the practice side, and content analysts on the product outcome side. To Lawrence, the former "are (appropriately) often more interested in studying the social organization of news production than in analyzing the product itself. Yet studying the product—news content—is where the rubber hits the road: Elegant conceptualizations of inter-organizational fields don't matter much if we cannot link them to what news organizations actually produce" (2006, p. 228).

Looking at only one side of the imitation coin hinders theory development by making it difficult to ascertain whether the production practices have any systematic effects on the resulting products. This approach also makes it hard to distinguish between the mechanisms that lead to the observed product outcomes or to adjudicate between competing explanations. Dobrev argues that, in sociology scholarship, "theoretical arguments explaining the specific mechanism that triggers imitation have been scant" (2007, p. 1271). Manski contends that in the economic analysis of social interactions—including imitation—the "outcomes of the population can usually be generated by many different interaction processes or, perhaps, by processes acting on individuals in isolation. Hence the findings of empirical studies are often open to an uncomfortably wide range of interpretations" (2000, p. 117).

In addition to looking at only one side of the imitation coin at a time, scholarship in communication, sociology, and economics shares additional shortcomings that arise from their lack of regard for technology and consumption issues. I will examine each of these shortcomings in turn.

To overlook the potential role that the development and use of artifacts might have in imitative practices and their resulting outcomes goes against widespread evidence that artifacts are consequential in news production, in particular (Boczkowski, 2004; Domingo, 2008a; Heath & Luff,

2000; Klinenberg, 2005; Sumpter, 2000), and in work, organizations, and markets, in general (Barley, 1986, 1990; Braverman, 1974; Knorr Cetina & Bruegger, 2002; Pinch & Swedberg, 2008; Rosenkopf & Tushman, 1994; Zuboff, 1988). In addition, recent studies provide examples of technology and imitation that resonate with phenomena examined in this book. The introductory chapter presented one such example from the account of online electoral campaigning provided by Foot and Schneider (2006). Shifting from politics to finance, in his account of the hedge fund Long Term Capital Management (LTCM), MacKenzie notes the following episode at a critical turning point in the fund's demise:

On September 2 [1998], [hedge fund head John] Meriwether faxed LTCM's investors its estimate of the August loss. [The] fax, intended to be private to LTCM's investors, became public almost instantly: "Five minutes after we sent our first letter . . . to our handful of shareholders, it was on the Internet." [One consequence of this dissemination was] an immediate effect on the prices of assets that LTCM was known or believed to hold. . . . The price of hurricane bonds fell 20 percent, even although there had been no increase either in the probability of hurricanes or in the likely seriousness of their consequences.   (2006, PP. 233–234)

Beneath the diversity in the social worlds studied by Foot and Schneider and by MacKenzie lies a shared pattern that is central to understanding why any account of imitation is potentially incomplete without an examination of technology. Actors took advantage of the Web's capabilities for easy access to and rapid dissemination of information to constantly monitor their competitors. In turn, knowledge acquired through monitoring was often utilized to imitate the actions or products of these competitors. Without the combination of these technical capabilities and the decision by the actors to take advantage of them, imitation would not have taken place in the way it did in either case—and perhaps not at all. This means, not that technology always plays a role in imitation, but that it can. In other words, neither the presence nor the absence of this role should be taken for granted. Therefore, rather than the indirect omission that characterizes the existing scholarship, a direct consideration of whether technology is implicated in the particular imitation phenomena examined better serves the analysis of imitation.

Scholarship about imitation also neglects the role of consumption. Accounts of the production and products of imitation remain silent about how consumers appropriate these products and experience a situation in which they are exposed to a decreasing variety of options. In addition to presenting an incomplete depiction of the imitation life cycle, overlooking the role of consumption has important drawbacks in terms of explaining how and why imitation happens and assessing its broader cultural and political consequences. To begin, most studies on imitation assume explicitly or by omission that the factors that explain the variance in production or products are not related to consumption trends. Perhaps it is mostly the case, as Darnton claims when describing his days at the *New York Times* and the *Newark Star-Ledger,* that journalists "really wrote for one another" (1975, p. 176). H. White argues more generally that "producers watch each other within a market. . . . Markets are not defined by a set of buyers, as some of our habits of speech suggest, nor are the producers obsessed with speculations on an amorphous demand" (1981, p. 518). But to assume that journalists and other kinds of economic actors are always self-referential and that consumption trends do not contribute to shape their behavior runs the risk of turning what should be an outcome of the inquiry process into one of its premises. Furthermore, communication scholarship often adopts a normative perspective on the negative consequences that a homogenized news supply has for society. This perspective yields important views, but it fails to anchor them in an analysis of how people actually appropriate homogenized news. In turn, this hinders the analyst's ability to reconcile normative claims with the possibilities and constraints of everyday life, thus limiting not only the assessment of consequences but also the conception of realistic reform strategies.

In sum, in this book I develop a theoretical framework that builds on relevant imitation scholarship in communication, sociology, and economics. This scholarship has complementary strengths but also shared limitations. To overcome these limitations and take advantage of the empirical analysis for theoretical development, this framework adopts four innovations. First, it studies both production practices and product outcomes. Second, it examines the situational and structural factors that affect imitation and the interplay between them. Third, it actively inquires into the role of technology in imitation dynamics. Fourth, it broadens the dominant focus on production and product to also include consumption processes.

How the Research Was Done

As mentioned in the introduction, the research design for this book consists of four studies, undertaken between 2005 and 2007, of the arch that goes from production to product to consumption. The remainder of this section describes the studies with enough information to situate the findings that will be presented in chapters 2–6. (A more detailed and more technical depiction of each of these studies is provided in appendix A.)

An Examination of Imitation in the Production of News

The first study focuses on imitation in news making. It is based on a field study of editorial work at Clarín.com and interviews with journalists at *Clarín, La Nación,* and Lanacion.com. The field study was undertaken in 2005 and included three months of observations in the Clarín.com newsroom and forty face-to-face interviews with staffers who represented all hierarchical levels of newsroom full-time employees and all beats. In addition, twenty-seven face-to-face interviews at the three other newsrooms were conducted between December 2006 and March 2007. Interviewees represented hierarchical levels that ranged from deputy managing editor to reporter and a wide array of beats from national to sports news.

Clarín and *La Nación* are Argentina's leading dailies, with 36% and 14%, respectively, of market share at the time when research for this book began.[4] (Additional information about the news industry and recent history of Argentina that is relevant for the purposes of this book will be presented in the following section.) *Clarín* has a tabloid format, targets a broad audience, and has a centrist-populist outlook. *La Nación* is the country's only broadsheet of national circulation, aims at consumers with a higher socioeconomic status, and has a conservative ideology. In the first quarter of 2006, *Clarín* had an average daily circulation of more than 420,000 and an average Sunday circulation of more than 807,000; the relevant figures for *La Nación* were more than 165,000 and 251,000, respectively (Instituto Verificador de Circulaciones, 2006). *Clarín's* average daily circulation decreased by around 30% from 1995 to 2005, but full-time newsroom staffing levels remained relatively high, and its profit margin stayed strong (Roa, 2007). During this period, the circulation at *La Nación* stayed relatively flat.

Clarín.com and Lanacion.com are the country's top online newspapers and, according to Albornoz (2007), two of the leading news sites in the Spanish-speaking world. They were launched just three months apart—in March 1996 and December 1995, respectively. The traffic and revenues of both online newspapers have grown steadily every year since their debut. For the month of August 2006, Clarín.com had 6.2 million and Lanacion.com 2.3 million unique users (Internet Advertising Bureau—Argentina, 2006a). Their respective staffing levels reflected the ups and downs of the Internet boom and bust as well as the financial crisis that hit Argentina in 2001 and 2002. By the time the field study of Clarín .com took place in 2005, its newsroom had approximately fifty full-time staffers, and that number continued to grow through the period of data collection. The newsroom of Lanacion.com had approximately twenty-five full-time staffers by the end of 2006. The online newsrooms of both newspapers were operationally autonomous from their respective print counterparts since their founding and until the end of data collection for this book.

The contemporary situation of these two rivals in the print and online arenas has evolved from very different historical trajectories and is tied to divergent cultural profiles and distinct places in the public imagination.[5] *La Nación* was founded in 1870 by former Argentine president Bartolomé Mitre and has been controlled by prominent families in the country since then. It has had a consistent conservative ideological tone and a loyal following among the country's upper and upper-middle classes. In recent decades, the newspaper company expanded to become a medium-sized, privately owned media conglomerate, with significant presence in the newspaper, magazine, and Internet sectors. *Clarín* was founded by Congressman Roberto Noble in 1945 and had significant connections to the centrist-nationalist Partido Desarrollista during its first decades of existence. It remained a midsized daily until the 1970s, when its rather-populist editorial orientation and aggressive business strategies launched it to the top of the circulation ladder. It then became the political and economic engine of a commercial expansion that allowed its privately owned, corporate parent, Grupo Clarín, to become Argentina's top media conglomerate, with a strong position in the newspaper, printing, broadcast and cable television, radio, Internet service provision, and online content markets.

Two markedly divergent cultural profiles have evolved from these historical trajectories. There is perhaps no better metaphor of this divergence than the offices of the two newspapers. *La Nación*'s print and online operations occupy several floors of a sophisticated high-rise building that also houses the offices of leading corporations. The building is in the heart of the Montserrat neighborhood in a location popular among top business enterprises. It is within walking distance to the area known as Micro-Centro—the locus of financial activity in Buenos Aires—and the Puerto Madero neighborhood, an expensive zone of urban renewal with fancy restaurants, top-of-the-line real estate, and a mix of tourism and business activity. In contrast, *Clarín* occupies a building that is also used by other units of the conglomerate, including its corporate headquarters, and is located in the working-class neighborhood of Barracas just blocks

away from a major public children's hospital and the Constitución transportation hub. Barracas is quite similar in demographics to the San Cristóbal neighborhood, where the Clarín.com offices were located during
fieldwork, as will be described in chapter 2. *Clarín's* building is large and
imposing, especially in the context of the surrounding real estate, yet its
exterior façade and interior design are simple and unsophisticated.

The two newspapers also have distinct places in the public imagination. *La Nación* elicits a rather self-effacing, intellectual, and subdued reaction among average citizens. Its readers like the elegance of its prose
and the steadiness of its ideological position. Even among many of those
who do not like the paper, their dislike tends not to be very passionate.
In contrast, *Clarín* inhabits a stronger and more central space in popular
consciousness and often generates a more passionate response among
proponents and opponents alike. Its readers appreciate the accessible style,
the extensive coverage of topics such as sports and crime, and the centrist-
populist ideological positions. But many people who do not read it are
nonetheless not indifferent to it and commonly express disagreements in
rather emotional ways. The different places that these newspapers occupy
in the public imagination were reflected in the reactions of people—from
academics and business executives to taxi drivers and doormen—
when I told them about my research. Whereas my interlocutors rarely
wanted to know something about *La Nación* or talk about its coverage,
many had questions about whether I had seen a specific journalist at
Clarín, or they commented, often in a passionate mode, about its general
editorial stance or a particular story published by the paper.

An Analysis of the Homogenization of News Products

The second study is devoted to examining the potential effects of imitation in news production on the resulting news products. It consists of a
content analysis of the top stories of the day in print and online newspapers. These are the stories that appear on the front page or top portion
of the homepage, respectively. For two reasons, top stories provide a suitable test of whether imitation in news production systematically affects
the resulting news stories. First, top stories receive the highest and most
careful level of attention from reporters and editors, including the top
editorial decision makers, since these stories have an important role in
setting the news agenda. Second, consumers devote more attention to
reading front-page and homepage material than to stories that appear
"inside" the paper or the Web site. Thus, when a news organization tries
to attract the attention of consumers, it is reasonable to believe that it

might focus its differentiation efforts more strongly on its front page or the top portion of its homepage than on other parts of the product.[6]

For print newspapers, the data come from samples of front-page stories in *Clarín* and *La Nación* at four points in time between 1995 and 2005. The first period is from September to December 1995, immediately before *La Nación* launched its online edition later in December of that year. The period provides a baseline level in terms of similarity of news products between these two newspapers before the emergence of their online counterparts. The second period is from July to October 2000, immediately before online news sites began increasing the volume and frequency of publication. This period was chosen to see whether there were any changes in print newspapers related to the existence of news sites that mostly replicated previously published print content. The third and fourth periods were selected to ascertain any possible consequences for print news of this increase in online publishing. They are from September to December 2004 and from September to December 2005. These periods took place four to seven and sixteen to nineteen months after the design, editorial, and organizational changes that Clarín.com unveiled in May 2004 (mentioned in the introduction) and that marked a major intensification of this trend across the industry.

For online news sites, data were collected from samples of top stories on Clarín.com and Lanacion.com, as well as those on a third site—Infobae.com—between September and December 2005, coinciding with the fourth period of study of the print outlets. Infobae.com, an outgrowth of the small financial daily *Infobae,* was included in the study because it added realism to the analysis: actors considered it to be a strong third player in the online news environment. For example, chapter 3 will show several instances of personnel at Clarín.com and Lanacion.com monitoring and imitating its content. Unlike its print counterpart, Infobae.com was not focused on financial news but published all kinds of content. It acquired a strong position in the online news space, in part, by being very aggressive in its efforts to publish constantly during the day. It also tended to feature a stronger component of sensationalism than Clarín .com and Lanacion.com.

Data from online news sites were gathered in the morning, afternoon, and evening to see how the news evolved as the day unfolded. The data consisted of each online newspaper's first nine stories, counting from left to right and from the top down in a gridlike manner. These stories often were what would appear on the first screen when viewing the site on a fifteen-inch monitor using the Microsoft Explorer browser to display the normal size of the Verdana font—a common configuration in Argentina at the time of the study. Thus, they represented an online equivalent of a print paper's front page.

Accounting for the Consumption of an Increasingly Less Diverse News Supply

The third and fourth studies focus on the consumption of homogenized news. The third study analyzes fifty semistructured interviews with online news consumers that were conducted face-to-face in Buenos Aires and its neighboring towns between November 2006 and April 2007. The interviews took place at a location chosen by the interviewee and lasted for an average of forty-five minutes. Interviewees were selected using a snowballing sampling approach. Initially, a handful of relatively distant acquaintances of either one of two research assistants were invited to be interviewed. The acquaintances were chosen to constitute a diverse group of people in terms of gender, age, and occupation. These interviews were considered preliminary for the purpose of analysis and were not included in the final pool. At the end of each of the initial sets of interviews, people were asked to list five acquaintances who fulfilled three criteria: regular use of the Internet; diverse in terms of gender, age, and occupation; and belonging to relatively different social networks. A randomly selected group of these referrals was contacted. Those who replied positively were interviewed and asked to provide contacts who met the above-mentioned criteria. The process continued until a pool of fifty people was formed. All of the fifty interviewees included in the analysis routinely "surfed" the Web, consumed online news as part of this activity, and relied mostly on newspaper sites for obtaining the news online.

In terms of gender and age, this pool loosely mirrored the adult population who accessed the Internet in Argentina at the time of the study. The gender distribution was 24 women and 26 men (thus, 48% female and 52% male). To assess age distribution, interviewees were divided into three age groups: 18 to 29 years ($n = 23$, 46%), 30 to 49 years ($n = 23$, 46%), and 50 years and older ($n = 4$, 8%); each group was quite evenly divided in terms of gender. Most interviewees were in the workforce at the time of the interview. They represented a broad spectrum of occupations, from traditional managerial and clerical roles and liberal professionals to self-employed copy editors, graphic designers, and computer technicians. A few others were college students, people seeking jobs, or retirees.

The fourth study is designed to complement the ethnography of online news consumers with an account of the most popular stories on Clarín.com, Lanacion.com, and Infobae.com. It looks at the top ten most-clicked stories on these sites and a control group of stories from each site—two randomly selected stories from the top one-third of the home-page, two from the middle section, and two from the bottom third. Data for this study were collected for fourteen weeks from July to November 2006—seven days per week, from Monday through Sunday, for a total of 70 days, or 10 instances of each day of the week. Information about the most-clicked stories was made publicly available on Lanacion.com and Infobae.com during this study. For reasons not relevant to this book, Clarín.com made public the information about its most-clicked stories in the years before and after but not during the period in which this study was conducted. However, I was given access to this information for research purposes. Thus, during the fourteen weeks of data collection, a research assistant visited the offices of Clarín.com once or twice a week and obtained access to the information about the top ten most-clicked stories earlier in that week.

For twenty-eight of the seventy days, data about Lanacion.com and Infobae.com were captured five times a day—at 7:00 AM, 11:00 AM, 3:00 PM, 7:00 PM, and 11:00 PM—to ascertain the evolution of possible patterns as the day went on. For the remaining forty-two days, data about these two sites were collected at 11:00 PM. Because of the above-mentioned access arrangements with Clarín.com, data about that site were collected once a day at the end of the day for all of the seventy days. At the time of the study, the three online newspapers recorded site traffic as it accumulated during the day and reset the counter at midnight of each day. Thus, when the data from the three online sites are compared, only the 11:00 PM figures from Lanacion.com and Infobae.com are used. Although the information collected from Lanacion.com and Infobae.com did not include site traffic between 11:00 PM and midnight, the volume of site usage was normally low at that time of the day, and the analysis procedure allowed for comparing data for twenty-three of the twenty-four hours of the day.

Context Matters

As mentioned in the introduction to this book, there are particular spatial and temporal coordinates that locate the inquiry. They are important because they allow consideration of the potential resonance of the empirical findings in other settings and periods and provide boundary conditions for the applicability of the theory development efforts. Yet the specificity of these coordinates does not preclude the analysis from making contributions that illuminate related empirical dynamics and theoretical problems. Thus, to continue making sense of what might be unique to this spatial and temporal setting and what might be shared across other settings, in the remainder of this section I will present an overview of national and industrial factors of particular relevance to this book's object of inquiry. To put the Argentine situation into comparative perspective, this is followed by a summary of the available evidence about the consumption of online news at work, the expansion of imitation in news production, and the homogenization in the resulting news products in the United States and Western Europe.

Notes on the Recent History of Argentina and Its News Industry

Argentina is located in the Southern Cone of the Americas, together with Bolivia, Brazil, Chile, Paraguay, and Uruguay. At the start of fieldwork in 2005, the country had a population of more than 38 million, which was concentrated in the large urban areas, especially the city of Buenos Aires and its neighboring towns (World Bank, 2008).[7] That year, Argentina had a gross domestic product in excess of $183 billion—55% of which was contributed by the service sector of the economy, 36% by the industrial sector, and 9% by the agricultural sector—and a high level of income inequality (World Bank, 2008).[8]

The country has a relatively modern media system, with more than ten national newspapers and many regional ones, five broadcast television networks, and a multitude of radio stations (Ulanovsky, 2005a, 2005b; Ulanovsky, Merkin, Panno, & Tijman, 2005a, 2005b).[9] The newer media technologies, such as cable television and mobile telephony, have diffused rapidly in recent years, and 28% of the adult population had access to the Internet by 2005 (D'Alessio—IROL, 2006).[10] The newspaper industry is mostly national in scope—with all national newspapers based in Buenos Aires—and its ownership is highly concentrated. As of 2005, *Clarín* and *La Nación* accounted for half of the national market, and the top five players accounted for two-thirds of it (Standard and Poor's, 2005). Furthermore, as Waisbord maintains, the industry shapes the broader media landscape since "morning papers . . . set the agenda for television and radio news" (2006, p. 278). From the vantage point of the developed nations, the Argentine press resonates with what Hallin and Mancini (2004) have called the "Mediterranean" media system of France, Greece, Italy, Portugal, and Spain. Like its Mediterranean counterparts, Argentine newspapers are deeply implicated in the political life of the country, with ideological positions quite identifiable by the citizenry. They have lower levels of professional development than in other countries and are caught between market demands and long-lasting economic and regulatory ties with national and provincial governments.

A distinctive aspect of the Argentine media system is that journalists who have a full-time employment relationship enjoy a comparatively higher degree of employment stability than workers in other occupations, thanks to a labor protection agreement that entitles them to very high compensation in case of "unjustified dismissal."[11] Because massive layoffs of journalists are very costly to news organizations, this has endowed the newsrooms of the leading Argentine print newspapers with higher levels of full-time personnel stability than their counterparts in other nations. In turn, this higher level of stability lessens the feasibility of resource-based explanations of imitation in news production and homogenization in the resulting news products, which have dominated political-economy approaches (Bagdikian, 2004; Baker, 1994, 2002; Klinenberg, 2007; Rosenstiel, 2005).

Although the first few decades of the twentieth century found Argentina in an enviable economic situation, the remainder of that century witnessed a decline in the economy and high instability in the institutions of government, punctuated by recurrent military interventions. The country's most recent military dictatorship lasted from 1976 to 1983. It had devastating effects, such as decimating the country's industrial infrastructure while exploding its foreign debt and severely damaging the cultural fabric of society through a virulent regime of state terrorism. It was also a dark hour for the press, marked by a general stance of complacency toward the military government among the leading media organizations, the disappearance of eighty-eight of the country's journalists, and the incarceration and forced exile of many more of their colleagues (Blaustein & Zubieta, 2006; Comisión Nacional sobre la Desaparición de Personas, 1984; Malharro & López-Gijsberts, 2003; Muraro, 1988; Postolski & Marino, 2005).

Democracy returned to the country in 1983, and with it came an overall sense of hope for an era marked by respect for the rule of law and a trend toward economic prosperity. The administration of President Raúl Alfonsín (1983–1989) largely delivered on the former but was unsuccessful on the latter. For the press, this period meant a progressive awakening to an environment of freedom of speech (Blanco & Germano, 2005; Com, 2005; Landi, 1988; Muraro, 1988; Zuleta-Puceiro, 1993). It also meant a gradual shift that Alves (2005) has aptly called "from lapdog to watchdog," that was also present in the transition to democracy of other Latin American nations during this period, and that strengthened the quality and stability of democratic reforms throughout the region (Benavides,

2000; Hallin & Papathanassopoulos, 2002; S. Hughes, 2006; Lawson, 2002; Skidmore, 1993; Waisbord, 2000, 2006).

This watchdog role reached its zenith during the administration of President Carlos Menem (1989–1999). A seemingly endless stream of corruption cases characterized this administration, and the media played a very aggressive role in bringing this matter to the public's attention (Lavieri, 1996; Peruzzotti, 2005; Ulanovsky, 2005b; Waisbord, 2006). The Menem presidency was also marked by a sweeping neoliberal project based on transferring the ownership of state enterprises to private hands, substantively opening the national economy to the flow of foreign capital, and undertaking bold measures to quell the hyperinflation it had inherited from the previous administration. Paradoxically, given how much the press undermined its power by systematically unveiling instances of corruption among its highest-ranked officials, the Menem presidency triggered a major wave of horizontal consolidation in the media industry by allowing companies with holdings in one sector of the industry to acquire privatized assets in other sectors (Albornoz & Hernández, 2005; Baranchuk, 2005; Fox & Waisbord, 2002b; Martini & Luchessi, 2004; Mastrini & Becerra, 2006; Rossi, 2005). Aided by these privatization and policy choices, *Clarín* transformed itself from a newspaper company to a conglomerate with a dominant position across the media landscape.

Despite a few years of economic growth in the middle portion of his two-term administration, President Menem's neoliberal project ended in massive failure, leaving the country with a high level of unemployment, an increase in foreign debt and budget deficit even though the state had shed numerous large assets, rising insecurity in urban areas, and an overall social discontent with what was widely perceived to be systemic corruption in government. An alliance of opposition parties headed by President Fernando de la Rúa took office in 1999, but it failed to stop the deterioration of the economic and social situation. As a result, the country nearly imploded in late December 2001, triggering its worst economic and political crisis in history. This led to, among other things, a default in the nation's foreign debt, a contraction of 11% in the gross domestic product in 2002, a collapse of the financial system, a succession of five presidents in less than a month, a wave of social unrest, and a collective mood of anger and despair (Auyero, 2007; Blustein, 2005; Garay, 2007; Levitsky & Murillo, 2005a; Mustapic, 2005; Romero, 2002). A transitional administration, headed by President Eduardo Duhalde (2001–2003), took power and managed gradually to bring the economic system to normalcy and contain social unrest.

Presidential elections were held again in 2003. Néstor Kirchner won and remained in office for his full term, through 2007. Fieldwork for this book was conducted during this period. The Kirchner administration enjoyed the upswing in the economy that had started during his predecessor's term, with the gross domestic product increasing at an annual average rate of nearly 9% between 2004 and 2007 (Corporación Latinobarómetro, 2008). Furthermore, the political and financial institutions gradually resumed normal functioning, social unrest decreased (but did not disappear), and a general sentiment of relief and moderate optimism was palpable, both on the street and in the news organizations in which fieldwork was conducted. Of direct relevance to this book is the evidence that during the Kirchner administration there was a tightening of the flow of information from government agencies to the press, and that the government sought to manipulate the press by arbitrarily distributing state advertisement as disincentives for publication of critical news (Blanck, 2007; Blanco & Germano, 2005; Centro de Estudios Legales y Sociales, 2007; Halperín, 2007; Open Society Institute, 2005; O'Donnell, 2007; Reinoso, 2007).[12] Chapter 4 will offer an empirical examination of whether this distinct feature of the press-politics relationship could explain the observed homogenization of print stories during the Kirchner administration.

A Comparative Lens

The phenomenon of news at work appears to be quite prevalent in the United States and Europe. For instance, the 2007 edition of the *State of the News Media* report noted that in America "the Web has gradually become a part of the working day. . . . Workers log on for the bulk of the day [and] come across news and information from time to time" (Journalism.org, 2007). A recent study of "networked workers" indicates that an increasing number of these workers in the United States are using the Internet throughout their work routines (Pew, 2008a). The 2008 edition of the *Pew Research Center Biennial News Consumption Survey* found that "a third of those who regularly go online at work say they get most of their news through the internet on a typical weekday, compared with 12% of those who do not regularly access the internet at work" (Pew, 2008b, p. 30).

Across the Atlantic, an examination of online news consumption during the 2005 general election in the United Kingdom showed that "63% of the total Internet election news audience looked at news during the working day" (Schifferes, Ward, & Lusoli, 2007, p. 12). A study of Internet consumption at work in France, Germany, Italy, Spain, Switzerland, and the United Kingdom conducted in 2007 concluded that "visiting news and information sites is the number one reason European at work users access the Internet" (Online Publishers Association—Europe, 2007, p. 11). Like their peers in Argentina, journalists in other parts of the world seem to be aware of the news-at-work phenomenon and how it affects traffic to their sites. For instance, in his account of how online journalists in the United Kingdom take advantage of site traffic data, MacGregor states, "When spikes in user numbers occur at local lunchtimes around the globe, inferences are made that office workers are the primary site users" (2007, p. 287).

The recent intensification of preexisting monitoring and imitation habits also seems to apply to newsrooms outside Argentina. Commenting about the contemporary media landscape in the United States, Rosenstiel argues that "the explosion in [news] outlets has not meant more reporters doing original shoe-leather reporting. Instead, more people are involved in taking material that is secondhand and repackaging" (2005, p. 701). Thus, he concludes, "This emphasis on synthesis is the new pack journalism" (p. 706). In his ethnography of editorial work on German news sites, Quandt shows that "the journalists constantly monitor the output of their . . . competitors in order to check their news in relation to what the others offer" (2008, p. 90).

In light of this intensification of monitoring and imitation, and as was discussed in a previous section, it is not surprising to find some evidence of homogenization in the resulting news stories. To Schudson, "The stories one reads in one publication are likely to bear a stronger resemblance to the stories in the next publication than they would have in the past" (2003, p. 109). Surveying the recent evolution of the news industry in the United States, the 2008 *State of the News Media* report concludes that "2007 became a year notable for the narrowness of the news agenda" (Journalism.org, 2008). This narrowness is such that a year earlier, in the 2007 edition of the report, we read: "Visitors could spend the good part of a day just following the links for a single news story. If someone were to actually do that, though, the value might be disappointing. With no editing process, related stories automatically pop up from all different outlets. In some cases the reports are nearly identical wire stories carried in different outlets" (Journalism.org, 2007).

Thus, it is not surprising that a study of all the outlets that produced local news in print, broadcast, and online media in the city of Baltimore during one week in June 2009 found out the following:

Much of the "news" people receive contains no original reporting. Fully eight out of ten stories studied simply repeated or repackaged previously published information. And of the stories that did contain new information nearly all, 95%, came from traditional media—most of them newspapers. These stories then tended to set the narrative agenda for most other media outlets.   (JOURNALISM.ORG, 2010, PP. 1–2)

The indication that the main phenomena addressed in this book are not necessarily confined within the Argentine borders does not mean that the local context is irrelevant. On the contrary, it is essential for the analysis to attend to the key features of the country's news industry and of its broader social, cultural, and political environment that are, in principle, most directly related to the purposes of this book and to empirically examine whether they make a difference and, if so, how. Thus, it is possible that the book's main findings are shaped by the industry's national scope, its role as a strong political player, and its levels of ownership concentration, horizontal consolidation, and full-time personnel stability. It is also feasible that *Clarín*'s and *La Nación*'s separation of their print and online newsrooms during this study have had an impact on the findings. It is also possible that the everyday practices and interpretive strategies that people living in Argentina enact to cope with an unstable context and the memories of a recent political and financial crisis have affected the results of the inquiry. Thus, the empirical analyses that follow will be attentive to the potential influence of these and other aspects of the spatial coordinates of this inquiry and, more generally, make sense of the findings from a comparative perspective.

Having laid out the theoretical, methodological, and contextual foundations of this book, the empirical journey begins in the next chapter with an exploration of how the discovery of the news-at-work phenomenon led to some key changes in content production at Clarín.com. These changes, in turn, are critical for making sense of subsequent increases in the rate of monitoring and imitation activity across online and print newsrooms, which will be the subject of chapter 3.

TWO

The Divergent Logics of Hard- and Soft-News Production

Located just a few blocks from Plaza Miserere (and the Once transportation hub, one of the busiest in Buenos Aires), in the heart of the working-class neighborhood of San Cristóbal, the building at the corner of Moreno and La Rioja is quite ordinary. The gray exterior, modernist design, and absence of highly visible corporate logos make the building quite self-effacing. It is virtually impossible for people passing by to know that during the period of fieldwork for this book, it housed the Internet businesses of Argentina's largest and most influential media conglomerate, Grupo Clarín, including Clarín.com. By the end of 2005 this online news site had approximately fifty editorial employees, who occupied most of the fifth floor of the building. The newsroom had a typical configuration of open spaces for the reporters and section editors and a few offices for the senior editors. It was organizationally divided into two units: Ultimo Momento (Latest Moment), devoted to breaking and developing news coverage, and Conexiones (Connections), charged with producing feature stories. The spatial arrangement of the workspace replicated this organizational division. People entered the newsroom through a reception area and, after walking a few steps, could take either a right turn and go to the Ultimo Momento sector or a left turn to the Conexiones one. An approximately twenty-foot-long hallway separated these two units, but the distance that separated their respective material and social environments is far more significant.

The Ultimo Momento sector was materially dense and socially intense. People worked in a relatively small space that housed three rows of desks; each row had six workstations that were quite close to each other. Some desks had multiple screens, and on the sector's periphery, there were several television sets that were nearly always on. The space was cramped and tight but relationally open: people moved around constantly and often shared desks and machines. One person was on call between midnight and 5:00 AM, but most personnel arrived in the morning. During the week, the sector was in full swing by 10:00 AM, with about fifteen people working frantically. The number of personnel began to decrease around 6:00 PM, although a sizable group remained in the newsroom until midnight; staffing levels were lower on the weekend. This was a high-energy work setting during peak hours; most people simultaneously focused on their workstations while talking—and, many times, shouting—to each other. The mix of talking and shouting, the sound from the television sets, and the music coming from the speakers of some computers created a loud and amorphous sound that enveloped the space. There was a climate of tension and stress but also of fun in this sector.

In contrast, the Conexiones sector was materially sparser and socially more relaxed. Most of its personnel worked in a more spacious subdivision that had two rows of workstations that were farther from each other than those at Ultimo Momento. A few of their peers worked in a contiguous subdivision that had a similar layout. In the entire sector, there were few additional machines and only one television set, which was rarely on. The space was more private than that in Ultimo Momento, and people tended to remain at their desks and have a proprietary stance toward their machines. During weekdays, staffers arrived at midmorning and few were present after 6:00 PM. Proportionally fewer workstations were occupied than at Ultimo Momento. Even at peak hours, it was quite calm and silent; people worked individually at their desks, listening to music through headphones and talking to each other far less than their Ultimo Momento counterparts did. A relatively relaxed and subdued work atmosphere prevailed in this sector.

The differences between the material and social environments of the two units are merely the tip of the iceberg of two divergent logics of content production. It is important to examine this divergence because it is critical to understanding the central dynamics involved in the news-at-work transformation. Making sense of these dynamics, in turn, contributes to setting the stage for subsequent analyses of imitation in work practices, the resulting news products, and their appropriation by consumers, topics to be addressed in chapters 3–6. But before moving forward with an account of these divergent logics of content production, it is important to examine how they originated and unfolded prior to the start of the fieldwork period.

The Evolution of Content Production at Clarín.com

As stated in chapter 1, Clarín.com operated largely autonomously from its print counterpart from its inception through the end of this study.[1] But during its first few years, the site's content production efforts were focused on providing an online window into the news that appeared on the pages of the print paper every morning. According to Marcelo Franco, editor of Clarín.com, "We worked a long time in digitizing what was our news heritage [*herencia noticiosa*]" (personal communication, December 14, 2005). This focus was common among the online ventures of traditional media in this period. Most of the online editorial work followed the same temporal patterns of the print newsroom—the period of highest intensity was from midafternoon until midnight. Most of the staffers concentrated on preparing the print content for dissemination in the online environment and then handling its actual publication. According to a Clarín.com journalist, during those years, "To publish was to move the print paper onto the Internet" (personal communication, October 11, 2005).

During the second half of the 1990s, the business environment for new media in Argentina and the world was marked by a seemingly endless stream of resources available to the actors and an incentive to pursue a wide array of projects with the hope that one or more of them would become huge successes. This environment influenced the development of Clarín.com. According to Guillermo Culell, who led the site from its founding until 2006, there was a "need to do almost anything just because we could do it" (personal communication, December 16, 2005). During this period, staffing levels increased, and many innovative endeavors were pursued.

The global burst of the Internet bubble coincided with a serious deterioration of the Argentine economy that culminated in 2001 in the worst financial crisis in the history of the country. In this context, Clarín.com streamlined its newsroom and shifted its content efforts from reproducing the print product and pursuing innovative projects to finding a bottom-line-oriented editorial mix. Culell dubs this stage in the evolution of the site the "phase of rationality," in which "we said, 'Let's focus on what works . . . let's discover what our niche is, what our public is, and work for them'" (ibid.). During the site's early years, usage normally peaked during the morning—in the hours shortly after the content of the print paper was made available online—and decreased substantively thereafter. Inspired in part by a project that delivered news alerts to pagers, by the end of 1990s the site began to provide an incipient stream of news updates during the day. When Culell and his colleagues started to systematically track the patterns of site usage, looking for clues about audience behavior, they "discovered" that after "our offer of news updates increased, the [site usage] curve [began to] plateau in the afternoon" (ibid.). They subsequently increased the volume and frequency of publication during the day, which led to an expansion of the hours when site usage was heavy. There was also an overall growth in traffic. Site usage remained at a much lower level between the late-evening and early-morning hours. Moreover, unlike what usually happens with print newspaper circulation, site traffic was substantially lower during the weekend.

These findings led Culell and his colleagues to conclude that their "niche" was people who were at work—expressed by the Monday-through-Friday, morning-through-afternoon temporal patterning of site traffic. This realization was a defining moment in the evolution of the site "because we began to imagine our public. Before that moment, our reader did not have a profile. . . . It was a milestone [*hito importante*]: now the reader ha[d] a face, a culture, a location" (Guillermo Culell, personal communication, December 16, 2005). These coordinates meant that, as a Clarín.com staffer put it, "Our prime time is 10 AM to 6 PM . . . people who are working, and the only way of being informed is via a Web page" (personal communication, August 26, 2005). They reasoned that consumers looked at online news sites in the midst of their busy work routines and seemed to be driven by an interest in having a quick summary of what was going on in the world and some attention-grabbing content for a moment of break from work.[2] They came to this second conclusion after seeing the high level of demand for short and snappy television chronicles that began to appear on the site.

In May 2004, to address a public that was believed to get the news at work, the top editors at Clarín.com launched a design, organizational, and editorial transformation that created the division between Ultimo Momento and Conexiones. The homepage was redesigned by dividing it into the two sections: Ultimo Momento was placed on the left side of the screen and received 60% of the space, and Conexiones occupied the remaining 40% on the right side (fig. 2.1).[3] Organizationally and editorially, the newsroom and news output were restructured into two units with these respective names. Ultimo Momento was allocated the majority of full-time personnel, who were tasked with producing an updated and comprehensive supply of news. Conexiones had a smaller number of full-time employees, who were charged with creating eye-catching feature stories that did not require urgent dissemination. Clarín.com staffers often resorted to notions of opposites when talking about this division between Ultimo Momento and Conexiones. The most recurrent notion was the idea that the news of the former was "hard" and that of the latter was "soft." For instance, in response to a question about cooperation between journalists in the two units after this division took place, a Clarín.com writer stated, "There isn't much possibility of exchange because [Conexiones] is much softer [news] and Ultimo Momento is much harder [news]" (personal communication, August 12, 2005).

The main parameters taken into consideration to separate the work of Ultimo Momento and Conexiones, and the representations used by the actors to make sense of this separation, converge with scholarly discussions about the distinction between hard and soft news. That is, in the present case this distinction is a construct of both the actors and the analyst. This distinction has been approached from a number of traditions of inquiry, including social history of the press (Curran, Douglas, & Whannel, 1980; H. Hughes, 1981; Ponce de Leon, 2002; Schiller, 1981; Schudson, 1978), sociology of news production (Fishman, 1980; Tuchman, 1978; Turow, 1983), studies of discourse and narrative (Bird & Dardenne, 1988; Gamson, 2001; Marley, 2007; P. White, 1997), and political communication (Baum, 2003; Delli Carpini & Williams, 2008; Patterson, 2000; Plasser, 2005). Although scholars have characterized the distinction in various ways (Baum, 2007; Bennett, 2003; Carroll, 1985; Fishman, 1980; Patterson, 2000; Tuchman 1978), a common denominator of most research is the notion that what distinguishes hard and soft news is found not in the essence of the reported events but in the social factors that shape news making. B. Zelizer concludes that in the initial waves of news production studies, "hard and soft news . . . were distinguishable not because they reflected inherent attributes of news but because they made scheduling more predictable and manageable" (2004, p. 66).

Scholars also assert that the difference between hard and soft news is partly one of temporality (H. Hughes, 1981; K. H. Jamieson & Campbell, 1983; Schudson, 1986; D. Scott & Gobetz, 1992; Smith, 1990). According to Tuchman, "The structuring of time [in the newsroom] influences the

2.1 Top portion of the homepage of Clarín.com, May 6, 2004. © *Clarín*.

assessment of occurrences as news events" (1978, p. 51). Thus, researchers have shown that a distinctive trait of hard news is news makers' understanding that they must communicate about a particular event within the news cycle they are working on—or, in Tuchman's words, the "urgency of dissemination." In contrast, "soft news stories need not be timely" (Tuchman 1978, p. 51) because journalists see them as open to communication in various news cycles without detriment to their newsworthiness. These temporal patterns are the constructions of actors: whether to treat an event as hard or as soft news depends somewhat on how actors frame their coverage in relation to the temporal rhythms of their work practices. In his study of a local television station, Turow found that coverage of an event can move from hard to soft, or vice versa, partly as a result of temporality shifts: "A few staffers noted that sometimes soft news could be 'turned' into hard news by 'the handling,' that is, by making it seem urgent" (1983, p. 117).

In relation to this issue of temporal patterns, the volume and frequency of publication of breaking and developing news at Clarín.com increased during the first few years of the 2000s and greatly intensified after the May 2004 transformation. "Speed was an imperative . . . that emerged naturally over time; it was like a snowball," commented Guillermo Culell, adding that "for competitive reasons, we [also] began to see who published first" (personal communication, December 16, 2005). This was because constant publication during the day had become the industry norm circa 2005. A Clarín.com editor stated, "Since the launch of the Ultimo Momento section, the temporal factor is key, the famous 'immediacy' . . . is [part of] the rules of the game in any online news site now" (personal communication, December 19, 2005).

Interviews with staffers at Lanacion.com confirmed that constant publishing of news stories during the day became the norm in the Argentine online news landscape. For instance, Alejo Vetere, sportswriter at Lanacion.com, recalled that when he joined the site in 2000, the homepage was "an index of the print edition. There was a small box that fitted a couple of lines of rotating breaking news. . . . Throughout the day we could put 15 stories [in that box], with no content other than headline and lead." This was because publishing breaking news "was not assigned any importance. . . . We were ten, twelve staffers [in the online newsroom]. We started around noon, already focusing on the next day's print edition. . . . There were one or two people devoted to updating the site during the day." In contrast, in 2006, "We are around twenty-five journalists in the online newsroom. Twenty-one of us are devoted to updating the site [during the day and] creating original content, and only four staffers work on putting the [next day's] print edition online during the evening" (personal communication, December 19, 2006).

Vetere's remarks describe a trajectory in the evolution of hard-news production that encapsulates some themes that are important in this chapter. In the first few years of online news, the temporal patterns of work replicated those of print journalism, and most work during the day was in support of publishing the print newspaper content, which in turn took place once a day and at a fixed and predictable time. A few years later, the temporal patterns of work were extended by starting in the early-morning hours; the hours of high activity shifted from midmorning to late afternoon and coincided with the peak of access during regular business hours; most of the content published was not coming from the print paper; and the act of publishing became continuous, its frequency unfixed and its timing unpredictable. The next section describes this transformation in greater detail.

The Production of Hard News at Ultimo Momento

The pace of work is relentless at the Ultimo Momento unit: journalists author most stories in less than half an hour, and each journalist is expected to produce six or seven new stories every eight-hour working day and update any of those stories when new relevant information surfaces. This high speed is tied to intersecting beliefs about the obsolescence of hard news, the pace of the online medium, and the expectations of the intended public. Journalists hold the notion that hard news "begins aging after two hours [on the Web] . . . and in four hours it has aged completely" (personal communication, July 28, 2005). This notion is linked to more general assumptions about the medium: "The Internet equals speed . . . and checking to see what is happening now" (María Arce, personal communication, November 2, 2005). In turn, these ideas are coupled with a belief that the public looks at the site repeatedly during the day and wants updated information on each new visit. For instance, "Supposedly the person who went out for lunch . . . goes back to the office and wants to see if there is anything new [on the site]" (personal communication, July 28, 2005). "There are people at work who are hitting the F5 'refresh' [key], so we have to change [the news] constantly" (personal communication, October 11, 2005). Sports editor Facundo Quiroga says that constant publishing is important to "demonstrate to the person who consumes our product that there is movement and change." He adds that "I have the chance to rotate, change, and create a journalism of vertigo, movement, and give [the public the equivalent of] fifteen newspapers at the same time. . . . If you demonstrate cleverness, movement, and change, you gain the respect and the trust of the [public]" (personal communication, December 15, 2005).

In this context, speed becomes both an editorial criterion and an evaluation metric. Speed is an editorial criterion because immediacy is an important factor in determining the newsworthiness of a story. According to an Ultimo Momento writer, "I look for what's new. . . . It's what's happening now. . . . It has this plus that you are not telling the news after it took place but at the same time the event is taking place. . . . To the person who's leaving his office, it won't matter if there was a train or bus accident two hours earlier; what matters to him is if he'll be able to go on the street and undertake his commute" (personal communication, July 5,

2005). As Clarín.com founding director Guillermo Culell stated above, speed also becomes an evaluation metric, because journalists assess their performance in part by regularly checking to see whether the competition has published a given story before they do. Competing by time acquires such intensity that sometimes journalists set the publicly available time of publication of a given story ahead of the actual publication time by ten minutes or so. Furthermore, journalists maintain that the competition engages in this practice too. When asked whether she looks at the competition after publishing a story, Ultimo Momento's María Arce says, "Time of publication is the first thing we look at. But on some sites . . . the time of publication is not the real time. It has happened to me to look at a site at 10:30 AM, and a story is not published. I look again at 10:40 and the story is published with a 10:05 [time of publication]" (personal communication, November 2, 2005).

The combination of high speed of publication and high volume of output contributes to the generation of significant levels of stress at Ultimo Momento. Staffer Daniel Accornero says that his job "wears you out mentally. . . . At the print paper the only stressful moment is when you have to publish, which is once or twice a day. . . . Here it is constant. Something happens and it has to be published as soon as possible" (personal communication, September 12, 2005). In addition, the material and social environments—marked by the important presence of media artifacts, a significant level of ambient noise, and a high-adrenaline atmosphere—further add to increased levels of stress among workers. This is more noticeable among new staffers. One writer says, "When I started I said [to myself]: I can't stand three television sets, the radio. . . . I was going crazy, I couldn't write" (personal communication, July 5, 2005). She adds that, like many of her peers, she became accustomed to working in this environment over time. But there seems to be a residual level of stress that does not disappear with adaptation to the work conditions and that has to do with the difficulty of slowing down. "You are never well, because when there is nothing going on, you want something to happen" (editor, personal communication, December 15, 2005).

The pace of work at Ultimo Momento leaves little time for the conventional information-gathering and story-authoring practices of traditional journalism. Most of the information featured in Ultimo Momento stories does not come from sources, or even from the print *Clarín*, but from other media. Staffers rely largely on wire copy and add content gathered through constant monitoring of television, radio, and online outlets. Furthermore, this content is used as a source for ideas about what stories to write and how to do it. Sources are contacted sporadically and to confirm uncertain or contradictory evidence rather than to gather new data or generate a new angle. Once the information for a given story is gathered, authoring efforts focus primarily on the parts of the story published on the homepage, namely, the headline and the lead. Ultimo Momento personnel believe that the headline and the lead are the main vehicles for conveying a distinct editorial message and for differentiating themselves from their competitors, in addition to keeping their coverage fresh and complete. This is related in part to the belief among staffers that the consumer of hard news on the Web wants only to glance at an extensive spectrum of headlines and leads in a couple of minutes or less and has little time to devote to reading those stories. Marcos Foglia, the unit's editor, claims, "Few people really read what's published; they read the headlines and that's it" (personal communication, December 13, 2005). Thus, not surprisingly, there is comparatively less energy devoted to the body of the text. Furthermore, most of the authoring practices involved with the body of the text consist of editing already-existent copy, "stitching" materials from multiple media into a coherent whole, and updating the content after new events take place without altering the rest. The following vignette illustrates typical content-gathering and authoring practices:

Editor tells reporter by instant messenger (IM) to update a story about [an airline company's] pilots who will go on strike tomorrow. Reporter gets the existing Clarín .com story from the homepage, copies, and pastes it into a Word file. . . . Then he gets two more stories from the wires. He combines them and writes a few sentences to unify their texts, then writes the lead and the headline, and sends them by IM to the editor. While he waits for the editor's response, he rereads the existing Clarín.com story and looks for additional wires. A few minutes later, the editor sends a new headline and lead by IM, and the reporter changes them in his Word file. Then, he goes to the publishing system, looks for the existing story, and copies and pastes the new headline, lead, and body of the text. One minute later the editor sends him the following message by IM: "They just canceled the strike. F——!" Reporter curses by IM, too, and asks, "What do we do now? Do I change this and write the text again?" Editor replies: "Just put that they canceled tomorrow's strike." Reporter then modifies the headline and the lead in the publishing system. Then he goes back to the Word file and makes changes—mostly having to do with verb tense—in only two paragraphs. This is now an old story, and the news is that the strike has been canceled. The rest of the text remains the same.
(FIELD NOTE, JUNE 5, 2005)

In addition to showing the primacy of other media in information gathering and the focus on the headline and the lead regarding story authoring, this vignette also sheds light on the important role played by IM in the communication infrastructure that supports work in the Ultimo Momento unit. Staffers use IM constantly to share information about stories such as alerts about new and potentially newsworthy items. IM is frequently mixed with oral exchanges to the point that at the beginning of fieldwork, the research assistants could not understand the meaning of many oral exchanges until it was determined that utterances were in reply to statements that had been made seconds earlier via IM. The use of this tool is so prevalent that when a virus transmitted via IM infected several computers at Clarín.com and forced a temporary interruption in its use, the frequency and volume of publishing decreased dramatically. This is because IM is crucial for fast and multidirectional information sharing in the newsroom. An Ultimo Momento staffer addresses the issue of speed by noting, "Although we have an [email] folder with stories that are gathered so that there is a record [of their existence] . . . the immediacy of news forces us to use a faster system . . . such as IM" (personal communication, November 28, 2005). One of his colleagues comments on the issue of multidirectionality: "[IM] is key, precisely because it brings a text simultaneously to five people without having them hover around a single computer or even move around, which is critical to us because it means time savings" (personal communication, July 28, 2005).

These patterns of work at Ultimo Momento are shaped in part by the processes of news production at *Clarín* and the variations in the supply and demand of information at different times of the day and days of the week. Although the Ultimo Momento unit is operationally autonomous from the relevant desks in the *Clarín* newsroom, like all of Clarín.com, the unit feels the presence of the print paper directly and indirectly. Furthermore, this relationship is marked by a tension between alignment and differentiation. On the one hand, and especially in relation to national and international public affairs stories, Ultimo Momento staffers try to "maintain the same line as the 'mother medium' [*la misma línea que el medio madre*]" (Marcos Foglia, personal communication, December 13, 2005). On the other hand and within this constraint, they also aim to assert their distinctive take on the news based on the premise that they publish in a different technological medium and are accessed by a public with expectations adapted to it and to the distinctive "at work" dominant consumption circumstance.

This tension is manifested differently at various times of the day. During the week, staffers leave the Ultimo Momento unit at midnight and close the day by preparing a news budget for the following day. The next person to arrive in the unit does so at 4:00 AM and is charged with updating the budget in relation to events that occurred after midnight.

The print paper's content dominates the editorial offerings of Ultimo Momento during the early-morning hours, in part in relation to its own journalistic importance and in part because there are very few new national news items in television, radio, and the wires by then. The influx of people into the newsroom begins to increase gradually toward 7:00 AM. The dual focus of the editorial work at that time illustrates the tension between alignment and differentiation mentioned above. On the one hand, there is an attempt to follow up on any stories published in the paper about events that are still unfolding during the morning hours. A staffer who works the early-morning shift reports, "If the paper opened a story . . . we have the obligation to close it, regardless of the value we assign to the topic. . . . It is a way of sewing [*surcir*] the relationship . . . between the two media" (personal communication, July 28, 2005). But, on the other hand, a key goal at that time of the day is to begin publishing new stories that did not appear in the print paper. Thus, the same staffer also says, "There is a concern to try to get our own or new lead story during the early-morning hours. The idea is that the lead story from the paper will not be the lead story of the site beyond 9:00 or 9:30 AM" (ibid.).

During the week, the time period from midmorning to midafternoon is the most intense one at Ultimo Momento because most staffers are present; most information is available through the wire services, television, radio, and the Web; and more site usage takes place then than at other times during the day. Because this triple increase in personnel, information, and audience coincides with a period during which the news agenda is only beginning to form in the print newsroom, it is not surprising that Ultimo Momento's differentiation efforts are at their peak then. An Ultimo Momento editor usually attends the print newsroom "noon meeting," but because the next day's top print stories are still in an embryonic stage, the information that emerges from this meeting has relatively limited impact on the online agenda at that time.

The hours from midafternoon until midnight see a gradual decrease in pace, a change of focus, and a progressive alignment of the top stories with their counterparts slated to appear in the next morning's print paper. The Ultimo Momento newsroom begins to empty as fewer newsworthy items show up on the wires and other media and the bulk of the public goes home from work and decreases their consumption of online news. Fewer stories are published during these hours than in the earlier periods of the day, with the exception of news about sports events that take place in the late afternoon and early evening. Thus, editorial efforts are partly refocused on "closing" stories that had been left open earlier in the day. "We try to close them in the sense that if there was a picket [*un piquete*] during the day, by 8:00 PM the story does not say 'picketers [*piqueteros*] interrupt the traffic on this street,' but the text instead says 'picketers interrupted the traffic from this to that hour'" (staffer, personal communication, October 20, 2005).

The other major marker of this period in the day has to do with the print paper. An Ultimo Momento editor attends the "afternoon meeting" of the print newsroom and reports back to his online colleagues about the anticipated editorial offer in the next morning's paper. This information exerts an indirect influence on online staffers, who pay attention to it and avoid deviation from the framing and content of the relevant print stories. Furthermore, in the case of news that the print newsroom deems particularly sensitive or that deals with events still unfolding and about which there is uncertainty about important facts, the influence is sometimes more direct in that it is channeled through conversations between print and online editors.

These weekly work patterns change during the weekend. There are fewer people in the newsroom, and the overall volume of news production decreases accordingly. This coincides with a considerable decrease in site usage during the weekend. Moreover, the published content changes in character too: it is dominated by news about sports events—in particular, soccer. Unlike during the week, when the ideal-typical consumer is imagined to access the site while at work, the weekend consumer is thought to access from home during breaks from leisurely activity. Staffer Miguel Middono says, "Things change over the weekend. . . . Most people look at the site from their homes. . . . On Sunday lots of people go out in the afternoon, so perhaps they look at the site in the evening to see the results of the sports games, the rest of the headlines, and that's it. One story that is always among the most viewed [on Sunday] is a kind of summary of the [sports] results over the weekend" (personal communication, October 18, 2005).

Although this logic of content production characterizes Ultimo Momento, a remarkably different one dominates the work of staffers located on the other side of the hallway.

The Production of Soft News at Conexiones

Consider the following description of a segment of a typical content production sequence at Conexiones:

10:30: Reporter #1 is writing a story on umbilical cord blood banks. She has already written about four pages in a Word file. She types a new paragraph, stops, reads what she's written, and continues writing. She had conducted interviews at a pediatric hospital the previous day and had begun writing the story this morning at 9:00. . . .

11:00: She continues reading the text, adding information, and making changes. . . .

11:35: She gives the story to reporter #2 for feedback. A physician whom she had interviewed calls to double-check the accuracy of technical information. "I'll publish it at 1:00 PM, so I'm sending it to you right away by email." She then approaches the graphic designer to see if the story illustration is ready and sends the story to her editor. Then she does a Google search for "*fecunditas,*" "biocell," and "bio cell." . . . Reporter #2 gives her feedback, and they discuss options for the headline. . . . Physician calls back to suggest changes, and they talk about them. When the conversation is over, she inputs some of the changes and sends the revised version by IM to reporter #2. They work together on the final version. **(FIELD NOTE, JUNE 13, 2005)**

This opening vignette provides a glimpse of how different the work practices among Conexiones staffers are from those of their Ultimo Momento counterparts. In this case, those differences are evident with respect to speed of production, volume of output, and information-gathering and story-authoring routines. First, Conexiones journalists author most stories in more than one workday, and each staffer is expected to produce two or three new stories every week. Moreover, these stories are rarely updated. Thus, someone who can produce a story in four hours is "very expeditious" (Conexiones writer, personal communication, August 12, 2005); an article that takes only two hours is "published in record time" (former Conexiones staffer, personal communication, October 13, 2005); and "what [Ultimo Momento staffers] can do in half an hour or fifteen minutes takes us a whole day" (former Conexiones editor, personal communication, December 21, 2005).

Timeliness does not shape newsworthiness or work schedules at Conexiones, and the stories are usually considered "atemporal." Editors and reporters believe that their public wants appealing stories, regardless of their ties to that day's occurrences. Moreover, there is a two-step fixed publication sequence during the day. First, an initial set of stories is published at midnight for consumption the following morning. Then, a second batch is published between noon and the early-afternoon hours in an effort to target consumption practices that take place between the lunch break and the end of the workday. In addition, once a story is ready, it is not uncommon to change its planned publication date, depending on the story inventory. As the vignette above demonstrates, all of this contributes to create an environment in which a staffer has time to do research, interview sources, and write a long story.

These patterns of speed of production and volume of output are tied to interrelated ideas about what the public of Conexiones wants from its stories and the character of this section as an editorial product. Conversations with Conexiones staffers reveal two different traits that the imagined public is believed to expect from the stories: appealing and entertaining material in some cases and subject expertise and thematic depth in others. Thus, for instance, a former Conexiones editor defines readers as "people between twenty and forty years old who are in their [work] offices or are students" and notes that "the stories are 'lighter' than the hard news [of Ultimo Momento]" (field note, June 9, 2005). But the consumer is sometimes also represented as someone with specific topical interests and a certain level of expectation regarding the thematic expertise on the part of the writer.

This mix of entertainment and depth in terms of consumer expectations is coupled with an analogy encountered in many conversations with Conexiones staffers. Their section is, as one editor put it, "like the magazine of Clarín.com" (personal communication, August 2, 2005). Like the Sunday magazine of a print newspaper, Conexiones mixes an array of light pieces and a handful of deeper features. Staffers comment about the magazine analogy when referring both to design and to content issues. Jimena Pique, a designer at Clarín.com, says, "In the Conexiones [part of the homepage], the [May 2004] redesign gave much more importance to the brand by means of a magazine vibe [*onda de revista*], to differentiate it well from what is the hot news [of Ultimo Momento]" (personal communication, September 15, 2005). A Conexiones writer comments, "This magazine imprint shelters us [*el impronte de revista nos ampara*] and allows us to play with a certain margin [of action] or certain things that in [the case of] the purer news it is not possible [to do]. They [referring to Ultimo Momento staffers] can't [do that] because they have to fulfill their obligations regarding the present time [*tienen una actualidad que cumplir*]" (personal communication, December 13, 2005).

In light of these patterns of speed of publication and volume of output and the relatively fixed and predictable production schedule, Conexiones personnel experience a much higher degree of control over when to author and publish than their Ultimo Momento peers. For instance, a Conexiones writer says, "I would never like to work at Ultimo Momento. . . . I don't like to rush. . . . They can't move from their seats [during their shift], and we can. I manage my own time" (personal communication, October 20, 2005). This, in turn, contributes to comparatively lower levels of stress among the staffers. A former editor reflects on the climate in the unit by noting, "On our side there is a satisfaction [that arises from] enjoying our kind of work, the style we can have, the freedom we have. Ours is a nice way of practicing journalism" (personal communication, December 21, 2005).

The information-gathering and story-authoring practices of Conexiones resemble those of print journalism. In terms of information gathering, although staffers rely to a significant extent on content that originated in other media, they also undertake conventional sourcing practices on a regular basis, as the vignette above shows. They have to have at least three sources per story that are seen as key suppliers of new information in addition to having a confirmatory role. The regular use of sources is coupled with a slower speed of production than at Ultimo Momento. Marcela Mazzei, a former Conexiones staffer, states, "At Conexiones . . . there was a demand that each story have several quotes . . . which is why there was more time to [write them]" (personal communication, October 13, 2005). For other media, Conexiones staffers mostly use online search engines to find additional data about a specific issue rather than to collect copy or come up with story ideas. Furthermore, these other media are accessed based on authoring needs and not on a constant basis.

In terms of story authoring, Ultimo Momento staffers focus mostly on the elements featured on the homepage. Their Conexiones peers—like most journalists in traditional media—concentrate largely on the body of the story, which is accessed by clicking either on the homepage or on a referring link. They spend a smaller but important part of their effort on the headline. But, unlike their Ultimo Momento peers, the key goal in constructing the headline is to find a phrase that entices the site users to view the main body of the story rather than to condense the main editorial message into a few words.

The relationships with the relevant units in the print paper are different in two ways from those prevalent at Ultimo Momento. Whereas the latter navigates a fine line between alignment and differentiation that begins with trying to gain a sense of what their print colleagues are up to at critical points during the workday, Conexiones personnel intentionally avoid contact with their print colleagues: "With the print paper, zero [relationship]" (Conexiones staffer, personal communication, August 2, 2005). Furthermore, those in charge of hard-news production feel an obligation not to deviate markedly from the print paper coverage—especially regarding sensitive issues. But their online counterparts who produce soft news aim at the opposite, to the point that "if [a story] is published by the print paper, it will not be featured [in Conexiones].

Once, the Municipality of the City of Buenos Aires put together an exhibit of the 1940s. I visited it [to gather information for a story] . . . on a
Friday, but on Saturday there was a story [in *Clarín*], so I did not do one
[for Clarín.com]" (Conexiones staffer, personal communication, October 20, 2005).

Finally, there are also significant differences between the production
practices at Conexiones and at Ultimo Momento in the use of IM and
the temporal structuring of work. As the vignette above illustrates, Conexiones staffers also utilize IM in their daily routines. However, they do
so less extensively than their Ultimo Momento colleagues. Moreover, as
additional analyses in the next section will show, when they do use IM,
they use it less for editorial purposes and more for social purposes. These
include exchanging information about personal and professional matters
that have no connection to specific news production tasks. Furthermore,
as stated at the beginning of this chapter, most staffers are present between the midmorning and midafternoon hours, from Monday to Friday.
It is quite unusual to find Conexiones personnel in the newsroom during
the early-morning or late-evening hours or on the weekend. In light of
the prevailing speed and volume patterns of production and the fixed
publication schedule, it is possible for the staffers to actually avoid being
present in the newsroom at these less socially desirable times and days.

The Divergent Logics of Content Production

Two markedly divergent logics of content production emerge from
the accounts of the social and material organization of work at Ultimo
Momento and Conexiones. The work in the two units exhibits substantive differences in a wide array of dimensions, including the temporal
patterns of editorial production, the material and social environment,
the information-gathering and story-authoring practices, the representations of the intended public, the uses of IM as a critical newsroom communication tool, the relationships with the relevant units in the *Clarín*
newsroom, and the varying rhythms in relation to time of day and week
versus weekend. Such a divergence in the logics of news production suggests two very different kinds of journalism within a single organization
and site.

Quantitative analyses of the field notes were performed to more precisely determine the magnitude of the differences between Ultimo Momento and Conexiones in four of the dimensions of work examined
above: temporal patterns of content production, provenance of infor-

mation, parts of the story worked on by journalists, and use of IM. (See appendix A for more details on the procedure.)

First, each recorded instance in the field notes that provides information about how long it took for a story to become authored—from assignment to publication—was identified. The analysis reveals that 85% of Ultimo Momento stories took less than thirty minutes to author, and 79% of Conexiones stories required more than one workday (table 2.1). Furthermore, whereas 96% of the stories at Ultimo Momento were produced in less than two hours, only 6% of the Conexiones articles were authored so rapidly, which is a significant[4] ($p < .01$) difference of ninety percentage points.

Second, every field note that indicates that a piece of information was used for a story was analyzed for whether the information came from a source, other media, or *Clarín*. Most information-gathering practices relied on other media in both cases, but Ultimo Momento personnel used sources more than six times less often than their Conexiones peers—a significant ($p < .01$) twenty-one percentage points less (table 2.1).

Third, when a journalist is recorded as working on a story, each mention in the field notes of whether she was working on the headline, the lead, the suprahead, or the main body of the story was identified. The contrast is remarkable: when Ultimo Momento staffers worked on a story, they dealt with homepage material nearly nine out of ten times, in contrast to slightly more than three out of ten for their Conexiones colleagues, a significant ($p < .01$) difference of fifty-seven percentage points (table 2.1).

Fourth, when there is a mention in the field notes of a journalist using IM, the analysis examined whether she used it for editorial purposes (to exchange story content, links, and files), for social ones (to chat about noneditorial issues), or in a fashion that did not permit the analyst to distinguish between the two options. Ultimo Momento staffers used IM editorially significantly ($p < .01$) more often than their Conexiones peers: 70% versus 41% of the time, respectively (table 2.1). Even if one assumes that all of the unclassifiable instances of IM use by Conexiones staffers were editorial uses—thus increasing the proportion of editorial IM use by those staffers to 56% (the sum of 41% and 15%)—the contrast with the 70% editorial use of IM by Ultimo Momento staffers is still significant ($p < .01$).

In light of how markedly the two logics of content production diverge at Clarín.com, it is not surprising that the staffers are aware of the differences between them. They mention these differences in observations and interviews and in relation to my rendition of their situation during

Table 2.1.   Quantitative Differences in Hard- and Soft-News Production at Clarín.com

	Ultimo Momento	Conexiones
Temporal patterns of content production (amount of time utilized for story completion)		
Up to 30 minutes*	85% (105)	2% (1)
More than 30 minutes but less than 2 hours	11% (13)	4% (2)
More than 2 hours but less than a workday	3% (4)	15% (8)
More than a workday*	1% (1)	79% (41)
Total	100% (123)	100% (52)
Provenance of story information (origin of the content used for authoring tasks)		
Sources*	4% (17)	25% (49)
Other media*	88% (340)	70% (138)
Clarín	8% (30)	6% (11)
Total	100% (387)	101% (198)
Time spent by journalists on different parts of the story		
Headline, lead, and suprahead*	88% (365)	31% (32)
Main body of the story*	12% (49)	69% (70)
Total	100% (414)	100% (102)
Newsroom communication tools (how journalists utilize instant messenger)		
Editorial use*	70% (281)	41% (46)
Social use*	28% (114)	44% (50)
Analyst cannot distinguish	2% (7)	15% (17)
Total	100% (402)	101% (113)

Note: Rows that have an asterisk indicate significant ($p < .01$) differences between the two units. Numbers in parentheses are counts.

and after talks when preliminary findings were given in the newsroom. For instance, during an interview with an Ultimo Momento staffer two days after giving a presentation of preliminary findings to several of the site's editors (which included an earlier version of table 2.1 but without the quantitative data), he says, "The little table is great [*el cuadrito está bárbaro*]; [the two units] are very different. The only point of connection is that all the work and all the content come together on the same page. There is no other point of contact" (personal communication, July 28, 2005).

Actors' awareness of the differences between the units is often expressed through metaphors of opposites. In addition to the widespread representations of hard and soft news and the already-mentioned analogy of Conexiones as the "magazine" of Clarín.com (which was tied to the implicit notion that Ultimo Momento was the equivalent of the site's "newspaper"), they often refer to the news of Ultimo Momento as "hot," distinguishing it from that of Conexiones, which is "cold." In the same metaphor of hot and cold, Clarín.com staffers commonly refer to the part of the homepage allocated to Ultimo Momento as the "warm zone" (*la zona cálida*) and to the Conexiones one as the "cold" or "gray zone" (*la zona fría o gris*).

These representations evoke gender differences between Ultimo Momento and Conexiones that have both demographic and symbolic dimensions. In traditional media organizations hard-news desks tend to have more male than female journalists, a pattern that is reversed somewhat among their soft-news counterparts. This also applies to Clarín .com, where Ultimo Momento has a greater proportion of male journalists than Conexiones. These gender differences, as in traditional newsrooms, also manifest themselves symbolically. On the one hand, the work at Ultimo Momento deals with "hard" subjects, and the pace of the work requires a degree of fortitude that tends to be associated with masculinity in everyday culture. Moreover, the informal exchanges among staffers at the end of the day, when the pace of work decreases and the ambience is more relaxed, sometimes acquire a tone that makes the two female research assistants feel uncomfortable. On the other hand, the tasks at Conexiones address topics in a "soft" way, and the very name of the unit stresses social connectivity—two traits often symbolically linked in the popular imagination to femininity.

Actors often elaborate on the character and consequences of the differences between Ultimo Momento and Conexiones. Some focus on content matters: "I always make a joke with the Conexiones people because, to me, both parties have a serious problem: we have the topics and they have the time to deal with these topics" (Ultimo Momento staffer, personal communication, July 28, 2005). Others link content to differences in practice. For example, "There is little professional relationship [between the two units] because the topics are totally different" (Ultimo Momento staffer, personal communication, October 18, 2005). Still others emphasize the practices: "[Ultimo Momento] has routines [*mecánica de laburo*] very different from the rest" (Clarín.com editor, personal communication, December 15, 2005). "There are two different kinds of journalism" (Ultimo Momento writer, personal communication, October 27, 2005). "[The routines] are completely independent. We don't send them a news budget nor do they send one to us" (former Conexiones staffer, personal communication, December 21, 2005).

These perceptions produce a situation in which most workers are quite comfortable with the two units remaining operationally separate. They lead also to the emergence of different cultures that sometimes have an "us versus them" flavor. An Ultimo Momento staffer comments:

There is a difference in the work, but also a jealousy matter. [Some Ultimo Momento workers] go to play soccer with [some Conexiones staffers], but each one has an image of the other that is not accurate. They might have their problems as much as we have ours, but . . . they see that we are a bunch of nervous wrecks [*histéricos*], highly anxious [*neurotizados*] about the immediacy of news, and we see that they are slugs [*un pachorraje*], that they make news whenever it pleases them. This is exaggerating, but these kinds of [opinions] exist. (PERSONAL COMMUNICATION, AUGUST 2, 2005)

Concluding Remarks

This account of Clarín.com shows that there are major differences between the two units devoted to the production of hard and soft news. These differences stand in contrast to a dominant strain in the literature that highlights the existence of shared practices and principles that cut across hard and soft news. This theme emerges when four ways in which scholars blur the boundaries that separate hard and soft news are pulled together. First, some sociological analyses underscore the political and cultural significance of soft news (Curran et al., 1980; A. Daniels, 1981; H. Hughes, 1981; Turow, 1983). Second, political communication scholars address a turn away from hard news and a trend toward a softening in the reporting of hard news (Bennett, 2003; Gans, 2003; Hamilton, 2004; Patterson, 2000; Sparks, 2000; Zaller, 2003). Triggered by such findings, studies have examined the circumstances in which soft-news outlets convey public affairs content—what some assume is at the heart of hard news—to consumers who are presumably uninterested in it (Baum, 2002, 2003; Brewer & Cao, 2006; Delli Carpini & Williams, 2001, 2008; Prior, 2002, 2007; Young & Tisinger, 2006). Third, scholarship has explored the importance of narrative configurations in both hard and soft news (Bird & Dardenne, 1988; Gamson, 2001). Fourth, researchers have also challenged a stark break between hard and soft news—and, by implication, generated the image of a common ground between them—by looking at shared traits not just between them but also with the fringes of mainstream media, such as talk shows and tabloid publications (Bird, 1992; Deuze, 2005; Ehrlich, 1996; Gamson, 1994; Grindstaff, 2002; Spragens, 1995).

Together, these four lines of research create the impression that the difference between hard and soft news rests against a background of commonalities. One way to frame this issue, formulated independently by two scholars, is that of "differences of degree but not of kind." Discussing hard- and soft-news programs in the context of political communication research, Baum states, "Clearly, at least in some instances, the difference between soft and hard news is one of degree rather than kind" (2002, p. 92). And to B. Zelizer, narrative analyses of hard and soft news "showed how all kinds of journalism were part of the same family and that the differences between them were differences of degree rather than kind" (2004, p. 131).

In contrast to the dominant image of differences of degree rather than kind from the scholarship on hard and soft news, my account of the differences between Ultimo Momento and Conexiones signals the emergence of divergent logics of news production at Clarín.com. The respective work routines in both units exhibit greater temporal differences than are commonly described in the literature. They show a parallel erosion of commonality in many other dimensions, ranging from the material environment to the representation of the intended public. To date, research has not identified major differences in how much and to what effect sources and other media are used, to which parts of a story journalists devote most attention, and the use of communication tools. If they exist, these differences should have surfaced, given the centrality of sourcing, authoring, and newsroom communication in studies of news work. Thus, the differences reported above signal a major decrease in common ground between hard- and soft-news production at Clarín.com. This combination of an accentuation of differences and a weakening of commonalities suggests the emergence of two kinds of journalism rather than different degrees of the same journalistic kind.

This analysis underscores the continued value of conceptualizing the distinction between hard and soft news as a construction of actors rather than as reflecting the content characteristics of the events being reported. Furthermore, it reaffirms the centrality that variations in temporal patterns play in the structuring of various modes of editorial work. More precisely for present purposes, as Mitchelstein & Boczkowski (2009) argue, studies of online journalism focus on the acceleration of news cycles on the Web (García, 2008; Klinenberg, 2005; Lawson-Borders, 2006; Pavlik, 2000; Quandt, 2008; B. A. Williams & Delli Carpini, 2000). But these studies often take this acceleration for granted and focus on its dynamics and consequences. Thus, in addition to its relevance for understanding the distinction between hard and soft news, the account offered in this chapter also contributes to research on temporality in editorial work. More specifically, it extends the findings reported in these studies by showing that acceleration in journalistic practice is not in the essence of online news but can vary greatly as a result of organizational and material factors, even within a single newsroom. In other words, time matters but always in relation to other relevant social and technological factors.

Although these conclusions are derived from the analysis of a single organization, it is worth noticing the dynamics of the contemporary journalism field identified in two recent lines of work that situate the present case study within patterns of practice that are somewhat more shared. Studies of news making in several countries depict phenomena similar to those examined here. They include the acceleration of production cycles for breaking news, the rise in the volume and diversity of features content, the availability of sophisticated newsroom tools, the decrease in conventional sourcing and increase in reliance on "third-party" content suppliers, the exploration of novel formats, and the emergence of complex relationships between the newsrooms of traditional and new media in multimedia conglomerate settings (Baisnee & Marchetti, 2006; Boczkowski, 2004; Domingo, 2008b; García Aviles & León, 2004; Klinenberg, 2005; Quandt, 2008; Reinemann, 2004; Rosenstiel, 2005; Sousa, 2006; Velthuis, 2006). This suggests that the conclusions of this study might be relevant in other contexts.[5] Furthermore, this is consistent with comparative analyses that suggest a trend toward the convergence of news media systems and products in recent years (Hallin & Mancini, 2004; Natarajan & Xiaoming, 2003; Shoemaker & Cohen, 2006).

The coexistence of divergent kinds of journalism points also to the changing character of editorial work. Although the Ultimo Momento routines run against canonical notions about sourcing and authoring, they are still editorial work in practice and in their consequences. Thus, they signal the need for a broader definition of what counts as journalism in some contemporary settings. The practices of Ultimo Momento personnel influence story selection and presentation—two critical elements of the editorial enterprise. These practices also have consequences for their peers and the overall media landscape, as will be shown in chapters 3 and 4. In addition, the ethnography of news consumption that will be reported in chapters 5 and 6 will show that consumers did not question the legitimacy of the news published in Ultimo Momento, even when they realized that competitors often carried comparable content.

Beyond its specific contributions to theorizing about hard- and soft-news production, the account presented above begins to shed light on the dynamics and consequences of the news-at-work transformation in the journalistic field. This transformation was significant in the emergence and evolution of these divergent logics of work in at least three ways. First, the initial increase in the frequency and volume of publication—critical to what subsequently became a defining trait of the hard-news logic—helped the top editors at Clarín.com to conclude that the public of online news had, as Guillermo Culell put it, a "face, culture, and location." As Culell maintained, "We discovered this phenomenon [referring to news at work] when we decided to generate [content] and create this bridge between the audience and the product" (personal communication, December 16, 2005). Second, the realization among top editors at Clarín.com of the existence of this phenomenon was the structuring principle that led to the design, organizational, and editorial changes that resulted in the division between Ultimo Momento and Conexiones. This, in turn, triggered a huge leap in the previously smaller differences between hard- and soft-news production. Third, once this change was in place, the idea of news at work became a critical component of the actors' representations of the distinctiveness of the online medium and the identity and temporal-spatial location of their public and of how this should be factored into the production of content.

The existence of Ultimo Momento and Conexiones meant that more news was available than before, not only for the public but also for journalists working in other organizations in the news field. Journalists have long had the habit of monitoring other outlets and sometimes imitating the stories first appearing in them. Whether this increase of news was related to changes in monitoring and imitation practices—prevalent not only in online newsrooms but also in those of their print counterparts—is the subject of the next chapter.

THREE

Monitoring and Imitation in News Production

On the afternoon of June 4, 2005, Argentina's national soccer team played against its counterpart from Ecuador. The following interaction had occurred at the Ultimo Momento unit of Clarín.com earlier that day:

Juan[1] says to Maria, "Have you seen the [lead] story on Infobae.com [a local news site]? They even quote *La Nación*." Maria says, "Yes, it is because they lifted that story from *La Nación*." Carla [overhears the conversation and] says that Infobae.com published [a story with] a statement that [Argentine soccer player Carlos] Tévez had made in an interview "with an important Buenos Aires daily." She asks Francisco [who covers the sports beat] about what Tévez had said. Francisco answers that it's a strong statement about the Argentine team, and that it didn't show up on the wires. Carla adds that it was part of an exclusive interview. They didn't know what newspaper had run the interview. Jose looks at *Clarín* and says that it had been published there. Carla complains, "They quote *La Nación* but not *Clarín*." Francisco goes ahead and publishes a story about [the statement by] Tévez. [An editor arrives in the newsroom later, looks at Clarín.com's homepage, and] tells Francisco, "We have two stories about the same [event]."[2] Francisco explains that they had run the second one because Infobae.com had published a story about Tévez quoting "an important morning daily." The second story is later withdrawn.   (FIELD NOTE, JUNE 4, 2005)

Because of its extraordinary character (it was unusual for Ultimo Momento staffers to duplicate stories about the same event on the homepage), this vignette vividly illustrates certain patterns of work that are central to this chapter. These patterns come into sharp relief when this vignette is juxtaposed with some related elements of the editorial routines of Inés Capdevila, deputy editor of the foreign desk at *La Nación*. In a regular work day, Capdevila typically leaves the newsroom around midnight. After a short, ten-minute taxi ride, the University of Missouri graduate reaches her home and turns on the computer "to see if anything [new] is happening" (personal communication, February 21, 2007), even though she left the newsroom only a short while ago. She goes to sleep a couple of hours later, with the television set turned to CNN with the volume on. "The day I realized that I was listening to the news while sleeping was when [Yasser] Arafat passed away in the early morning [Buenos Aires time]. I dreamed that Arafat had passed away [only to realize that it was not a dream]" (ibid.). When she awakens at around 7:00 AM, she spends between two and three hours scanning the news in a variety of media and organizations that include print newspapers, local television and radio stations, and approximately twenty news sites from countries around the world. She then takes a break from the news until she arrives in the newsroom at approximately 1:30 PM.

Once at her desk, Capdevila continually monitors what is happening in Argentina and the world by scanning the wires, television, and the Web. "It's an automatic, mechanical [practice]. . . . You get in and out of the Web constantly. . . . I probably look at the *New York Times* [on the Web] twenty times a day" (ibid.). This routine intensifies during the "dead period" between 4:00 PM and the time reporters and correspondents file their stories two to three hours later. Among other goals, during this period she looks repeatedly at the sites of Lanacion.com and Clarín .com "to see how they pursue" the main topics of the day in her area. "There was a period at 6:00 or 7:00 PM when Clarín.com [prominently displayed] on its homepage what were going to be the main stories of [*Clarín*] the following morning. . . . If we saw a headline that we did not have, we added [the story to the next day's edition. During that period] to us, Clarín.com was a window into the print *Clarín*" (ibid.).

There are a number of differences between the events reported in these two vignettes. They take place in competing news organizations (*Clarín* and *La Nación*), in the newsrooms of two media (online and print), and over different time spans (rapidly in the first case and during the course of a day in the second), and they involve a different number of actors (a group in the first and an individual in the second). However, three important common threads run through these vignettes. The first is the centrality, intensity, and mundane character that monitoring competitors and other players in the journalistic field has in the stated news production routines. Second, actors do not monitor others face-to-face but instead resort to a complex technological constellation of old and new media. Third, information learned through technologically mediated monitoring contributes to editorial decision making in a way that fuels imitation. This chapter addresses these three commonalities to provide an account of monitoring and imitation in news production.

This account reveals that the changes in online news production analyzed in chapter 2 had the unintended consequence of triggering a qualitative leap in the information that journalists had about stories deemed newsworthy by competitors and other members of their organizational field. It shows that whether journalists took advantage of this transformation depended fundamentally on the type of content they produced, to a much lesser extent on the medium for which they worked, and very little on the newspaper to which they belonged. First, journalists who produced hard news intensified their monitoring of the organizational field and increased the imitation of news stories learned through this monitoring, but their colleagues who created soft news experienced far less change in both monitoring and imitation. Second, there were some differences in the monitoring and imitation actions of print and online journalists, but they rested on a substantive basis of common ground. Third, there were no major differences in monitoring and imitation across organizational lines. The analysis shows that technology plays a critical role in enabling transformations in monitoring and imitation but does not determine this pattern of variance. By contrast, this pattern emerges from a combination of factors at the intersection of situated practices and contextual structures that will be explicated in the conclusion to this chapter. First, monitoring and imitation activities in editorial work will be depicted in the next two sections.

Monitoring

Because of their heavy reliance on other media and because the content of these media (especially the online news sites) changes constantly during the day, it is not surprising that Ultimo Momento personnel at Clarín.com monitor the news space pervasively and intensely, often several times an hour. For instance, one editor comments that he looks at competitors' sites "all the time. . . . I don't want to miss anything of what they have" (personal communication, December 15, 2005). Comparable monitoring practices are also an important component of the work routines of Lanacion.com journalists in charge of producing hard news. A staffer who writes about politics says, "I continuously look at Clarín.com and [local news sites] Infobae.com, Ámbito.com, and Perfil.com. . . . I have a lot of windows open [on the computer screen] and I keep looking" (personal communication, December 18, 2006).

Print journalists have long monitored the news space using wire services, television, radio, and print media as part of their news production processes. But journalists at *Clarín* and *La Nación* who are charged with producing hard news say that online media have increasingly had a larger and more important role in their monitoring routines. Most interviewees claim that this change began around 2002 or 2003 during a period when the tendency by Clarín.com and Lanacion.com to publish constantly during the day was already established and growing fast and has since intensified. Julio Blanck, one of three editors-in-chief at *Clarín*, recalls that he began to regularly monitor Clarín.com during the day when he assumed his position in April 2003. "I'd tell you that in this period [this habit] increased. . . . I don't know if it'll keep growing because I do it a lot now. I look at Clarín.com all the time to see what [news] it has" (personal communication, December 14, 2006). Echoing Blanck, Fernando Rodríguez, an editor on the metro desk of the print *La Nación*, says that he looks at local online news sites "every ten minutes. . . . I have [their window tabs] at the bottom of the screen and keep clicking" (personal communication, March 20, 2007).

Journalists monitor the news field for at least three reasons. First, they do it to keep abreast of the news. Thus, Alberto Amato, a journalist on the national desk at *Clarín*, says, "In general I look [at online news sites] to make sure that nothing has happened in the world and I didn't learn about it" (personal communication, February 22, 2007). Second, they monitor the news to look for information that might be useful in the daily routine. *La Nación*'s Fernando Rodríguez comments that he looks at Lanacion.com in part "to get a sense of the kind of information I can count on [for the following day's edition]" (personal communication, March 20, 2007). Third, journalists monitor to calibrate their actions vis-à-vis the competition at critical junctures of the news production process. As he recalls a developing story, an Ultimo Momento staffer says that "looking at the competition is inescapable. When we defined the headline and the lead we were going to use, the first thing we did was to look at the sites of Lanacion.com and Infobae.com to see theirs." He adds, "This is something that happens almost naturally. 'This is how we frame the story, in principle; let's see how the others do it'" (personal communication, July 28, 2005). Echoing these words, a political reporter at Lanacion

.com says that she often looks at the competition after publishing a story "as a form of control that is easily available. . . . If I see a framing very different from the one I used, I will not be alarmed but will keep an eye on the story because it might mean that I'm missing something" (personal communication, December 18, 2006). Furthermore, Fernando González, editor on the national desk at *Clarín*, notices that Lanacion.com put up the content of the print edition shortly after midnight: "On Saturdays at around 1:00 or 1:30 AM, I look at their site because the Sunday paper is an important one. I still have half of my paper to print because we [continue printing] . . . until 4:00 AM. And if there was something that I should change and do a second edition, I could do it. It would have to be very important, and it has never happened. But, yes, I do look at it" (personal communication, February 22, 2007).

Several of the journalists interviewed mention a certain sense of alienation associated with these monitoring practices. Susana Reinoso, a journalist at *La Nación* who specializes in media and culture, maintains that not only have the windows to the world of news and information accessed by journalists grown dramatically in recent years, but "I believe that if I don't open all these options, there is a part of reality that is going to escape me." She adds, "It's like a 'reality-fiction' game [*un juego realidad-ficción*] because I know, working in a news medium, that reality is re-created every day . . . but I still believe that I have to have all the windows open all the time" (personal communication, February 22, 2007). In a related vein, Adriana Bruno, editor on the entertainment desk at *Clarín*, comments, "Every time there is more energy spent on looking at what the others are doing. . . . I guess it began as a necessary thing . . . but it also reaches a point in which for an inertial [process] it begins to grow and becomes an intellectual exercise that stops having the reader as referent and begins to have the other media as referent. And we all get on the merry-go-round . . . and forget about the ring [*la sortija*] that was what we had" (personal communication, February 21, 2007).

In addition to these common features among journalists in online and print newsrooms, there are differences in how they enact the intensity and pervasiveness of monitoring, based on the distinct character of their respective media. For journalists working at online news sites, constant monitoring is tied to the high speed of news production—an issue introduced in chapter 2—and how this intensifies the race to be the first to publish a story. Ultimo Momento's sports editor, Facundo Quiroga, says that he looks at other media "all the time" because "they win and I like to beat them." Being first is "a journalist thing. I believe it doesn't matter to the public. But I love [winning], and I get really upset when I lose" (personal communication, December 15, 2005). Thus, it is common for staffers to look at the competition immediately after publishing a story, particularly one that just broke, to see if they "won." Consider the following interaction at Clarín.com: "A cable news channel announces the verdict of the Michael Jackson trial, which triggers a rush to publish the story. [Seven minutes later] the updated story is published. The editor [in charge of the story] immediately looks at the sites of [competitors] and says, 'We published it first.' The homepage editor congratulates him, shakes his hand, and says something to the effect of 'It's great to work with you'" (field note, June 13, 2005).

As stated in the introduction, the online and print newsrooms of *Clarín* and *La Nación* operated autonomously when the fieldwork for this book was taking place. Like the Ultimo Momento staffers of Clarín.com described in the previous chapter, personnel of Lanacion.com's newsroom attend the noon and afternoon meetings of its print counterpart and try to align their coverage with the perceived orientation of the print newspaper, especially in the realm of public affairs news. According to the site's deputy editor, Mariana Robin, "We have to . . . follow a certain [editorial] tendency of the print paper" (personal communication, February 21, 2007). But despite these efforts by the online newsroom and the fact that the two newsrooms are located in the same space (unlike *Clarín*'s newsrooms, which are housed in buildings that are two and a half miles apart), the news production routines of both newsrooms are largely independent. Lanacion.com's sports editor, Ariel Tiferes, says that this physical proximity "allows us to check stuff [with print journalists]. But . . . in the daily routines, there is no relationship; they do not call us and tell us 'This happened, publish it.' . . . We are two different newsrooms" (personal communication, December 14, 2006). The comments by Robin and Tiferes illustrate an asymmetry in the relationship of operational autonomy between the online and print newsrooms. Whereas the former try to align with the latter to a certain extent, the reverse is not true. As was described in chapter 2, this asymmetry and the larger dynamics of operational autonomy also characterize the ties between the online and print newsrooms of *Clarín*. For instance, according to a sports writer in that print paper, "There is not daily contact [with the online newsroom]. It has happened to me that I was following [soccer club] Boca [Juniors] in Brazil and . . . I had just talked to the coach, and we had the lineup they were going to use. At that same time, Clarín.com published a very different lineup from the one that was going to play [the match]. . . . And I thought that there is a person from *Clarín* here, [but] it is as if there were two different worlds" (personal communication, March 20, 2007).

Within the context of this operational autonomy between print and online newsrooms, a second distinctive aspect of monitoring by online journalists is their attempt to align their coverage with that of their counterparts in their respective print newsrooms. One direct monitoring practice that facilitates alignment is attendance at the noon and afternoon editorial meetings. A more continuous and less intrusive way is to use a software program that allows journalists to see on a computer terminal the composition of the next day's *Clarín* edition as it evolves during the day. Thus, for instance, Javier Domínguez, who writes about international news, says, "Regularly at 5:00 PM, I begin to see the [print paper's foreign news] section through [the software]" (personal communication, December 13, 2005). He often takes this information into account for the online international news coverage.

An issue distinct for print journalists is that the time spent looking at online news sites is, for many, at the expense of the time they previously devoted to scanning wire service copy. Daniel Miguez, who worked for several years on the national desk before becoming editor of *Clarín*'s suburban papers, states, "Since we all got Internet access on our computers [in the newsroom] some years ago . . . online [sites] have replaced the routine reading of wire services copy" (personal communication, March 22, 2007). Julio Chiappetta, his colleague on the sports desk, concurs by noting, "I look at the wires less because the latest [news] is on [Clarín .com]. It's faster than the wires. Before, the wires gave you the feeling that they were the latest; now with [Clarín.com] it's the latest of the latest [*lo último de lo último*]" (personal communication, March 20, 2007).

Monitoring is far less pervasive and intense among online and print staffers charged with producing soft-news stories than among their colleagues who are reporting hard news. For instance, at Clarín.com several hours might pass with no Conexiones staffer monitoring the sites of competitors. Former Conexiones writer Marcela Mazzei says, "I don't look much [at online news sites]" (personal communication, October 13, 2005). Furthermore, unlike their Ultimo Momento colleagues, who monitor the news field continuously in search of newsworthy items, Conexiones staffers do so far less often and sometimes only during a break from work. For example, Leo Bachanian, who writes about television, says he looks at the sites of competitors about once a day, "in the afternoon, after we [normally] publish our [television] story [of that day]" (personal communication, November 11, 2005).

A similar pattern of monitoring characterizes the work of print journalists who produce soft news. For example, Ricardo Sametband, a reporter for the weekly technology section of *La Nación,* comments that he looks at "Clarín.com very little, Lanacion.com a bit more." Sometimes a story that first appeared in Lanacion.com could "lead to a good idea . . . but because [his counterpart at Lanacion.com] focuses on urgent news and I focus on 'news you can use,' it is [usually] not a very useful idea for one of my stories" (personal communication, March 21, 2007).

Technology plays a vital role in the monitoring practices described above, and few would be possible without personal computers, television and radio sets, print newspapers and magazines, and a host of programs, devices, software protocols, and material infrastructure. The significance of the role of technology contrasts with the absence of theorizing about technology and monitoring in the news and imitation more generally. In studies of news production, the lack of work on technology in monitoring becomes prominent when it is contrasted with the attention devoted to factors such as colocated interpersonal networks (Bourdieu, 1998; Donsbach, 1999; Shoemaker & Reese, 1996; Tuchman, 1978; B. Zelizer, 1993). Researchers have argued that sustained, face-to-face interactions among journalists favor the emergence of social relationships that are in turn conducive to monitoring and being monitored. The quintessential situation of this kind is the campaign trail, which creates "womb-like conditions" (Crouse, 2003 [1972], p. 7) that increase monitoring.

In this study, the importance of this lack of emphasis in the scholarly literature on the role of technology is perhaps nowhere more salient than when attempting to understand the reinvention of the *cablera* (the "cable box") at Clarín.com. In print and broadcast newsrooms of Argentine media, this Spanish neologism is used to refer to the device that receives wire service copy. But after the May 2004 redesign at Clarín.com, the *cablera* was reinvented as a new position in the Ultimo Momento unit and a new space in this unit's section of the newsroom. One of the employees who occupies this position called himself a "news hunter" (*cazador de noticias*), hired "to fish all the news that comes along, be that via wire services, national and foreign online news sites, radio, television, pictures, any source of information that furnishes any news that is relevant [to us]" (personal communication, November 28, 2005). The pace of work is relentless, requiring the staffer to monitor "everything all the time" (ibid.) during the eight-hour work shift. The people who perform this function work in a space that is centrally located in the Ultimo Momento section of the newsroom and that includes "four monitors—two television sets and two computer screens—with their respective keyboards and mouses [and speakers. In addition, the staffer] has a remote control, a notebook replete with newspaper clippings, and a piece of paper with notes jotted down. . . . This space is virtually isolated from the rest of the newsroom. Two additional television sets become a sort of lateral wall, and the four monitors hide [the staffer]. It is the most private space in the newsroom" (field note, May 2, 2005).

In this technologically saturated location in the newsroom, *cablera* staffers utilize a wide array of tools to digitally capture interesting news items in a variety of media and relay information about them to their colleagues by instant messenger (IM). Normally, the editors screen these messages first and then assign the newsworthy items to the writers. But the writers also regularly look at the messages and proactively contact editors to ask if they can write a story about an item they consider appropriate. At Clarín.com's Ultimo Momento, IM plays an important function in monitoring. It enables a sort of indirect and more passive monitoring that is layered on top of the direct and more active practices undertaken by surfing the Web or listening to a newscast. For instance, according to Miguel Middono, a writer in the general-interest beat of the unit, "Sometimes you don't have time [to monitor] because you are working on a story, and fifteen minutes can go by without looking. So, we take advantage of what [*cablera* staffers] do. Because they send electronic messages, you can go back to them [after finishing a story]." He adds, "If it were different, if they just shouted things out loud, we would have to [interrupt the work flow and] jot down notes or otherwise we might forget" (personal communication, October 18, 2005). The monitoring implications of IM in the online newsroom are tied to the finding (reported in chapter 2) that Ultimo Momento personnel utilize IM for editorial purposes significantly more than their Conexiones peers. Using IM editorially contributes to having a more encompassing and multilayered monitoring gaze. In addition, it affords faster and multidirectional information flows, as was argued in the previous chapter. This is more important to journalists producing hard news than to their counterparts who are making soft-news content.

The account in this section reveals significant variance in monitoring linked to the type of news being produced, smaller and less important differences related to the specificity of the medium, and little divergence by organization. Differences in monitoring activities will be discussed further after an examination of the imitation dynamics tied to monitoring in editorial work.

Imitation

To a naive observer, the mundane character of imitation is an immediately salient feature of the practices undertaken by online and print journalists at *Clarín* and *La Nación*. That is, when confronted with the opportunity to imitate the coverage of other news organizations in the course of their daily routines, actors do not normally engage in a long and complicated reflexive process but undertake imitation in a relatively spontaneous, mindless, and matter-of-fact fashion. The two vignettes that opened this chapter illustrate this issue, as does the following, more ordinary news production sequence in Clarín.com's Ultimo Momento unit: "Reporter looks for new stories. She looks at her emails, the wires . . . Infobae.com, and Lanacion.com. She notices that on Lanacion.com there is a story about [former governor of Córdoba Province, Eduardo] Angeloz. She asks an editor if someone has already done this story [at Clarín.com]. The editor says 'No.' She tells him, 'I'll do it then.' [Half an hour later] reporter uploads the story [into the publishing system] and informs the editor by instant messenger" (field note, April 11, 2005).

Imitation practices are premised in part on a straightforward logic of replication in news production. In the words of a Clarín.com editor: "If a piece of news has been published by [the competition], then we also have to publish it. Perhaps it is not very important, so we lower it [referring to placement on the homepage], but we publish it anyway. If they have it, we have it too" (personal communication, July 28, 2005).

This logic affects the selection and construction of stories. Regarding the selection of stories for inclusion on Clarín.com, Miguel Middono notes, "If the two [main] cable television news channels are showing you the same [news story], you have to publish it too. . . . You have no other option [*no te queda otra*]" (personal communication, October 18, 2005). A sports journalist at *Clarín* observes that since the increase in the volume and frequency of publication by online news sites, "all the time you get stuff that you didn't get before. That alters your work routine." For example, "Lanacion.com has [a story] that tennis player X is injured. You don't have that piece of information in your newsroom because the person who covers tennis has the day off. . . . But when Lanacion.com publishes that story, the other sites do it too, which in turn alters your [news budget] for the next day" (personal communication, March 21, 2007).

The following two brief interactions at Clarín.com illustrate how this logic also affects the editorial construction of stories. It is April 28, 2005, and Radiotelevisione Italiana (popularly known as the RAI), Italy's national public service broadcaster, has just aired a video that Italian soccer star Fabio Cannavaro shot of himself when he played for Italy's Parma Football Club in the late 1990s. It shows him as he injects a performance-enhancing substance that was allowed for athletes at the time. In the video, Cannavaro mentions the nickname of a teammate who was present when this happened, and it is believed that he was referring to Juan Sebastián Verón, a well-known Argentine player. Thus, the story acquires prominence in the Argentine media. At 7:50 PM Buenos Aires time, when the story is still unfolding and it is unclear whether Verón was involved in the incident, the following dialogue takes place at Clarín.com:

Editor tells sportswriter to add links [on the story] to Italian media. Sportswriter says that they should add that [Verón] had been present.
Editor: "No . . . let's not go there."
Sportswriter: "But it's everywhere."
Editor: "Then, yes." (FIELD NOTE, APRIL 28, 2005)

A few weeks later the following exchange happens as three Clarín.com staffers are deciding on the positioning of stories on the homepage:

Staffer 1: "We could move up [a story about then Palestine president] Abu Mazzen and down [a story about the national soccer team of] Venezuela."
Editor: "Good." . . .
Staffer 1: "Because nobody is paying attention to [the story about] Venezuela, and everybody has the Abu Mazzen one."
Staffer 2: "Yes, [the latter] is Lanacion.com's top story." (FIELD NOTE, JUNE 4, 2005)

As with story selection, issues having to do with the content of the Verón story and the framing of the Abu Mazzen story are shaped in part by conforming to criteria expressed in decisions made by other news organizations.

These emergent and distributed dynamics of interorganizational consensus formation are reinforced by intraorganizational patterns of ties between the online and print newsrooms. These patterns acquire different shapes, depending on whether online or print is the starting point of the relationship. When the online newsroom tries to relate to its print counterpart, the intention to align with the known coverage or perceived editorial orientation of the latter enhances conformity processes. (Issues related to the countertrend of differentiation will be considered later in this section.) This alignment is manifest in actions such as attendance at print editorial meetings, calls to the print newsroom regarding highly sensitive stories, and the use of software tools to keep tabs on the print edition as it evolves during the day. Thus, when *La Nación's* Inés Capdevila notes that in the late afternoon Clarín.com becomes a window into *Clarín*—at least with respect to the foreign-news beat—it is because Clarín.com's staffer Javier Domínguez begins at 5:00 PM to use the intranet to check out the next day's configuration of *Clarín's* foreign-news section and takes this information into consideration for the news site. Alignment is also indirectly influenced by the mindfulness of staffers at Clarín.com and Lanacion.com of the editorial stance of their print counterparts and their subsequent attempts to avoid major deviations from it.

The intraorganizational patterns of connections between print and online newsrooms are different when the former is the initiating party. Although print journalists monitor a wide array of online news sites, it is quite common for them to look at their own online site more often than others. This has much to do with the simple fact that, at least at *Clarín*, the default opening homepage of the Web browsers on the newsroom computers is Clarín.com, and journalists cannot modify it by themselves. More important than this higher frequency of monitoring is a dual use that many print journalists make of their own paper's online site. They use it as an alert system that triggers searches for additional information and as a partial replacement for the wire services. *Clarín's* coeditor-in-chief Julio Blanck says that Clarín.com "replace[d] . . . the wire services. . . . I don't look at wire copy [anymore]." He adds that staffers at Clarín.com "see the wires, select them, and put them [on the news site] according to a very reasonable criterion that is not only convenient [to us] but [also] efficient. And they select some [news] that is interesting, that our journalists in the newsroom would not look at, such as stories on science and technology" (personal communication, December 14, 2006). Because an online news site publishes fewer stories than those available on the wires and often selects those stories following the lead of other media outlets, a potential first-order effect of this displacement of wire services is a double narrowing of the news net among the editors: there are fewer candidates for inclusion on the print paper and less diversity among these candidates.

Access to sources also shapes imitation practices. A sportswriter at *Clarín* comments, "There are days that I go to the training session of the [soccer team he regularly covers] and I come back [to the newsroom] absolutely sure of what I have, because I saw it, because I talked [to sources]. On that day, I don't need to check online news sites . . . so much." In contrast, "There are days that maybe you don't go to the training session. [Therefore,] you don't have so much information. That day maybe you [look at online news sites] more often. You look at 3:00 PM, then again at 5:00 PM. . . . It depends on how much information I have to fill a page" (personal communication, March 20, 2007). Thus, sourcing decreases imitation. However, at least among some journalists, opportunities for regular access to sources seem complicated by the quickening pace of work in the contemporary media environment. In the case of online news, chapter 2 showed how little sourcing took place among Ultimo Momento personnel amid high temporal pressures. Some print journalists mention the decreasing number of opportunities for sourcing as well. For instance, *Clarín*'s Fernando González complains: "I get 200, 300 emails per day and lose too much time deleting them, cleaning [my inbox]. Then you sort of live for that. . . . You get the best news by having a cup of coffee with [a source] and getting stuff out of him. By email, except when he has a predisposition to tell you something, you will not get an exclusive. And there is increasingly less time to sit down and have a cup of coffee [with sources]" (personal communication, February 22, 2007).

These practice dynamics are paired with evolving representations of the consumer among journalists. As was stated in chapter 2, the representation of the ideal-typical online news consumer began to mature only recently. In contrast, the ideal-typical print reader was long assumed to have known and stable behaviors and preferences that were taken largely for granted. But there is a sense among journalists that these behaviors and preferences have been changing rapidly in recent years and that consumption as a whole has become less predictable. According to Silvia Fesquet, coeditor-in-chief at *Clarín*, "The demand of people makes media [organizations] increasingly more attentive and in an evolution that, in the past, could take place over ten years and now has to be . . . faster. . . . Before, you had the reader more with you: your grandparents bought [the newspaper], then your parents, and you . . . didn't even know why you bought this newspaper or that magazine. . . . There was more [consumer] loyalty" (personal communication, December 15, 2006). In addition to this shared notion of an overall shift in consumption, the representations of the consumer relevant for the present analysis vary by medium.

Print journalists represent the contemporary consumer as someone who uses the Web during a regular day to acquire knowledge of more stories than in the past. This representation is based on the notion that a significant proportion of consumers learn about the news during their workday by looking at the same sites that journalists monitor. A crime news reporter at *Clarín* says, "People are informed of what happened during the day. They know the basic [facts] about the events" (personal communication, March 23, 2007). A colleague on the sports desk expresses similar ideas: "Unlike what happened not so long ago, many people who will read the paper tomorrow morning already saw [the news] today on the Internet" (personal communication, March 21, 2007).

This representation of the consumer helps shape print journalists' agenda because, according to *Clarín*'s coeditor-in-chief Daniel Fernández Canedo, it intensifies a tendency that already existed in the days of "old media." "On the next day the reader wants to see [in the newspaper] what he watched the previous day on television." This issue becomes particularly salient in the construction of a newspaper's most precious editorial asset—the front page. Fernández Canedo, who is one of a handful of newsroom employees directly responsible for *Clarín*'s front page, comments that when tomorrow's print paper reaches its readers, "everything is [already] known. This is the central difficulty, the central angst [*angustia*] that [the editors-in-chief] have: how do we break a story about a topic that is already known, but that, at the same time, we cannot [not publish]?" Premised on these ideas about the changing character of consumption, print journalists try to differentiate their coverage from that of competitors—in the same and other media—less by offering new information and more by interpreting it in an original way. They often refer to this as "*la mirada*," loosely translated as "the look" or a perspective on things. According to Fernández Canedo, "We are working a lot on *la mirada* more than the news [story] in itself, [to] find a new *mirada* about the things that are happening" (personal communication, December 14, 2006). *Clarín*'s Fernando González points out that the headline of the lead story on the front page of the paper on the Sunday (February 18, 2007) before our interview is "highly illustrative" of attempts to differentiate via *la mirada:*

"[They] speed up the Buenos Aires [mayoral] election: June 3rd" [*Apuran la elección porteña: 3 de junio*].[3] "Speed up" is the [distinctive] element, because by 2:00 PM [of the day before publication] it was known that the election was going to take place on June 3rd, and "speed up" means that the election was moved ahead of schedule. . . . The print media, in particular *Clarín,* increasingly works on . . . giving an interpretation to the news because the competition with television and radio and now online media is very strong and wearing, and most people are already informed [about the news when the print paper reaches them]. This has greatly intensified in recent years. Now there are practically very few news [stories] for which [print coverage] can be enhanced or differentiated. (PERSONAL COMMUNICATION, FEBRUARY 22, 2007)

Different concerns permeate the representations about consumers among online journalists. Congruent with the beliefs of their peers at Clarín.com, staffers of Lanacion.com also conceive of their ideal-typical consumer as someone "at work." According to Ariel Tiferes, the site's sports editor:

Seventy percent [of the consumers] are people who . . . log on when they arrive in their [workplaces], and if they have time, they log on [again] to see what's new and [then] keep working. Maybe they log on again at lunch when they have some time. . . . They are people who maybe can't listen to the radio and [so] visit our site. . . . We realize that this is going on also with the live sports Webcasts. [When they take place] during regular business hours, their [traffic] increases by 300%.
(PERSONAL COMMUNICATION, DECEMBER 14, 2006)

In addition to this common notion about the primacy of the news-at-work phenomenon, journalists at Clarín.com and Lanacion.com also share the belief that consumers expect two main elements from hard-news coverage online: timeliness and comprehensiveness. The concern that if consumers do not find up-to-the-minute coverage, they might stop visiting a site was addressed in chapter 2 in the context of Clarín .com. A similar concern is also prevalent among Lanacion.com staffers. This belief is paired with the idea that consumers of online sites might also abandon a site if its hard-news coverage is not as complete as possible. For instance, during an Ultimo Momento team meeting, an editor argues that a consumer "can have several windows opened [on the screen], and if he doesn't find something on one site he goes to another one" (field note, April 21, 2005). Lanacion.com's Mariana Robin expresses a similar thought: "If tomorrow [Britney Spears] says she is pregnant, we have to put it [on the homepage] because maybe the person who found out about this on the radio would visit . . . our site, and if she doesn't see it, she'll leave" (personal communication, February 21, 2007). The aim of providing updated and thorough coverage contributes to expanding imitative practices among journalists who are producing hard-news online. The speed of production reduces the time to search for unique content, and the desire to offer a comprehensive rendition of current events increases the likelihood of replicating news stories published elsewhere.

In chapter 2, it was argued that the actors make sense of the divergent logics of production between the Ultimo Momento and Conexiones units at Clarín.com by resorting to analogies of opposites, such as hard-soft, newspaper-magazine, hot-cold, and warm zone–gray zone. The news site as a gas station is an additional popular metaphor among the site's journalists. It provides a window into their representation of consumers as well as their own experience of the construction of similarity and difference in news production. Clarín.com's editor, Marcelo Franco, describes the metaphor as follows: "You need to fill the tank of your car. . . . You don't choose the gas station . . . for the price or quality of the gas. . . . Basically there is no major difference in either the service or the cost. . . . To us, hard news is like people coming [to the site] to fill their tank during the day. . . . Therefore, the possibility of differentiating ourselves from the competition is minimal. . . . Thus, we invented the light mechanic service [*el servicio de mecánica ligera*] while the customer fills the tank" (personal communication, December 14, 2005).

This "mechanic service" is the soft news published in the Conexiones section of the site. Echoing Franco's thoughts, Clarín.com's director Guillermo Culell says, "We had to add something so that it would be possible to distinguish one site from the other, to say where our personality was. . . . And we gambled on the Conexiones format, which are stories that are not in the agenda of the print paper and that are originally produced by us" (personal communication, December 16, 2005). Thus, the consumer of hard news is represented as someone who expects updated and comprehensive coverage to satisfy a basic information need—akin to the basic car's need to be satisfied with gas. The consumer of soft news, either the same or a different person, is imagined as someone who expects some original added value for spending time satisfying this basic need—similar to checking the air pressure of the car's tires or buying a soda at the gas station's store.

In this metaphorical construction, hard news becomes a generic commodity, and soft news the vehicle for content differentiation. But for the actors, the commoditization of hard news does not mean that it has secondary status relative to soft news. Hard news is considered the type of content that attracts consumers to the site in the first place—just as gas is what brings people to a gas station. Once they are there, they purchase other products and services. Also, hard news is considered superior to soft news in setting the news agenda, which fulfills a critical mission of a news organization. According to Marcos Foglia, Ultimo Momento's editor, "Beyond the differentiation that the soft [news] sector brings to a site, the hard [news] sector continues to shape the topics on the country's news agenda, even despite the fact that the information is a commodity" (personal communication, December 13, 2005).

In addition to representations of consumer preferences as expressed in the gas station analogy, the comments by Franco, Culell, and Foglia illustrate how actors' experiences matter in the imitation process. These experiences differ by medium. The overall sense among online journalists is of strong content homogenization when it comes to hard news. A reporter at Clarín.com comments, "There is a reality, and it is that all [online] newspapers . . . have the same [news stories]" (personal communication, October 5, 2005). Reflecting on his own practice, Lanacion.com's sportswriter Alejo Vetere says that looking at "Clarín.com [and] Infobae .com, you realize that [imitation has taken place] because they have the same mistakes that the wire copy has. . . . We all [participate] in a circle: they lift [the story] from there, we do it from here, and everything feeds [into the circle]" (personal communication, October 5, 2005).

Online journalists charged with producing hard news do not like this state of affairs because it conflicts with their core occupational values and sense of self. One does not usually go into the field of journalism to replicate someone else's stories. Thus, they try to differentiate their output somewhat within a very narrow maneuvering space. According to a Clarín.com editor, "We try to give [the news] our own perspective [*mirada*], within the constraints of what is possible, because these are Internet times, as you well know" (personal communication, December 15, 2005). One manifestation of these efforts to be different is the utilization of information gathered through monitoring to change one's framing of an already-published story that is presented quite similarly by a competitor.[4] According to Lanacion.com's Mariana Robin, "We try to use different headlines [from those used by other news sites]. . . . It's very funny because sometimes it happens that . . . we publish at the same time two very similar headlines, and if there is a plan B, we perhaps make the decision to 'well, let's change it,' especially if [the other site] is Clarín .com, and perhaps they have the same idea and change it too" (personal communication, February 21, 2007).

There is less uniformity among print journalists about whether there is increased similarity in the stories published by competing newspapers, in particular *Clarín* and *La Nación*. During my interview with Ricardo Roa, deputy managing editor of *Clarín*, I mention my impression that the coverage of these two papers has become increasingly similar in recent years. He responds, "Yes, the difference was clearer before, as you say. . . . I also notice this" (personal communication, March 23, 2007). A colleague of Roa's on the sports desk expresses a related thought: "A phrase that you hear frequently in newsrooms is that today everybody has the same [news stories]" (personal communication, March 21, 2007). But this is not a universal view. For example, when I ask *La Nación*'s metro editor, Fernando Rodríguez, whether he thinks that his paper and *Clarín* have become more alike in recent years, he replies, "No. We're like a kind of

DNA chain" (personal communication, March 20, 2007). When *Clarín*'s crime reporter, Virginia Messi, is asked a similar question in relation to her beat, she answers, "In general, *La Nación* and *Clarín* have quite different visions of crime news. A leading story for *Clarín* is a void in *La Nación*. Or what *La Nación* gives prominence to, we don't even publish" (personal communication, February 23, 2007).

Issues about the management of reputation also shape imitation in hard-news production. Economics scholarship has generated important insights about the role of reputation in imitation (Bikhchandani & Sharma, 2001; Choi, 1997; Ottaviani & Sorensen, 2000; Scharfstein & Stein, 1990, 2000; Zwiebel, 1995). In an argument that resonates with Keynes's phrase that "it is better for reputation to fail conventionally than to succeed unconventionally" (1964, p. 158), Scharfstein and Stein show how a "sharing the blame effect" might drive imitation among actors in charge of investing on behalf of principals. According to them, when the reputation of a manager is tied to the actions of her peers, this manager is likely to "simply mimic the investment decisions of other managers, ignoring substantive private information. [This behavior] can be rational from the perspective of managers who are concerned about their reputations in the labor market" (1990, p. 465). Studies of the media elicit similar dynamics in the case of news production (Breed, 1955; Crouse, 2003 [1972]; Hamilton, 2004; Kiernan, 2003). Dunwoody maintains, "Each journalist knows that his editor is watching the competitive newspapers and wire services and is evaluating what he produces *in relation to* what the competition publishes. If he produces something different, he may be in trouble; at the very least he will have to defend his choice. But if all competitors produce the same story for the day, then each editor assumes his reporter has done a good job" (1980, p. 17, emphasis in original).

For print and online journalists interviewed for this study, these reputation dynamics add to imitation in the production of hard news. One online journalist says, "There is a general [tendency] among journalists . . . to go with the flock, and there is a great fear to be different" (personal communication, February 21, 2007). This increases the likelihood that a journalist will publish a story about an event that is also covered in other media. According to an editor at Clarín.com, "There is a criterion that says that we have to provide [consumers] with everything that the others [referring to competitors] have and more. . . . So we have to offer them the same news that the others have" (personal communication, July 28, 2005).

This constellation of practice, representation, experience, and reputation factors that contributes to imitation in hard-news production is not present in the production of soft news. To begin, the monitoring practices of soft-news journalists are less intense and pervasive than those of their hard-news counterparts. This means, at least in principle, that they have less knowledge of the output of their competitors and other players in the news space. In turn, this translates into fewer story candidates to be imitated. Moreover, some of the intraorganizational practices that increase imitation among hard-news journalists are absent or acquire a reverse sign among their soft-news peers. Thus, Clarín.com Conexiones staffers do not routinely follow the coverage of their counterparts, and when they learn about it, they try not to duplicate it. Furthermore, journalists who produce soft news seem to have more sustained access to sources than their hard-news colleagues. This is in part because they have more time to work on each story and, in the case of Clarín.com, have a mandate to quote a certain minimum number of sources per story. As noted in chapter 2, Conexiones staffers utilize information gathered from sources more than six times more often than their Ultimo Momento colleagues, which, in turn, reduces the likelihood of similarity in news production.

The final practice concerns a fundamental difference in the type of content used by hard- and soft-news journalists. The timeliness of hard news is a major factor that orients the efforts of journalists in a way that restricts the spectrum of newsworthy events. Journalists monitor each other to make sure that they miss nothing that is relevant, which contributes to increasing the likelihood of similar outputs. In contrast, the content of soft news is far less timely, which in turn reduces the chances of imitation. *La Nación*'s Ricardo Sametband, when asked about similarities between his weekly technology supplement and the comparable one published by *Clarín,* answers, "Because 90% of the stories that we produce are atemporal, only once in a while do the two of us [have] the same story" (personal communication, March 21, 2007).

Hard- and soft-news journalists also differ in their representations of the consumer, at least in the case of online news. As argued above, consumers are believed to want unique stories when it comes to soft news. Therefore, it makes little sense for the journalists who produce them to imitate the competition. This representational configuration is tied to reputation forces that, unlike those of their peers who are charged with producing hard news, reward journalists for the originality of their output rather than for its speed and comprehensiveness in relation to the output of peers in other newsrooms. This also then becomes a disincentive for imitation in news production.

Finally, there is an important experiential difference between journalists producing hard and soft news. The hard-news journalists convey a sense of an "event push" in their work routines. This is particularly prevalent among online journalists. An assertion commonly made by journalists reporting on hard news is that the "[news] agenda is imposed on us." According to *La Nación*'s Inés Capdevila, "Maybe we don't establish the agenda, but the agenda is established for us [*se nos establece a nosotros*]" (personal communication, February 21, 2007). Ariel Tiferes, her colleague on the sports desk of Lanacion.com, expresses a similar thought: "On the Web, the news is [already] there, and you have to take it" (personal communication, December 14, 2006). The soft-news journalists, in contrast, share the feeling of having to "pull events" into their editorial offerings. Journalists charged with producing soft news share a sense of greater freedom in choosing the editorial offering, marked by the commonly heard expression of "having to go outside the newsroom to get the story." Clarín.com Ultimo Momento's María Arce sums things up by saying that in her unit "you always depend on a third party, because we are not on the street but [in the newsroom]. And the information comes to you from the television, the radio, the wires, the Web, the phone, but always from a third party." At Conexiones, "I generate the information. . . . I go out and research a topic that I came up with" (personal communication, November 2, 2005). The news that other outlets are reporting exerts pressure on hard-news journalists to make their work conform to that of their hard-news peers. In contrast, soft-news journalists experience greater agency in constructing their stories, which places a wider array of potential stories at their disposal.

Concluding Remarks

In this chapter I have examined issues of monitoring and imitation in the online and print newsrooms of *Clarín* and *La Nación*. My analysis reveals a greater intensity and pervasiveness in the monitoring practices and a larger reliance on technology in these practices among journalists who produce hard news than among their soft-news counterparts. It also reveals that journalists who make hard news utilize the information learned through monitoring to imitate other players in the organizational field significantly more than do their colleagues who make soft news. In addition, the account demonstrates that the monitoring and imitation actions of hard-news journalists sometimes acquire different manifestations depending on whether they work in an online or print newsroom. These manifestations appear to be local adaptations to the character of the medium that rest on a substantive basis of common ground between online and print workers rather than qualitative cleavages between these two media. Finally, despite differences in ideological stance, editorial style, historical trajectory, and cultural profile between *Clarín* and *La Nación*, there is an absence of major variance in monitoring and imitation across organizational lines.

How are we to account for these patterns of variance? It is important to consider three sets of issues: the processes by which transformations unfolded across the organizational field; the role played by technology; and the interplay between situated patterns of practice and larger structural formations. The actors did not plan, intend, or foresee the changes that reverberated across the journalistic field and that were triggered by the increase in the volume and frequency of publication by online news sites. It is important to recall that, at least at Clarín.com, the decision to increase production was somewhat improvised and gradual and aimed at satisfying perceived changes in consumption. Moreover, this increase in volume and frequency emerged as a strategy of hard-news production only after the actors became convinced of its contribution to bottom-line success in terms of site usage. Because the other leading online news sites, such as Lanacion.com, were doing the same, this modus operandi was institutionalized (Berger & Luckmann, 1966) across the organizational field. For reasons described in this and the previous chapters, many actors did not like some core elements of the emergent logic of hard-news production. But because of the "cultural-cognitive" (W. R. Scott, 2001) dimension of institutionalization ("the shared conceptions that constitute the nature of social reality and the frames through which meaning is made" [p. 57]), actors experienced the situation as taken-for-granted. This contributed to their perception of field-level change as beyond their reach.

Within these process dynamics, the transformations in monitoring and imitation emerged as unintended consequences of certain modes of appropriating the technological "affordances" of the Web.[5] The low cost of information gathering, replication, and dissemination and minimal publishing delays enabled the actors to greatly increase the volume and frequency of publication, especially of hard-news stories. But this does not mean that these transformations were technologically determined.[6] The relevant technical infrastructure already existed during the first several years of Clarín.com and Lanacion.com, but during this initial period, online journalists did not take advantage of it in the ways described in chapter 2. This, in turn, meant that there were few changes in monitoring and imitation in both online and print newsrooms and in the resulting news products. Analyses of these products in chapter 4 will further illuminate this. Moreover, if technology had a determining role, there would have been no major variance between hard- and soft-news production. Having no determining role, however, should not be equated with having no role at all. Although counterfactuals are always complicated, it is reasonable to believe that the transformations examined above could not have happened without the affordances of digital networked computing. Thus, technology should be considered a necessary but not sufficient condition for increased monitoring and imitation in contemporary news work.[7]

Two dimensions of technology and technical practice are important for understanding the materiality of monitoring and imitation. First, actors did not resort to the use of a particular artifact but rather to an emergent constellation of hardware, software, and connectivity devices and their links to large-scale systems that are best characterized under the rubric of "infrastructure" (Bowker & Star, 1999; Edwards, 2003; Jackson, Edwards, Bowker, & Knobel, 2007; Star & Bowker, 2002; Star & Ruhleder, 1996). The notion of infrastructure emphasizes that technologies are often socially consequential not in a self-contained fashion (i.e., *this* computer program, *that* television technology) but in complex bundles of artifacts, protocols, and standards with the predisposition and skills to use them in particular ways. For instance, this infrastructural character becomes evident when considering the technological configuration of the *cablera* space at Clarín.com. This example also points to the second dimension. This configuration is primarily an infrastructure for *seeing* the organizational field and enabling news production at the intersection of localized newsrooms and distributed information flows. Thus, it is akin to the "scopic systems" described by Knorr Cetina and her colleagues in their analyses of technology in financial markets (Knorr Cetina, 2003, 2005; Knorr Cetina & Grimpe, 2008; Knorr Cetina & Preda, 2007). But unlike the case of finance work—which tends to rely on all-inclusive scopic systems that actors *must* use to do their jobs and thus exhibit low levels of variance in their use—there were substantial differences in whether and how journalists appropriated these scopic infrastructures in their news production routines.

The centrality of these scopic infrastructures in the account presented in this chapter points to the value of paying attention to technology in imitation. In chapter 1, I argued that most scholarship has proceeded as if imitation happened in a world devoid of artifacts. However, overlooking the role of technology would make it impossible to explain the intensification of monitoring and the expansion of imitation. Simply put, such an analysis would not have been able to make sense of the character and timing of the trend. In addition, a focus on technology helps us to rethink the roles of certain critical factors, such as social networks, in shaping changes in the degree of imitative activity. As stated above, media scholars have long seen tightly interrelated and colocated social networks as the prototypical incubator of pack journalism. This has parallels with a major stream of organizational sociology that underscores the role of interorganizational networks, such as interlocking boards of directors, as conduits for imitation (Davis & Greve, 1997; Galaskiewicz & Wasserman, 1989; Gemser & Wijnberg, 2001; Haunschild, 1993; Haunschild & Beckman, 1998). The account presented in this chapter suggests that interactions among journalists of different newsrooms, and social networks in general, might not be as central a factor driving imitation in contemporary settings as it appears to have been in the past. The role previously played by social networks in channeling information seems to have been displaced, at least in part, by the extensive use of technology. This is also consistent with findings by Knorr Cetina and her colleagues that indicate that reliance on scopic systems in financial work is inversely correlated with the prevalence and efficacy of interpersonal networks.

The changing patterns of technological infrastructures and practices also help to illuminate how monitoring and imitation emerge at the intersection of situated practices and contextual structures. In chapter 1 I argued that although communication analyses of imitation focus on the dynamics of practice, sociological studies of interorganizational mimicry concentrate on broader structural formations. The same can be said of analyses of monitoring, which is a critical precursor of imitation— that is, it is impossible to imitate without knowing what the relevant others do.

On the one side, scholarship on imitation in the media has yielded textured accounts of the prevalence of monitoring practices in news production (Breed, 1955; Crouse, 2003 [1972]; Donsbach, 1999; Noelle-Neuman, 1973; Reinemann, 2004; Shoemaker & Reese, 1996). Schudson argues that "news institutions monitor one another all the time" (2003, p. 109). Moreover, to Bourdieu, this is because journalists often operate under the assumption that "to know what to say, you have to know what everyone else has said" (1998, p. 18). Thus, for instance, in his ethnography of reporting at a summit of the World Trade Organization, Velthuis states that he and his colleagues routinely and "eagerly check[ed] electronic media sources to see what our competitors wrote, how much space they were granted by their editors, and how prominently their articles were published" (2006, p. 137).

On the other hand, taking a cue from H. White's dictum that "markets are tangible cliques of producers observing each other" (1981, p. 543), sociological studies of imitation in economic action devote considerable attention to examining the structural conditions that shape actors' observations of their competitive field. Two streams of this scholarship are particularly relevant for the issues addressed in this chapter. First, studies of interorganizational imitation often focus on how variations in social structure alter the "observability" of an organization's environment and subsequently shape the rate of imitation (Dobrev, 2007; Greve, 1996, 1998; Guillen, 2002; Haunschild & Miner, 1997; Labianca & Fairbank, 2005). For example, "An organization tends to imitate its counterparts because competitive pressures stemming from these counterparts in the market make them more visible and comparable to the focal organization" (Rhee, Kim, and Han, 2006, p. 503). Second, accounts of "public measures" attempt to ascertain how the emergence of widely available and legitimized knowledge, such as rankings, affects the social structure of observability and conformity in organizational fields (Anand & Peterson, 2000; Elsbach & Kramer, 1996; Espeland & Sauder, 2007; Sauder & Lancaster, 2006; Zuckerman & Sgourev, 2006). One consistent finding from this line of research is that the presence of rankings is often accompanied by an effort from organizations to conform to the evaluation metrics of better performers, which in turn increases the level of similarity across the organizational field.

From the vantage point of journalists, the growth in volume and frequency of publication in online news triggered a qualitative leap in the observability of their organizational field. When an actor monitored her competitors, it became easier for her to see what they were up to. For instance, *La Nación*'s Inés Capdevila could get a glimpse of what *Clarín* was planning for the next day's edition just by looking at Clarín.com in the late afternoon. This qualitative leap in observability had a potential "public knowledge" effect among news organizations that was akin to the effect of the introduction of rankings into an organizational field. Not only could actors observe more and better than before, but they knew that their competitors had, in principle, access to the same legitimized knowledge. However, whether journalists took advantage of this increased ability to observe the organizational environment and were affected by the "publicness" of its knowledge depended on the monitoring practices whereby they made this environment visible to themselves. The observability of the environment and the publicness of its knowledge can be of little or no consequence to an actor if, for whatever reason, she does not or cannot gather this information or it is not meaningful for her or both. An example is the far less intense monitoring undertaken by journalists producing soft news in comparison to their hard-news counterparts. Thus, the intensification of monitoring—and its subsequent contribution to the expansion of imitation—should be understood as emerging at the intersection of transformations in social structures and situated practices. Structural conditions in this case are shaped by the observability and publicness of the organizational environment. Issues of practice are signaled by differences in factors, such as editorial routines, intraorganizational relationships, and representations of the public. In turn, these factors affect the monitoring undertaken by the actors to render changes in structural conditions into workable input for news production.

Likewise, the dynamics of imitation are also affected by structural alterations in the technological, competitive, and audience dimensions of news work. But these alterations do not suffice to explain major differences in the enactment of imitation by type of news and comparatively minor differences in the enactment of imitation by medium. The major variance between hard and soft news arises from divergent patterns in sourcing practices, alignment processes between online and print newsrooms, representations of the public, ideational and affective experiences, and reputation management. The comparatively more minor variance by type of medium is an artifact of differences in technological affordances, editorial routines, and levels of awareness among the actors about the increasing similarity in the news. Moreover, the efficacy of these factors is also moderated by the countervailing forces of differentiation attempts pursued by actors in online and print newsrooms. To ascertain the consequences that these production factors—and the parallel differentiation efforts—have in shaping the resulting product outcomes, in the next chapter I present an analysis of patterns of similarity in the selection, presentation, and narration of online and print news.

FOUR

The Homogenization of News Products

I asked for suggestions when I was deciding whom to interview at *Clarín*. A friend who knows the Argentine media scene well said, "Make sure you talk to Alberto Amato." He added, *"Alberto te va a cantar la justa"*—a turn of phrase in *porteño* Spanish akin to "he calls it like he sees it" in English. A journalist for more than thirty years and a veteran of many newsrooms, Amato replies promptly and positively to my request for an interview. "Let's get a cup of coffee," he suggests when we meet, and we begin talking as we walk to the small bar on Tacuarí Street at 1700s that counts many *Clarín* personnel among its regulars. Passionate about his trade, Amato is eager to share his views about the state of online news; he even brings along several printouts as illustrations of issues that concern him. I ask whether he has noticed any changes in the similarity of the stories supplied by the Argentine media in recent years. He looks directly at me, pauses for a few seconds, and responds with a gesture of frustration as follows.

Amato: Well, today the three newspapers [referring to *Clarín*, *La Nación*, and the small leftist daily *Página/12*] published the same picture on [their respective] front pages. All three newspapers! . . . This means that print journalism doesn't think differently [*el periodismo gráfico no piensa diferente*]. We are so attentive to what *La Nación* and *Clarín* are going to publish. And let's not be in the situation of not having it.

Interviewer: Has this changed over time?

Amato: Yes, it got worse. (PERSONAL COMMUNICATION, FEBRUARY 22, 2007)

The picture to which Amato refers is of Argentina's president at the time, Néstor Kirchner, and his Venezuelan counterpart, Hugo Chávez, taken on the occasion of the launch of a joint endeavor between the two countries (fig. 4.1). Amato fails to mention that the front pages of *Clarín* and *La Nación* also feature two other headlines about similar events (an incident in a Buenos Aires slum and a transportation accident), and both *Clarín* and *Página/12* have headlines about a political crisis in Italy. In other words, at least half of the front-page news stories in each daily are about an event reported in at least one of the other two. The remainder of this chapter examines the extent to which this fragment from the interview with Amato resonates with systemic patterns of similarity in the news supplied by the leading Argentine online and print media in recent years. This is a unique window into how transformations in monitoring and imitation in editorial work affect the resulting news products.

To this end I draw on a content analysis of the top stories of the day in print and online newspapers. (This study was succinctly mentioned in the introduction and is more fully described in chapter 1 and appendix A.) By top stories of the day, I mean those that appear on the front page or on the top portion of the homepage. Print data were collected from *Clarín* and *La Nación* for four ten-week periods in 1995, 2000, 2004, and 2005. Online data were gathered from Clarín.com, Lanacion.com, and a strong online competitor, Infobae.com, three times a day for a ten-week period in 2005—coinciding with the fourth print period. The analysis examines which stories are *selected* for inclusion on front pages and homepages, how the content of these stories is *presented* on these front pages and homepages, and how the stories are *narrated* "inside" the pages of their respective print newspapers and news sites.

The analysis reveals four key findings. First is an increase in the similarity in the selection of news and its front-page presentation for print newspapers that coincides with the timing of the growth in the volume and frequency of online news publishing. Second is a high level of similarity in the selection of stories for print and online outlets in the contemporary scenario. Third is a high level of similarity in the narration of stories for online sites. Fourth, these patterns apply only to hard news. The longitudinal increase of similarity in print, the timing of this increase, the recent high level of similarity across the print-online divide, the differences between print and online outlets, and that these patterns apply only to hard news are consistent with the account of news work offered in chapters 2

4.1 Front pages of *Página/12*, *Clarín*, and *La Nación*, February 22, 2007. © *Página/12*, *Clarín*, and *La Nación*.

and 3. Thus, drawing on these findings, in the conclusion of the chapter I elaborate on the heuristic value of looking at the production and product stages of the imitation life cycle. In light of idiosyncratic characteristics of the Argentine context described in chapter 1, I end the analysis with a coda about whether the increase in similarity in the news might be an outcome of the political relationships between the government and the press during the presidency of Néstor Kirchner (2003–2007).

Selecting the News

Consider the front pages of *Clarín* and *La Nación* on August 8, 2000 (fig. 4.2). Two pairs of stories about the same events were selected for inclusion on both front pages: a piece about an Argentine military officer captured in Europe (the lead story in *Clarín*) and an article about a popular march to a church that takes place every year. Contrast these front pages with those on November 23, 2005 (fig. 4.3). In this case, there are three pairs of stories about the same events featured on both front pages: an article about statements made by the then-minister of the economy (the lead story in both newspapers), a story about an ongoing criminal trial with significant political connotations, and a piece about Argentine tennis player David Nalbandian's return to his hometown after winning the 2005 Shanghai Master's Tournament. In addition to the increase in the number of pairs of stories about the same event, the immediate impression received when comparing figures 4.2 and 4.3 is of a loss of front-page "real estate" with any differentiation in terms of story selection.

Next, take a look at the homepages of Clarín.com, Lanacion.com, and Infobae.com on the morning of November 17, 2005 (fig. 4.4). Before delving into issues of similarity in story selection, the very similar design of the homepages is noteworthy, especially the division in the placement of hard and soft news.[1] In all three cases, hard news was placed on the left side of the screen, and soft news and other kinds of content on the right side. (These soft-news and other kinds of content were removed from fig. 4.4 to enhance readability of the hard-news stories on these homepages.) With respect to the hard-news stories—which in the morning shift averaged only two-thirds of the top nine stories included in the sample—three triads of stories about the same event were featured on the three homepages. First, the lead story on all sites—located at the top-left corner of the screen—was about a confrontation between Argentina's then president and the country's bishops. Second, the three sites also published stories about tennis player David Nalbandian's passage to the

4.2 Front pages of *Clarín* and *La Nación*, August 8, 2000. © *Clarín* and *La Nación*.

4.3 Front pages of *Clarín* and *La Nación*, November 23, 2005. © *Clarín* and *La Nación*.

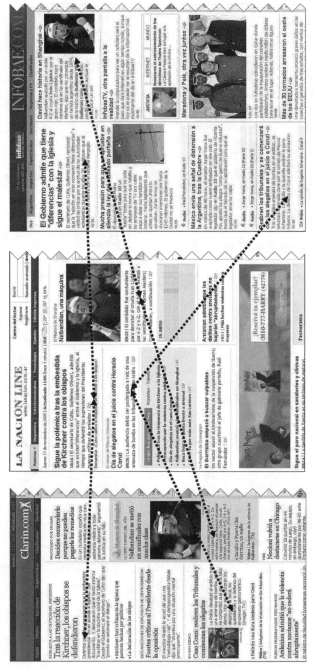

4.4 Top portion of homepages of Clarín.com, Lanacion.com, and Infobae.com, November 17, 2005. © Clarín.com, Lanacion.com, and Infobae.com.

semifinals of the Shanghai Master's Tournament, and they illustrated it with remarkably similar pictures. As noted above, this developing story also deserved inclusion on the front pages of *Clarín* and *La Nación* six days later, after he had won the tournament (fig. 4.3). Third, there was coverage of an ongoing crime investigation in all of the online newspapers. A cursory glance at the portion of the three homepages devoted to hard news yields a striking degree of similarity.

The comparison of these front pages and homepages illustrates a clear trend toward increasing similarity in the selection of print news in just a decade and an equally high level of similarity between print and online news in the contemporary setting. To measure similarity, the analysis examines whether a story published in one of the print newspapers or online news sites addresses an event that is also the subject of a story in the other print newspaper or at least one of the other online news sites, respectively. To ascertain the possible influence of the format and subject matter of each story, the analysis looks at two other questions. The first is whether a story is hard news or soft news or another, less common type of format. This is important for establishing links between the production dynamics analyzed in the two previous chapters and the product outcomes that are the focus of this one. The second question is whether the main topic addressed in the story is a public affairs issue (articles about politics, economics, business, and international news) or a non–public affairs one (articles about sports, crime, science, technology, medicine, natural disasters, accidents, and the like). Answering this question will help to determine the existence of thematic patterns in online and print news data. But, more important, it is critical for assessing possible cultural and political consequences of homogenization in the news.

As mentioned above, four different samples were collected for the print newspapers and one for the online newspapers. For analytical purposes, the data were consolidated by sample instead of by newspaper because variance across samples applies to all newspapers, and the main findings become visible from comparisons across these samples. Idiosyncratic outcomes that apply to a particular paper in one or more samples will be noted whenever appropriate.

The analysis yielded two general results. First, all of the print cases of overlap and all but three of the online cases concern hard-news stories. This finding is consistent with the divergent logics of hard- and soft-news production and the major variance in imitation by type of content examined in the two previous chapters. Second, in all samples, the majority of the stories were hard news (table 4.1). Moreover, in the case of the print samples, although the proportion of hard news relative to the total

Table 4.1.   General Characteristics of the Print and Online Data Sets Used for the Content Analysis of News Products

	Print Data Set				Online Data Set		
	1995	2000	2004	2005	Morning	Afternoon	Evening
Sample size	208	235	237	247	540	540	540
Mean number of stories per front page	5.2	5.9	5.9	6.2	N/A	N/A	N/A
Content type							
Hard news	91% (190)	89% (208)	81% (192)	84% (207)	66% (359)	71% (383)	82% (441)
Soft news	9% (18)	10% (24)	16% (38)	10% (25)	21% (112)	9% (48)	10% (55)
Editorials, interviews, and op-eds	0% (0)	0% (1)	3% (7)	4% (10)	2% (11)	11% (57)	7% (40)
Entertainment prescheduled news	N/A	N/A	N/A	N/A	11% (58)	10% (52)	1% (4)
Other	0% (0)	1% (2)	0% (0)	2% (5)	0% (0)	0% (0)	0% (0)
Content overlap							
Hard-news stories with overlap	70	70	80	98	181	197	241
Proportion of hard news with overlap relative to all hard news	37%	34%	42%	47%	50%	51%	55%

number of stories decreased over time, the absolute number of hard-news stories stayed relatively unchanged. This is because although the number of front-pages stories grew (e.g., the 2005 sample has 19% more stories than its 1995 counterpart), it appears that most of the increase was allocated to other content types. Therefore, the proportion of hard-news stories with overlap to the total number of hard-news stories is used in this and the following sections as the main metric of similarity in story selection. This helps to control for variation in the total number of stories and in the proportion of hard-news stories across samples. In addition to these general findings, specific results apply to patterns of similarity between the print newspapers, among their online counterparts, and across both media.

Regarding the print newspapers, there is an increase in the level of content overlap between *Clarín* and *La Nación* that goes from 37% in the 1995 sample to 34% in the 2000 sample and then increases to 42% and 47% in the 2004 and 2005 samples, respectively (see table 4.1). Because the 1995 and 2000 samples were before the intensification of constant publishing of online newspapers and the difference between them is not significant, they are combined into a *Before* period. Similarly, the 2004 and 2005 samples are merged into an *After* period. Comparing these two periods reveals a significant ($p < .01$) increase of ten percentage points in the proportion of hard-news stories with content overlap (see table 4.2). That the timing of the increase in the similarity of print newspapers' front pages from the *Before* to the *After* periods coincides temporally with the growth in volume and frequency of publication by news sites supports the notion that a consequential expansion in the imitation activities of print journalism is tied to the changes in online sites. Furthermore, the increase in the level of content overlap is also tied to a thematic variation: a significant ($p < .01$) rise of sixteen percentage points in the proportion of public affairs stories with content overlap from the *Before* to the *After* periods (table 4.2). This increase took place even though both the proportions of public affairs and non–public affairs stories and the proportion of overlapping non–public affairs stories stayed relatively unchanged.

Concerning the online newspapers, the analysis shows a high level of content overlap, averaging 52% across the three shifts. Moreover, this already high level of overlap increases moderately as the day unfolds: from 50% in the morning to 51% in the afternoon and 55% in the evening—the latter being the lowest level of differentiation in story selection of all samples, print and online. Because the difference between the morning and afternoon samples is so small, for analytical purposes they were aggregated into a single sample and contrasted with the evening

Table 4.2.   Homogenization in the Selection of Hard News

Print	Before period (398 stories)	After period (399 stories)	Variation
Content overlap	35%	45%	+10%***
Content focus			
All public affairs stories	60%	56%	–4%
Stories with overlap only	33%	49%	+16%***
All non–public affairs stories	40%	44%	+4%
Stories with overlap only	38%	39%	+1%

Online	Morning and afternoon (742 stories)	Evening (441 stories)	Variation
Content overlap	51%	55%	+4%
Content focus			
All public affairs stories	63%	57%	–6%
Stories with overlap only	51%	53%	+2%
All non–public affairs stories	37%	43%	+6%
Stories with overlap only	51%	64%	+13%***

Print-Online	Print 2005 (207 stories)	Online 2005 (744 stories)	Variation
Content overlap (*Clarín* and *La Nación* only)	47%	47%	0%

***$p < .01$.

sample. This comparison yielded an increase of four percentage points in the level of similarity (table 4.2).

In addition to the high level of similarity in story selection among these three online news sites, there are also two sets of important thematic variations that take place as the day unfolds. First, there is a growth of six percentage points in the proportion of non–public affairs stories from the combined morning-afternoon shifts to the evening shift, resulting mostly from sports news that breaks in the latter part of the day (table 4.2). More important, there is also a significant ($p < .01$) increase of thirteen percentage points in the level of similarity of non–public affairs stories from the morning and afternoon to the evening. Second, the analysis examines whether a story that had overlap in one shift also had overlap in at least one of the other two shifts that day. The results show that the proportion of stories that appear in only one shift registers a significant ($p <$ .01) growth of twenty percentage points from the morning-afternoon to the evening shift (table 4.3). Furthermore, whereas the thematic mix of the overlapping stories that appear in more than one shift remains unchanged throughout the day—with two-thirds devoted to public affairs and one-third to non–public affairs—the proportion of non–public affairs stories among the more ephemeral stories with overlap shows a significant ($p < .01$) rise of twenty-three percentage points toward the end of the day.[2] Taken together, these thematic variations converge with issues of differentiation raised in the two previous chapters. First, news sites differentiated their coverage from their print counterparts mostly regarding non–public affairs stories. But this does not mean greater differentiation among online players, because they pursued their differentiation efforts in the same direction, that is, toward their non–public affairs coverage. Second, it appears that the tension between alignment and differentiation with the print newsroom that is experienced often among online staffers might also have a thematic aspect. The former tendency is seen in public affairs stories, and the latter is stronger in non–public affairs news.

Table 4.3. Daily Evolution of Online Stories with Overlap in Relation to Their Durability

	Morning and Afternoon (378 stories)	Evening (241 stories)
Durability		
Yes (stories that appear in at least two shifts)*	64%	44%
No (stories that appear in only one shift)*	36%	56%
Content focus		
Stories with durability		
Public affairs stories	67%	67%
Non–public affairs stories	33%	33%
Stories with no durability		
Public affairs stories*	61%	38%
Non–public affairs stories*	39%	62%

Note: Rows that have an asterisk indicate significant ($p < .01$) differences from the morning and afternoon to the evening shifts.

In my examination of homogenization across print and online news, my analysis draws on the online data of Clarín.com and Lanacion.com in 2005 in the absence of print *Infobae* data.[3] The analysis reveals three sets of findings. A comparison of the stories with overlap within the print and the online samples shows no difference in the level of similarity across media (table 4.2). This finding is consistent with news production dynamics analyzed in chapter 3 and underscores the claim made in that chapter that the variance between media is less salient than that having to do with type of content.

The two other findings are about important patterns that connect the print and online newspapers of the same company at two key points in time during the evolution of the 24-hour news cycle. They are the transition from the print edition to the online homepage in the morning of the same day and the bridge between online evening coverage and the print front page of the next day. Regarding the first moment, 47% and 46% of the hard-news stories in *Clarín* and *La Nación*, respectively, are about events also featured on the homepages of their online counterparts in the morning.[4] Furthermore, there are also substantive ties between the stories published on the front page of one newspaper and the home-page of its competitor. Forty-five percent of *Clarín*'s hard-news stories are about events also featured in the morning homepages of Lanacion.com, a figure that goes down only slightly to 41% for hard-news stories from *La Nación* to Clarín.com. There is also a high level of similarity in story selection within the print-online pairs of the same newspaper organization in the transition from the end of one day in the online environment to the following morning's print edition.[5] The hard news on the evening homepages of Clarín.com and Lanacion.com anticipate 58% and 51% of the hard news of the next day's front pages of *Clarín* and *La Nación*, respectively. There are also substantive levels of overlap across media and companies: Lanacion.com's evening homepage anticipates nearly one-half (48%) of the front page of the next day's *Clarín*, whereas Clarín.com's evening homepage anticipates a bit more than one-third (36%) of the next day's *La Nación*. This lower level of overlap between Clarín.com's evening homepage and *La Nación*'s print front page is related in part to the high level of non–public affairs reporting in the former and the much lower level of this kind of content in the latter.

These findings about the evolution of similarity in story selection across media and organizations reinforce at least four aspects of the production dynamics analyzed in previous chapters. Despite the historical, strategic, editorial, and cultural divisions between *Clarín* and *La Nación*, there is little difference in terms of the connections between the print and online editions of each of these organizations. This product outcome is consistent with remarks made previously about a parallel lack of difference between the two companies regarding imitation in news production. Second, the similarity in story selection between a print paper and the morning edition of its online counterpart is the expression of the widespread inclination among online journalists to follow up on the stories introduced by their print paper. Third, the high level of anticipation of the next day's print front page by the previous day's online evening homepage is tied to two elements of the online and print production processes. One is the intensification of alignment efforts among online staffers as the day comes to an end. The other is the pressure to conform that is experienced by print journalists with respect to the growing "publicness" of news knowledge during the day. Although it is not possible to establish which of these two elements has a stronger influence on the observed product outcomes, it is likely that each contributes to the creation of a strong cross-media convergence in story selection during the transition from one day to the next. Finally, the substantial cross-media, cross-organizational continuities further underscore the impression of a densely interconnected web of homogeneous story selection patterns in the current Argentine media scene.

Chapter 3 includes quotations from journalists in which they acknowledge the increasing difficulty they face in differentiating their news products by the selection of stories. *Clarín*'s coeditor-in-chief Daniel Fernández Canedo mentions that because they are aware of this trend, he and his colleagues resort increasingly to what they call *la mirada*, or a singular perspective on the news, to distinguish themselves from their competitors and other players in the broader media landscape. But to what extent does *la mirada* make a difference? In a situation of increasing sameness in terms of *which* stories are told, do journalists differentiate their coverage by *how* they tell these stories? The next two sections will answer these questions.

Presenting the News

Two additional analyses were pursued to answer these questions. They were conducted on the subset of stories that displayed content overlap in the selection patterns reported above. The first analysis dealt with the presentation of information on front pages or homepages. Each print story was contrasted with the other one in its dyad and assessed regarding the use of textual (main subject, verb, and rest of the headline) and visual (placement and illustrations) elements of editorial construction as well as a measure of interpretive likeness. A similar analysis was performed on dyads and triads of online stories—with the exception of visual elements because differences in use of visual resources introduced systematic biases in the comparison of Clarín.com, Lanacion.com, and Infobae.com homepages.[6]

The headlines of the dyads and triads with overlap in story selection in figures 4.2–4.4 provide an opening glimpse into issues of similarity in the presentation of print and online news. The front pages in figure 4.2 have two pairs of stories with content overlap. The first pair, about an Argentine military officer arrested in Europe, has the following headlines: "An Argentine military [officer] was detained in Italy" (*Clarín*) and "[They] detained a retired military [officer] upon a request from France" (*La Nación*). Both headlines share the verb but not the subject or the rest of the sentence. They also have a medium level of similarity in issues of placement, illustration, and interpretation. The second pair of stories is about an annual march to San Cayetano Church in Buenos Aires, which is undertaken by many people who are unemployed. *Clarín*'s headline is "San Cayetano, more than a million," and *La Nación*'s is "A multitude asked for jobs in San Cayetano." These headlines do not share the subject, verb, or remainder of the sentence and have a relatively low level of similarity in matters of interpretation. However, both stories have pictures on their front pages—albeit different ones—and exhibit a medium level of similarity regarding placement.

The front pages in figure 4.3 have three pairs of stories with content overlap. The first pair, about a statement by Roberto Lavagna, minister of the economy at the time, regarding budget issues in public works, has the following headlines: "Lavagna denounced extra costs in public works" (*Clarín*) and "Lavagna urged the limitation of expenditures on public works" (*La Nación*). Both headlines have a high level of similarity regarding subject, placement, and illustration; a medium level in the rest of the sentence and in interpretation; and a low level in choice of verb ("denounced" vs. "urged"), which is the main marker of difference in the editorial positions of the newspapers about this story. The second pair of stories is about an investigation into a fire that killed more than a hundred people in Cromagnon, a Buenos Aires concert venue, a year earlier. The headlines are "Cromañón: a girl said she knows who shot the flare [which ignited the fire]" (*Clarín*) and "Polemic testimony in the Cromagnon [judicial] case" (*La Nación*). The headlines have a high level of similarity in placement and illustrations, a medium level in interpretation, and a low level regarding all three textual elements. The third pair deals with a visit to his hometown by tennis player David Nalbandian, after winning that year's Shanghai Master's Tournament. The headlines are "The idol, at home" (*Clarín*) and "From China to Córdoba, a party for Nalbandian" (*La Nación*). The similarity of both headlines is high for issues of placement, illustration, and interpretation, medium in terms of verb choice, and low concerning the subject and rest of the sentence.

The homepages presented in figure 4.4 have three triads of stories with content overlap. For the purpose of analysis, each of these triads is unbundled into three dyads, which are examined separately. The first triad, and the lead story on each site, is about a confrontation between Argentina's president at the time and the country's bishops. The respective headlines read: "After [President Néstor] Kirchner's reaction, the bishops defended [themselves]" (Clarín.com), "The polemic continues after the attack of Kirchner against the bishops" (Lanacion.com), and "The government admits 'differences' with the Church and the malaise continues" (Infobae .com). The headlines in the dyad of Clarín.com and Lanacion.com have a low level of similarity in the choice of subject and verb and a medium level of similarity in the rest of the sentence and interpretation. The similarity between the headlines of Clarín.com and Infobae.com is low in all four categories. It is also low between Infobae.com and Lanacion.com, with the exception of a medium level in interpretation. This results from the mild convergence of meaning between the notion of a "polemic" and the feeling of "malaise" between the parties.

The second triad—about tennis player David Nalbandian's passage to the semifinals of the Shanghai Master's Tournament—features the following headlines: "Nalbandian got into the semifinals with a lot of class" (Clarín.com), "Nalbandian, a machine" (Lanacion.com), and "David makes history in Shanghai" (Infobae.com). With the exception of the use of the similar subjects—Nalbandian or David—in all three dyads and a medium level of similarity in interpretation issues between Clarín.com and Infobae.com, the rest of the elements exhibit remarkably low levels of similarity across the board. The third triad is about an ongoing judicial investigation: "Conzi case: The Courts reopen and the hearings [*alegatos*] begin" (Clarín.com), "Day of hearings in the trial against Horacio Conzi" (Lanacion.com), and "The Courts reopen and the argument hearing in the Conzi trial will begin" (Infobae.com). The three headlines have a high level of similarity regarding issues of interpretation—they primarily convey the occurrence of a particular phase in the trial—but whereas Clarín.com's and Infobae.com's headlines are nearly identical, Lanacion .com's is quite different.

Table 4.4. Homogenization in the Presentation of Hard News with Overlap

Print	Before period (140 stories)	After period (178 stories)	Variation
Level of similarity of all stories	33%	49%	16%***
Level of similarity by content focus			
Public affairs stories only	34%	49%	15%**
Non–public affairs stories only	32%	50%	18%**
Level of similarity of all stories by type of variable			
Textual variables (subject, verb, and rest of headline)	20%	37%	17%***
Visual variables (illustrations and placement)	52%	63%	11%**
Interpretation variable	36%	56%	20%***

Online	Morning and Afternoon (378 stories)	Evening (241 stories)	Variation
Level of similarity of all stories	33%	28%	5%
Level of similarity by content focus			
Public affairs stories only	34%	32%	2%
Non–public affairs stories only	33%	25%	8%
	Durability (349 stories)	No durability (270 stories)	
Level of similarity of all stories by durability	28%	36%	8%**

Print-Online	Print 2005 (98 stories)	Online 2005 (350 stories)	Variation
Level of similarity (*Clarín* and *La Nación* only)	49%	35%	14%**

***p < .01. **p < .05.

The headline that summarizes the patterns of presentational similarity suggested by these front pages and homepages is "Similarity of Print News Grows over Time and Surpasses That of Online News." The remainder of this section provides a more detailed analysis of these patterns.

An examination of similarity on the front pages of *Clarín* and *La Nación* between 1995 and 2005 reveals a sizable and significant ($p < .01$) increase of sixteen percentage points, from 33% in the *Before* period to 49% in the *After* period (table 4.4). This increase affects public affairs and non–public affairs stories to a comparable degree—fifteen and eighteen percentage points, respectively. This finding suggests that the expansion of imitation shapes not only *which* stories are selected for inclusion on front pages but also *how* they are presented. The size of the increase and the fact that it applies to all kinds of stories indicate that this is a strong trend.

The increase in similarity from the *Before* to the *After* period is more pronounced in the textual elements of content presentation (subject, verb, and rest of the sentence) than in the visual elements (illustrations and placement). Thus, whereas the textual elements register a significant ($p < .01$) rise of seventeen percentage points, the visual elements show six percentage points less, or a significant ($p < .05$) growth of eleven percentage points (table 4.4). This is noteworthy because these two sets of elements are often used to emphasize different aspects of editorial construction. The textual elements tend to be used to convey an editorial viewpoint about the story, and the visual ones often signal the importance assigned to the story in relation to the other stories featured on the front page. This suggests that the main effect is less about what kinds of news are considered particularly important and more about how a given story is editorially framed. One manifestation of this greater increase in the similarity of textual elements is the increase in the number of very similar textual constructions of headlines between *Clarín* and *La Nación* since 1995. There are several instances of either identical or nearly identical pairs of headlines in 2005—and none in the 1995 sample. For instance, on September 27, 2005, both newspapers published two overlapping front-page stories. The first pair of stories, about Antonio Boggiano, then a Supreme Court judge, had these headlines: "Boggiano affirms that the government betrayed him" (*Clarín*) and "Boggiano says that the government betrayed him" (*La Nación*). The headlines of the second pair, about statements made by then U.S. president George W. Bush, were "Bush emphasized the leadership of Brazil in Latin America" (*Clarín*) and "Bush emphasized the leadership of Brazil in the region" (*La Nación*).[7]

Much lower levels of presentational similarity characterize the online news landscape. The analysis reveals an average level of similarity of 31%

across all shifts and a small and nonsignificant decrease of five percentage points from 33% in the combined morning and afternoon shifts to 28% in the evening shift (table 4.4). This decrease is due primarily to a drop of eight percentage points toward the end of the day in the non–public affairs stories, which converges with findings that online staffers put their differentiation efforts more intensely into non–public affairs stories than into public affairs stories.

An analysis of durability provides another window into the dynamics of similarity in online story presentation. In chapters 2 and 3, we saw that stories that lasted for more than one shift were often modified during the day when relevant events took place. The analysis reveals that stories that lasted more than one shift had a 28% level of similarity, whereas those stories that had content overlap in only one shift had a 36% level of similarity, or a significant ($p < .05$) difference of eight percentage points between these two types of stories (table 4.4). Furthermore, an examination of the stories with durability in consecutive shifts shows a decrease of similarity over time. Stories that appeared in the morning and the afternoon had levels of similarity of 35% and 25%, respectively. Those that appeared in the afternoon and the evening had levels of similarity of 35% and 27%, respectively. This examination of durability signals that stories that had repeated opportunities to be updated exhibited a decrease in similarity levels in the presentation of content on the homepage. As shown in chapter 3, Lanacion.com's Mariana Robin noted that she and her colleagues sometimes modified the headline of a story if they saw that it was too similar to that featured by one or more competitors. More generally, these patterns of durability are consistent with the notion that online journalists were aware of the rise of content homogeneity, disliked this trend, and tried to move away from it within their sense of what was feasible in light of their work conditions.

To compare the print and online data of *Clarín* and *La Nación* in 2005, the visual elements were not taken into account in the recalculation of levels of similarity in the print sample because these elements were not coded in the stories of the online sample. The analysis reveals that whereas stories in the print sample had a 49% level of similarity, their online counterparts had a 35% level, or a significant ($p < .05$) difference of fourteen percentage points (table 4.4). It is worth stressing at least three issues related to this large difference in levels of similarity. First, from a technical standpoint, it is much less costly to change the homepage of an online news site—or nearly any page of a site—than the front page of a daily newspaper. On the one hand, the affordances of the Web make it quite easy for a journalist to modify a particular page. The convergence between the ethnographic and product data on durability dynamics shows that online journalists took advantage of these affordances, at least to a certain extent. On the other hand, as we saw in chapter 3, even though some journalists, such as *Clarín*'s Fernando González, might use the online sites of their competitors to monitor forthcoming print editions in the event they have to change a front page, they rarely act on this information to print a second edition of their paper. Second, although interviews with print and online journalists revealed that neither group liked the homogenization of news, online journalists were more aware of it. In turn, this might have fueled greater differentiation efforts. Third, in light of online journalists' focus on the headline and the lead, it is not surprising that these differentiation efforts might have been disproportionately targeted at their homepages.

In sum, and to go back to the question of whether—as suggested by print journalists interviewed for this book—*la mirada* offers a way to differentiate editorial content, the findings presented in this section indicate that *Clarín* and *La Nación* failed to substantially distinguish their front pages from each other. Instead, there was a marked increase of presentational similarity within the pairs that already exhibited similarity in story selection. Furthermore, and consistent with the ethnographic analysis provided in chapters 2 and 3, the construction of homepages featured a comparatively lower level of presentational similarity. But there is more to news content than what is conveyed on front pages and homepages. Thus, the next section continues the examination of homogenization in the news by looking at the narration of stories.

Narrating the News

To get at these issues, another analysis was conducted. It aimed to ascertain degrees of sameness and difference in the narrative construction of content on front-page and homepage stories with content overlap. Each print story was compared to the other one in its pair and evaluated with respect to the writing of stories, the use of sources and illustrations, and an overall metric of interpretive similarity. A similar procedure was followed to examine dyads and triads of online stories—with the exception of visual elements, for the same reasons given in the analysis of presentational matters.

The analysis of print stories with overlap reveals levels of similarity of 23% and 30% for the *Before* and *After* periods, respectively (table 4.5). These are much lower levels of similarity than those observed for the

Table 4.5.   Homogenization in the Narration of Hard News with Overlap

Print	*Before period* (140 stories)	*After period* (178 stories)	Variation
Level of similarity of all stories	23%	30%	7%
Level of similarity by content focus			
Public affairs stories only	22%	34%	12%
Non–public affairs stories only	25%	29%	4%
Level of similarity of all stories by type of variable			
Textual variables (writing and sourcing)	27%	33%	6%
Visual variable (illustrations)	28%	34%	6%
Interpretation variable	13%	22%	9%

Online	*Morning and Afternoon* (312 stories)	*Evening* (196 stories)	Variation
Level of similarity of all stories	50%	46%	4%
Level of similarity by content focus			
Public affairs stories only	53%	55%	2%
Non–public affairs stories only	46%	39%	7%
	Durability (302 stories)	*No durability* (206 stories)	
Level of similarity of all stories by durability	47%	50%	3%

Print-Online	*Print 2005* (98 stories)	*Online 2005* (302 stories)	Variation
Level of similarity (*Clarín* and *La Nación* only)	32%	53%	21%***

***$p < .01$.

presentation of these stories on the front page—33% and 49%, respectively. However, there is still a nonsignificant increase of seven percentage points from the *Before* to the *After* periods. This before-and-after growth applies to both public affairs and non–public affairs stories, but it affects the former more strongly than the latter. Furthermore, this growth manifests itself evenly with regard to the textual and nontextual variables examined in the analysis.

The size and character of this before-and-after pattern are tied to several aspects of the news production routines described in chapter 3. First, it is not surprising that the increase in similarity is far less pronounced in narrative construction than in front-page presentation, because more editorial effort per story is spent on the former than on the latter. Second, although the pattern is neither large nor significant, it is still noteworthy because it affects all types of stories and all the elements of narrative construction included in the analysis. Third, the relatively small size of this effect is consistent with the attempts by print journalists, who consider it very difficult to differentiate coverage by the selection of stories, to utilize *la mirada,* or a singular perspective on the story that can best achieve differentiation by narrative means. However, the presence of an increase of similarity over time—even taking into account its relatively small size and statistically nonsignificant character—converges with the concerns expressed by some of these journalists about the rising limitations they experience in their ability to tell different stories. They tie these limitations to the expansion of imitation across the media landscape.

The increase in similarity of front-page stories is evident in several key components of the construction of journalistic narratives. Opening paragraphs become more similar over time. The writing style moves toward the adoption of shorter paragraphs and more direct language. Factual information becomes more dominant in the *After* period, whereas clear expressions of ideological positions become rarer. The use of anonymous sources decreases, and the number and diversity of viewpoints increase, but there is remarkable convergence in the selection of sources and quotations. That is, although there is an increase in the number of sources and quotations per story, both papers tend to overlap over time in the sources relied on and the quotations used. *Clarín*'s use of illustrations remained constant over time, but *La Nación* gradually approached that of its competitor. For instance, it replaced cartoons by graphs, which has long been one of *Clarín*'s distinct features. This leads to increased visual similarity. All these changes result in a decrease in content diversity. The following comparison of a pair of stories from the *Before* period with a pair from the *After* period illustrates this pattern of increased similarity in narrative construction.

In the fall of 1995, a summit of presidents from the Ibero-American region took place in Bariloche, located in southwestern Argentina. *Clarín* and *La Nación* sent special correspondents to cover the event. Both papers ran front-page stories about the summit on October 18, 1995. These stories are quite different in terms of editorial construction. In the sample paragraphs that follow, *Clarín*'s article opens with a critical statement about the Cuban embargo and mentions President Carlos Menem later in the article. In contrast, *La Nación*'s piece opens with President Menem's statements about a change in the position of the president of Cuba, Fidel Castro, and mentions the embargo later on. These paragraphs convey clearly the ideological positions of both papers. Whereas *Clarín* was critical of President Menem and the embargo, *La Nación* supported him on this issue and was not critical of the embargo.

Clarín	*La Nación*
First paragraph, about the embargo:	*First paragraph, about Menem:*
"In its strongest manifestation since its creation, but without abandoning the caution of addressing the subject in indirect form, the Ibero-American Summit rejected yesterday the commercial embargo that the United States [has] maintain[ed] against Cuba since 1962 for becoming a socialist country."	"President Carlos Menem noted as a fact [that was] plausible and 'promising of other changes, the recognition by Castro, regarding some type of improvements, toward the International Monetary Fund and the World Bank, made without euphoria and with austere words.'"
Later in the story, about Menem:	*Later in the story, about the embargo:*
"President Carlos Menem did not appear so content after Castro left the Llao-Llao hotel, where the fifth Summit took place. In a press conference that closed this fifth Summit and in response to a question from *Clarín*, he insisted on his old demand of 'democratization' of the socialist system in the island and about the respect of human rights" (Pazos, Santoro, & Viceconte, 1995, p. 2).	"However, later on, in response to the possibility that Cuba might have some system of political opening, in recognition of the support given by the Summit against the American embargo, [President Menem] said: 'We have talked informally (with Castro) and I do not see any possibility" (Bellando, 1995, p. 8).

Ten years later, on September 27, 2005, both newspapers published front-page stories about the national government's decision to replace the head of the Coast Guard. Unlike the previous pair, the opening paragraphs of these stories are nearly identical, which was extremely rare in 1995, emphasizing factual matters and mentioning the same facts. This makes it quite difficult to differentiate their ideological position on the event. It is noteworthy that each story has a byline. This indicates that there was substantive direct involvement by a reporter who was working on each story. These are the opening paragraphs of both stories:

Clarín	La Nación
"The government replaced the head of the Coast Guard, Pedro Pasteris, suspected of participating in operations [undertaken to] make people disappear during the military dictatorship, when he was responsible for the security of the international bridge that connects the Corrientes city of Paso de los Libres with Uruguayana, Brazil, at the beginning of the '80s" (Braslavsky, 2005, p. 3).	"The government replaced yesterday the head of the Coast Guard, Pedro Pasteris, after it became publicly known in a judicial investigation about his alleged responsibility in the disappearing of nine people when he was chief of the international bridge of Paso de los Libres, between 1980 and 1983" (Colonna, 2005, p. 6).

Unlike the print stories, the content of the online stories with overlap exhibits a high level of similarity that averages 49% across the three shifts.[8] This high level of similarity is consistent with the analysis of content production reported in chapters 2 and 3, specifically about issues of inadequate time allotted to staffers to source and find unique information and the presence of intense monitoring and imitation of competitors and other media players. Like the presentation of content on homepages, the level of similarity decreases slightly as the day unfolds, decreasing from 50% in the combined morning and afternoon shifts to 46% in the evening shift (table 4.5). The bulk of the change over time is driven by non–public affairs stories. This finding converges with evidence about news production at Clarín.com and Lanacion.com that reinforces the notion that most differentiation attempts tend to center on non–public affairs matters. Furthermore, the examination of durability provides another window into the issue of differentiation. The analysis reveals that durability plays a more limited role for narration than for presentation of content: stories with durability have a 47% similarity, whereas those without it have a 50% similarity (table 4.5). This is not surprising, because the work routines of online journalists who produce hard news afford less of an opportunity to modify the narrative of stories than the headline and the lead featured on the homepages.

This high level of similarity is an average across the stories in a given shift or content category. Thus, whereas in some cases the content of the stories in a dyad or triad is quite dissimilar, there are many instances of stories that contain many identical or nearly identical paragraphs. In most instances of nearly identical paragraphs, there is some difference in the text of one story in relation to the other in its dyad or the two others in its triad, which is evidence that the content was not republished automatically. Instead, the journalists at the relevant sites introduced some modifications before publishing the stories on their respective Web sites, but the bulk of the narrative remained unchanged. The following two examples—one that treats a public affairs subject and the other a non–public affairs story—illustrate the presence of nearly identical content and evidence of a journalist's intervention.

On November 11, 2005, Clarín.com and Lanacion.com published stories about some statements made by the minister of the economy, Roberto Lavagna, at an event organized by *Clarín*. The headlines are "Lavagna said that an agreement with the IMF [International Monetary Fund] 'is not indispensable' " (Clarín.com) and "Lavagna says that an agreement with the IMF is not indispensable" (Lanacion.com).[9] The first three paragraphs of the two stories follow.

Clarín.com

"The economy minister, Roberto Lavagna, affirmed this afternoon that 'it is not indispensable' to achieve an agreement with the IMF during 2006. However, he admitted that obtaining a 'reasonable' understanding [with the IMF] would be beneficial for the country.

" 'It is not indispensable, but with a reasonable agreement it would be easier,' maintained the head of the Palacio de Hacienda [the headquarters of the economy minister] at the end of his speech in a seminar series organized by *Clarín* to celebrate the 60th anniversary of its founding.

Lanacion.com

"The economy minister, Roberto Lavagna, affirmed today that 'it is not indispensable' to achieve an agreement with the IMF during 2006, but he admitted that obtaining a 'reasonable' pact [with the IMF] would be beneficial for the country.

" 'It is not indispensable, but with a reasonable agreement it would be easier,' maintained the head of the Palacio de Hacienda at the end of his speech in a seminar series.

"The minister underscored that 'we will put in all the effort [needed] to achieve [the agreement],' although he stressed that the central aspects of the current economic policies will not be negotiated" ("Lavagna dijo," 2005).

"The minister underscored that 'we will put in all the effort [needed] to achieve [the agreement],' although he stressed that the central aspects of the current economic policies will not be negotiated" ("Lavagna dice," 2005).

The similarity between the first paragraphs of these stories is remarkable. They are nearly identical, except for some stylistic differences and Lanacion.com's omission that *Clarín* had organized the event at which Minister Lavagna had spoken.

Eleven days later, on November 22, 2005, Clarín.com and Infobae .com published stories about statements made by former soccer player Diego Armando Maradona. Maradona, who became famous playing for the soccer team Boca Juniors, stated his strategic support for its archrival, the soccer team River Plate, in an impending match between the latter and the then tournament leader, the team Gimnasia y Esgrima de la Plata. Unlike the previous pair, the headlines of these two stories were quite different: "Maradona: 'On Sunday, I will support River [Plate]'" (Clarín.com) and "Diego moves far away from Boca [Juniors] for 90 minutes" (Infobae .com). But with the exception of some unique background and contextual information conveyed in the opening paragraph of the Clarín.com story, the first three paragraphs of both stories are markedly similar.

Clarín.com

"The end of the tournament is near and Boca, in second place, knows that to [win] it will need some help from River, its archrival. This is why, this Sunday, many *xeneizes* [Boca Juniors fans] will support El Millo [River Plate's nickname]. This will begin with [Boca Juniors'] number one referent: Diego Armando Maradona. El Diez [Maradona's nickname] made statements in the program *For a handful of dollars*, hosted by Juan Pablo Varsky on radio Spika (FM 103.1).

Infobae.com

"(NA)[10] Diego Maradona made surprising statements today when he emphasized that on Sunday he will support River for the first time in his life and made a request for Boca's coach, Alfio Basile, whom he asked to 'find the definitive lineup.'

"'On Sunday, for the first time in my life, I will have to support River,' said El Diez. 'Against [soccer team] Argentinos-

"'On Sunday, for the first time in my life, I will have to support River. Against Argentinos [Juniors] I supported 'El Bicho'

Juniors] I supported El Bicho [the team's nickname], because I can't forget everything that I experienced in La Paternal [the neighborhood where Argentinos Juniors is located],' added the greatest.[11]

because I can't forget everything that I experienced in La Paternal,' he said.

"In addition, he spoke about Boca: 'The time has arrived to make decisions, [its coach, Alfio] Basile has to find the definitive lineup,' and said that he still doesn't see as the champion a team from La Ribera [a popular name for the area where Boca Juniors is located]. 'The best team in Argentine soccer is Vélez, which plays nicely and is well put together" ("Maradona," 2005).

"About coach Alfio Basile, he stated: 'The time has arrived to make decisions. Coco [Basile's nickname] has to find the definitive lineup. The best team in Argentine soccer is Vélez, which plays nicely and is well put together,' he said despite the fact that Boca [Juniors] defeated it categorically in La Bombonera [Boca Juniors' stadium] last Sunday" ("Diego se aleja," 2005).

In light of the high level of similarity across the online sample and the much lower level of similarity in the *After* period of the print sample, it should come as no surprise that there was a sizable difference between the online and print editions of *Clarín* and *La Nación* in 2005. To calculate the exact magnitude of these differences, the visual elements of the print stories were not considered, because they were not coded in the online stories. The analysis reveals that whereas online stories had a 53% level of similarity, their print counterparts had 32%, or a significant ($p < .01$) difference of twenty-one percentage points (table 4.5). It is worth noticing that this is the largest difference of all comparisons within and across media. This difference is consistent with the evidence about the relevant processes of news production presented in chapters 2 and 3. Furthermore, its sheer size also speaks loudly about the divergent conditions of story authoring dominant in the newsrooms of these two media. Whereas online journalists who produce hard news work frantically to generate a large number of stories and update them whenever new relevant information becomes available, their print counterparts often author only one story in a single day. Whereas the online journalists rely heavily on information already existing in the media world and greatly limit their efforts at narrative construction, the print journalists try to find new facts and original quotations and are able to spend much longer authoring texts. Although there has been a longitudinal trend toward increasing similarity of content in the print domain, the high point of this trend in 2005 still exhibits a level of similarity below that found in the homogenized domain of contemporary online news narratives.

Having analyzed patterns of similarity in the presentation and narration of the news, it is time to pose the question again: to what extent does *la mirada* make a difference? The answer is: not enough to counter the effects of homogenization in news selection. Between the striking increase in the presentational similarity of print news, the remarkably high level of narrative similarity of online news, and the comparatively smaller but still consequential rise of narrative similarity of print news, the contemporary media landscape is marked not only by homogeneity in *which* stories are covered but also in *how* they are told. In the next section I discuss these patterns in depth. I draw on the analysis presented in this and the two previous chapters to elaborate on their theoretical and methodological implications for scholarship on imitation.

Concluding Remarks

This chapter has unpacked the consequences of imitation in journalistic work for the resulting news products. All cases of content overlap in the print newspapers and nearly all in the online newspapers had to do with hard news. This is a clear expression of the divergent logics of hard- and soft-news production and, especially, the much higher prevalence of monitoring and imitation in the former than in the latter. A glance at the main findings regarding content overlap in hard news across the three levels of analysis that are summarized in table 4.6 reveals a homogenization of print products over time and strong evidence for homogeneity of both print and online news in the contemporary context. Overall, the remarkable increase of content homogeneity in print from the *Before* to the *After* periods and the high level of homogeneity in both print and online news for 2005 are supported by three trends. First, similarity in the selection of print stories rises by ten percentage points over time and reaches a level of 47% for both print and online news in 2005. Second, the presentation of stories on front pages registers a sizable and significant increase in similarity. Third, in 2005, print has a similarity level of 49% for presentation, and online has a similarity level of 53% for narration. Thus, this analysis shows the power of the production dynamics examined in chapter 3 to generate substantive field-level effects for the resulting news product outcomes. Furthermore, although this analysis did not examine broadcast media, the available research mentioned in chapter 1 suggests that the agenda of these media is dependent on print news. Therefore, there are reasonable grounds to believe that the trend toward homogenization of print news might spill over into the media landscape.

Table 4.6. Summary of the Main Findings of the Content Analysis of News Products

	Selection level of analysis	Presentation level of analysis	Narration level of analysis
Print (*Clarín* and *La Nación*, 1995–2005)	Large increase in similarity in recent years	Large increase in similarity in recent years	Small increase in similarity in recent years
Online (Clarín.com, Lanacion.com, and Infobae.com, 2005)	Small increase in similarity as the day unfolds	Small decrease in similarity as the day unfolds	Small decrease in similarity as the day unfolds
Print and online editions of *Clarín* and *La Nación*, 2005	Print = Online Both have equally high level of similarity (47%)	Print > online Print: high level of similarity (49%) Online: medium level of similarity (35%)	Print < online Print: medium level of similarity (32%) Online: high level of similarity (53%)

However, against this background of remarkable homogeneity across print and online media, it is important to address the patterns of variance between both media and within the online medium. The main difference between print and online has to do with divergent patterns in the presentation and narration levels of analysis. On the one hand, in 2005 print had a level of similarity that was fourteen percentage points higher than online in the presentation level of analysis. On the other hand, in that same year, print had a level of similarity for narration that was twenty-one percentage points lower than that of online. This variance between print and online is attributable to differences in several of the situated-practice factors explored in chapters 2 and 3. The main locus of print journalistic practice is the story, and most of the daily practices of reporters and editors on issues ranging from sourcing to writing are devoted to the construction of the content that goes inside the paper. In contrast, the particular circumstances of hard-news production at Clarín.com described in chapter 2 mean that most online journalistic practices focus on the construction of the content that is featured on the homepage. Moreover, these differences in everyday practice are also related to the differences in level of awareness of news homogenization between print and online journalists. Online journalists had a more uniform and more heightened sense of homogenization than their print counterparts. Thus, even though both sets of journalists shared a dislike for the perceived trend toward homogenization, this greater level of awareness might have motivated the online journalists more than their print counterparts to differentiate their coverage within their particular conditions of production. This leads directly to issues of differentiation.

As stated in chapter 1, most media and communication scholarship underscores the homogeneity of news content. Cottle argues that "the differentiated nature of the news field to date has been under-theorized" (2003, p. 19) and calls for efforts to shed light on issues of heterogeneity in journalistic products. These efforts are pursued to a certain extent by economic studies of the media, usually under the rubric of "product differentiation" (Gal-Or & Dukes, 2003; George & Waldfogel, 2003; Spence, 1976; Spence & Owen, 1977; Steiner, 1952). These studies shed light on a number of supply- and demand-side factors that affect product differentiation outcomes in the market for news and information. This chapter focuses on the first type of factors; chapter 6 will examine the second kind.

At least two supply-side factors that positively affect product differentiation in the news are relevant to the present case. First, a decrease in the level of price competition can entice producers to intensify differentiation strategies that are not based on price. Free access to online news sites—including those examined in this book—was the norm in Argentine and in most countries during the period covered by this research. Second, an increase in market competitiveness can provide incentives for producers to increase preexisting levels of product differentiation to maintain profits and market share. The emergence and growth of online news meant a substantive rise in the level of competition in the Argentine media landscape during the study period.

Together, these factors suggest that actors should have engaged in substantive differentiation efforts and that these efforts should have resulted in greater product differences than previously. But the findings presented in this and the two previous chapters show that although actors pursued a variety of attempts to differentiate their hard-news products, the overall efficacy of these attempts was not enough to counter stronger imitation dynamics.[12] Thus, print journalists tried to seize opportunities to publish front-page stories that competitors would not publish and labored to find different *miradas*, or unique perspectives, on stories that competitors did not have. Their online counterparts, when updating a competitor's story, used that opportunity to change its presentation on the homepage. But in the aggregate, these attempts could not offset the powerful drive to sameness in news production accounted for in chapters 2 and 3. Furthermore, the existence of these differentiation and imitation forces highlights that the homogenized landscape of hard news that pervades the contemporary Argentine media scene arose in spite of attempts to create greater variety undertaken by some actors, with different degrees of intensity and conviction. That is, in addition to the presence of the rather impersonal forces of the market, the drive for product differentiation was also fueled by the personal preferences of journalists who disliked the substantive homogenization of news content. However, the expansion of imitation practices examined during the period of this study prevailed, despite the preferences of some of the actors performing them.

The research presented in this chapter, by itself and in combination with the evidence provided in the two previous chapters, overcomes limitations of scholarship on news homogenization in particular and on imitation in general. As stated in chapter 1, focusing on a single medium and at a single point in time has often hampered empirical studies of the homogenization of news. The approach adopted in this chapter shows the value of looking at homogenization in a longitudinal and cross-media fashion. On the one hand, had the data been collected at a single point in time, the analysis would have been unable to detect the temporal evolution of similarity in story selection over a decade for print and during a day for online. On the other hand, had the data been from a single medium, the analysis would have been unable to elicit the presence and absence of differences between print and online.

A more general benefit that emerges from this approach applies to studies of imitation by linking production and product data. As discussed in chapter 1, the existing scholarship tends to adopt an "either/or" stance by looking at either practices or outcomes; it rarely combines the two in a single study. This chapter shows the value of bridging the production-product, or practice-outcome, divide. Relying solely on production data would have made it impossible to make any claims about their systematic effects on the resulting products. Yet if the inquiry had examined only similarity in product outcomes, it would have been unable to elicit the practices that generated them. In contrast, a dual production-product approach enables the analyst to establish both the existence of similarity in outcomes of the production dynamics under study and the mechanisms that account for this. The next two chapters extend this perspective by examining consumption issues.

Coda

The increase in overlap and similarity of print news in the *After* period coincides with the administration of President Néstor Kirchner (2003–2007). Chapter 1 notes the evidence that during this administration there was a tightening of the flow of information from government agencies to the press and that the government sought to manipulate the press by arbitrarily distributing state advertisements as disincentives for publication of critical news. It is possible that this political environment could have directly and indirectly contributed to an increase in imitation of news stories in two complementary ways. *Clarín* and *La Nación* could have been directly motivated under pressure from the government to select a particular story for publication on the front page on a given day or to present or narrate it in a certain way or both. These newspapers could also have been influenced not to publish one or more stories on the front page on a given day or to avoid certain forms of presentation and narration or both. This would indirectly increase the likelihood for other possible stories to be published that day on the front page or for alternative forms of presentation or narration to be utilized or both.

If there was pressure from the government to publish or not publish certain stories, or to do so in certain ways, and if this hypothetical pressure contributed to increase the level of content overlap or similarity in the front-page stories published by *Clarín* and *La Nación* in the *After* period, this pressure would have been focused on national news. That is, the focus would have been on politics and economics, because these are the stories with direct implications for the business of government.[13] Therefore, to test whether all or some of the observed variance in news products examined in this and the previous chapters could be attributed to government pressure rather than to changes in imitation practices, a second analysis of the print samples was conducted to compare national news with all other categories of content focus. To this end, this analysis first contrasted the rate of increase in content overlap and similarity levels in the *Before* period and the *After* period in three scenarios:

a. when all stories are taken into account;
b. when only national news is considered; and
c. when only the other categories of news are examined.[14]

To estimate the proportion of the variance that could *not* be attributed to hypothetical pressure from the government, the rate of increase for the non-national news categories was applied to the *Before* sample in each of the three levels of analysis.

For the selection of stories for publication on the front page, the analysis shows that the rates of increase were 29% for the whole sample, 31% for the national news subsample, and 22% for the other news subsample (table 4.7).[15] When a rate of increase of 22% is applied to the growth from

Table 4.7. Hypothetical Influence of Politics on the Homogenization of News Products

Level of analysis	Before period (398 stories)	After period (399 stories)	Rate of increase from Before to After period	After period adjusted to rate of increase in other news	Difference between Before and adjusted After periods
Selection: proportion of hard-news stories with overlap	35%	45%	29%	43%	8%**
National news only	39%	51%	31%		
Other news only	32%	39%	22%		
Presentation: level of similarity of hard-news stories with overlap	33%	49%	48%	48%	15%**
National news only	32%	50%	56%		
Other news only	34%	49%	44%		
Narration: level of similarity of hard-news stories with overlap	23%	30%	30%	29%	6%
National news only	23%	31%	35%		
Other news only	24%	30%	25%		

$**p < .05$.

the *Before* to the *After* period for the whole sample, it yields an adjusted *After* period of 43%. The difference between the *Before* and the adjusted *After* periods shows a significant ($p < .05$) growth of eight percentage points, from 35% to 43%. Thus, the analysis indicates that if the larger increase in content overlap in the national news (and not in other news categories) was due to government pressure, this additional factor would account for only two of the ten percentage points of growth over time. In other words, this influence of the political system over the press would not be able to explain a significant 80% of the observed variance.

Concerning the presentation of stories on front pages, the analysis reveals that the rates of increase were 48% for the whole sample, 56% for the national news subsample, and 44% for the other news subsample (table 4.7). Applying a rate of increase of 44% from the *Before* to the *After* periods for the whole sample yields an adjusted level of similarity of 48%, or a significant ($p < .05$) increase of fifteen percentage points. As with the selection level of analysis, if the larger growth in the level of similarity for the national news and not for the other news categories was the result of government pressure, it would apply to only one of sixteen percentage points, or less than 10% of the observed variance.

A reexamination of the narration level of analysis shows that the rate of increase for the whole sample was 30%. The rates of increase for national and other news categories were 35% and 25%, respectively (table 4.7). When the 25% rate of increase is applied to the *Before* period level of similarity of 23%, it yields an adjusted level of 29% for the *After* period, or only one percentage point short of the original 30% level. As with the other levels of analysis, the presence of government pressure on the press could account for only a fraction of the before-and-after effect: one of the seven percentage points of increase in similarity, or a mere 14% of the observed variance.

Together, these results indicate that it is not possible to attribute the majority of the increase in overlap in the selection of stories and similarity in their presentation and narration to only the existence of hypothetical pressure from the government on the press during the *After* period. This does not mean that such pressure did not exist or was ineffective in contributing to the homogenization of news. Nor does it confirm that such pressure existed or was effective. If the hypothetical government pressure existed, it could perhaps by itself generate a larger fraction of the variance in national news coverage than was established in the preceding paragraphs. However, this analysis shows that there are reasonable grounds to assume that most of the observed variance would occur even in the absence of government pressure on the press. In other words, this analysis cannot elucidate whether the observed variance is overdetermined. But it can safely establish that the imitation forces that shape news production are consequential for the resulting news stories, regardless of the press-politics dynamics at play during the Kirchner administration.

FIVE

The Consumption of Online News at Work

Fabiana, a thirty-five-year-old clerical employee at a federal government agency, is a passionate consumer of online news. This sense of passion is evident in the enthusiasm she expresses when talking about online news and in the body language that accentuates the highs and lows of her discourse. It comes also into sharp relief within the context of an office setting that forcefully conveys the monotonous atmosphere of an archetypical, public sector bureaucracy. Fabiana began working in this agency when she was twenty years old, shortly after finishing high school. It was in this job that she discovered online news in 2000, when her agency launched its Web site and employees were given access to the Internet. Since then, in a progressive fashion, the Web has become her main source of news, displacing even the reading of the Sunday paper. "I stopped buying the Sunday *Clarín* about five months ago," she says (personal communication, February 20, 2007). By the time she is interviewed for this study, in an empty office just a few steps away from her desk, Fabiana has developed a steady routine of online news consumption, in particular during the workweek. These are some of the routine's salient features:

Every day I spend one and a half hours visiting news sites during the lunch break. I read three online newspapers [Clarín.com, Lanacion .com, and Infobae.com] at once. I first look at the entire homepage, from top to bottom, and then I go back to the top [of the screen] and start clicking [on stories. Then, at home] I reread superficially . . . to see

if anything happened [since the last reading]. I spend less time [on news sites] then. . . .
In general, when we sit down to eat [lunch], most of the people [in the office] read
[online] newspapers. My manager reads the [online] newspaper, and we comment [on
the news]. "Have you seen so and so?" . . . We are a group of five [in my sector], . . .
and there is always someone reading [news sites] and talking about them. If I don't
know the story [about which people are talking], I log on or say "tell me everything
about it." . . . What I like is to compare stories across sites. . . . We [in the office] talked
a lot about the [Nora] Dalmasso case [a murder with strong sexual overtones that was
at the top of the news agenda nationwide for weeks during the period of this study]. I
read it on Perfil[.com], on Lanacion.com. . . . She passed away, poor woman. But she
was partying before [that happened]. We wanted to know how [she died]. . . . We talk
about something and we have to laugh; otherwise, it is too boring.   (IBID.)

Although unique in some respects (only a small number of interviewees said they devoted ninety minutes to reading online news every
workday), Fabiana's story conveys certain characteristics of online news
consumption shared by many other people interviewed for this book. In
this chapter I analyze these characteristics with two related but distinct
goals. First, I probe the continued relevance of conceptual dimensions
of news consumption that are central in accounts of traditional media
audiences. I also take advantage of this analysis to rethink broader issues regarding the intersection of media and work in the contemporary
world. Second, I provide critical background to the next chapter's account
of consumers' appropriation of an increasingly homogenized content
supply.

To accomplish the first goal, I examine three conceptual dimensions
of news consumption: its sequence and dynamics, its spatial and temporal coordinates, and its connections to offline and online sociability.
Regarding issues of sequence and dynamics, the analysis reveals that this
consumption is a routine activity that often unfolds in a two-step sequence, and news sites are navigated somewhat habitually. In Fabiana's
case, this meant visiting news sites for the first time in the day on her
lunch break—reading the homepage entirely and then clicking on some
stories—followed by a subsequent visit later in the day. Moreover, in this
routine, the first visit of the day tends to be comprehensive, methodical,
and long, whereas subsequent visits are often limited, disorganized, and
brief. Concerning temporal and spatial coordinates, situational dynamics
influence the news consumption experience through the rhythms of office work and the role of interactions with coworkers, as clearly illustrated
in Fabiana's case. Regarding sociability issues, online news consumption
is embedded in existing relational networks. This sociability becomes

consequential in terms of the stories read and how they are discussed, which is also evident in Fabiana's vivid comments.

By making sense of discontinuities and continuities in these three dimensions, I will show that the news-at-work phenomenon is marked by the emergence of novel features of online consumption within the context of traits that have long marked traditional media consumption. In turn, understanding this combination of permanence and change in audience behavior will be essential for assessing the everyday dynamics that shape the appropriation of an increasingly homogenized news supply. Furthermore, this account also provides fertile ground for inquiry into ongoing transformations of the intersection between work and media. Thus, I conclude this chapter by reflecting on the meaning of news at work for the changing boundaries between work and home and between the instrumental and leisure purposes of media consumption in today's complex organizational and information practices.

Patterns of Online News Consumption

In chapter 1, I argued that at the time research for this book was conducted, the bulk of access to online news sites coincided with the time and place of work for the majority of the economically active population. Thus, it is not surprising that when asked about their online news consumption routines, most interviewees spontaneously make reference to the phenomenon of news at work. Echoing Fabiana, Julián, a twenty-four-year-old who has been working in an accounting firm since his college days, signals a sense of normalcy about this pattern. Asked whether consuming online news while at work was considered problematic at his workplace, he replies, "No. Maybe [my managers] gave me a bit of grief when I began doing this around 2001, because I think it wasn't common then. But nowadays it's very common that everybody at work has the instant-messaging software and the news sites opened [on their computer monitors]" (personal communication, January 4, 2007).

Like Fabiana, for those who already have a daily news consumption habit, getting online news at work is tied to an overall displacement of traditional media by digital media.[1] Several interviewees say that they have abandoned print newspaper reading because the main online news sites are free or because the consumption of online sites is integrated into the workday rather than happening during the part of the day devoted to family or leisure. Juan Agustín, a twenty-eight-year-old copy editor, says that he formerly read a print newspaper daily during his commute to work but switched to online news "when I got a computer. It's cheaper . . . and the truth is that you never read the entire [print] newspaper" (personal communication, February 8, 2007). Alexis, a thirty-seven-year-old psychiatrist, notes, "Between the lack of time and the Internet, I stopped buying [print newspapers]. I went from buying two newspapers per day, *Clarín* and *Página/12*, to buying one per day a few years ago. Depending on the day, I used to buy one or the other. Then, I started to buy *Clarín* only on weekends. Now, I don't even buy *Clarín* anymore" (personal communication, December 26, 2006). This replacement of print by digital in terms of the media artifacts used by interviewees does not mean that the print content is lost. On the contrary, as will be shown below, consumers often access the content of print media through their online counterparts.

Among the interviewees under the age of thirty, consuming online news at work is often the entry to regular news reading.[2] In other words, many of the youngest interviewees became socialized into the daily news consumption habit upon entering the workforce. They report more sporadic or occasional news consumption before then. Even those who were raised in households with computers connected to the Internet often comment that they did not routinely check the news online then. For instance, Julián, the accounting firm employee, states that he started to get the news regularly "when I began to have access during the day [at work]. Before, I was in high school until 5:00 PM and I didn't have access there. And then we had Internet at home, but we had an old modem, and it was difficult [to visit news sites]" (personal communication, January 4, 2007). When Stella, a twenty-five-year-old employee in a public opinion research firm, is asked whether she began reading online news at home or at work, she replies, "No, I began to read at work" (personal communication, March 5, 2007).

Because it displaces the material locus of the daily habit of news consumption from print to digital during the workweek or because it is a major entry to that habit, getting online news at work becomes consequential for most of the people interviewed for this study. Three distinct patterns in which this consumption takes place mark this novel phenomenon and are important antecedents that help us understand the practice and experience of consuming increasingly homogenized news. These patterns have to do with the sequence and dynamics of consumption, its spatial and temporal coordinates, and its connections to offline and online sociability. The remainder of this section is devoted to an analysis of each of these patterns.

Sequence and Dynamics

Studies of news consumption in print, broadcast, and digital media show that people's practices tend to be structured in relatively predictable sequential and dynamic patterns (Bogart, 1989; Gauntlett & Hill, 1999; Jensen, 1990; Lull, 1982; Tewksbury, Hals, & Bibart, 2008). Thus, it is not surprising that patterns of this kind also mark the consumption of online news at work. But whereas some aspects of these patterns resonate with those of traditional media and print in particular, others exhibit an important degree of novelty.

As with newspaper reading (Bogart, 1989), most interviewees visit online news sites more than once a day. However, a departure from the world of print is a sequence of consumption that sets the first visit of the day apart from all the subsequent visits in a series of important dimensions. Those who visit online news sites only once a day or less frequently tend to consume sites in a way that conforms to the parameters of the first visit of those who undertake multiple visits. This pattern of first versus subsequent visits applies to the workweek. The situation is different during the weekend, as will be explored in the next subsection.

The first visit to an online news site is undertaken routinely in a double sense: each individual usually conducts this visit during the same part of the day and looks at news sites according to a navigation process that varies little from one day to the next. For most interviewees, the first visit is in the morning, shortly after arrival at the office or when sitting in a workspace at home, but immediately before undertaking work tasks. Julieta, a twenty-three-year-old receptionist at a car dealership, says, "I get to work at 9:00 AM, turn on the computer, open my emails, and click on Página/12[.com]. I look at [the site] until 9:20 [AM] for sure, and that's enough to read the homepage news that interest me" (personal communication, February 28, 2007). Luis Ignacio, a thirty-five-year-old entrepreneur in the culture industry who works in his home office, comments that "I like to have about one hour and change, the first thing in the morning, to [visit multiple news sites]" (personal communication, December 13, 2006).

Another popular time of day for the first visit is around lunchtime. Fabiana, whose experience was mentioned above, does this and so does Cecilia, a twenty-one-year-old clerical worker at a cyber café. "I [look at news sites] from 1:00 to 2:00 PM, which is when there's nobody here" (personal communication, January 24, 2007). This prevalence of first visits in the morning and during lunch periods parallels print newspaper consumption. "Fifty-nine percent of those who read a paper on a given day read it before the end of lunch" (Bogart, 1989, p. 150). This practice also departs from the typical television-viewing behavior. "Television news [is] scheduled at the juncture between the work day and the free time of the evening" (Jensen, 1990, pp. 63–64).

Interviewees often note that during these first visits they navigate their preferred sites in a similar fashion day after day. This is consistent with traditional media consumption. For instance, in one of the first observational studies of television audiences, Lull concluded that "routines for viewing, even those operating during the first few weeks of the television season, occurred in a rule-governed, routinized fashion with apparently little conversation in most homes" (1982, p. 810). When consuming online news at work, although these navigation routines vary by individual, they all have a few elements in common. First, they are methodical and comprehensive, trying to canvass the main content of each Web site and then focusing on the stories or topics of interest. Second, the routines are aimed at acquiring general information about the world and specific content that might be directly relevant for work-related matters. There seems to be little effort to engage in the participatory spaces available on most of the news sites commonly visited, such as blogs and forums. Third, they last for a significant period of time. Although the actual duration varies by individual, most interviewees agree that these initial visits are much longer than subsequent ones.

These first visits often begin with an examination of the entire homepage, sometimes from top to bottom, others from bottom to top, and still others following quite idiosyncratic screen navigation paths. Viewers then click on a few stories that attract their attention. Martín, a twenty-five-year-old lawyer, says that he starts on the homepage and keeps "scrolling down, looking at the headlines and the leads" (personal communication, February 27, 2007). Marcela, a thirty-three-year-old worker in the advertising sector, concurs: "I read the homepage and then if there's something that interests me, I click on it" (personal communication, January 29, 2007). Ignacio, a thirty-three-year-old movie producer, echoes Martín and Marcela: "I look at all the headlines and then I [click] if I want to see a story" (personal communication, March 10, 2007).

Interviewees often say that they click on only a handful of stories during each of these first visits. In addition, unlike the homepage, which is usually seen in its entirety, these stories are rarely read in full. Natalia, a twenty-three-year-old college student who also has a clerical job, says, "I read a complete story only very few [times]" (personal communication,

December 18, 2006). Sebastián, a thirty-three-year-old television screen-writer, comments, "You don't have to read the full story to know what the news is about. This happens to me with all the stories on the Internet that are from newspapers. . . . They contain useless data all the time" (personal communication, January 15, 2007). When commenting about a story she clicked on during her most recent visit to a news site prior to the interview, Laura, a thirty-six-year-old marketing specialist, says, "I read one or two paragraphs and then I saw that it was more or less the same, and it bored me so I left [the story]" (personal communication, December 1, 2006).

In the case of online news sites with a strong print counterpart—which include Clarín.com and Lanacion.com and also the online editions of smaller but still somewhat popular national newspapers such as *Página/12* and *Perfil*—these initial visits are also marked by a sustained level of interest in the content first published by these print outlets. It is often the case that the content of the print newspaper has a strong presence on the homepages of Clarín.com and Lanacion.com sites during the first hours of the morning. Then, as was described in chapters 2 and 3, their respective online newsrooms begin to publish new stories. This process coincides with a displacement of the print stories from the top portion of the homepage and sometimes even a removal of them from the home-page. However, regular consumers of these sites seem to have no problem finding the print content, even later in the day. This is because they know where the main stories might be located. That the sites of Clarín.com and Lanacion.com offer a section with the entire content of their respective print counterparts also helps consumers to find this content.

Figure 5.1 provides evidence of the importance of the print newspaper content in the first visits to Lanacion.com. In the figure, the evolution of the provenance of the top ten most-clicked stories is contrasted with the stories in the control group as the day evolved, from Monday through Friday.[3] At seven in the morning, print stories constitute 42% of the stories on the homepage and 64% of the top ten most-clicked stories. Four hours later, these stories amount to one-seventh of those available on the homepage but two-thirds of the most popular ones. By three in the afternoon, the homepage is almost entirely populated by stories published first on the Web, yet print stories still account for one-half of those included in the top ten list. The popularity of print stories decreases as the day unfolds and reaches its lowest level, 17%, toward the end of the day. Because the clicks on the stories in the top ten list are cumulatively counted as the day unfolds and (as will be shown below) there is less clicking on stories during the subsequent visits than during the first one,

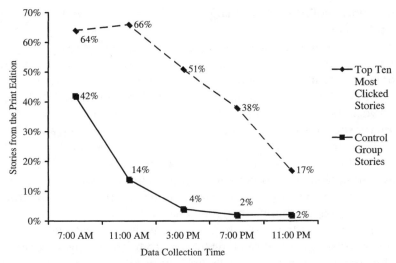

5.1 Proportions of print stories among the most-clicked and control groups on Lanacion.com.

it is likely that the data in figure 5.1 overestimate the importance of the print stories during the afternoon and evening hours. However, the difference of twenty-two percentage points between the stories in the most-clicked and control groups at 7:00 AM, when there is little of this carryover effect, and the large differences at the times of the day marked by the first visits (52% and 47% at 11:00 AM and 3:00 PM, respectively) support the notion of the importance of print content as part of the information intake during these first visits.

Subsequent visits differ from the initial visit in several dimensions. They take place at nonroutine times and intervals. They do not occur at fixed moments in the day—such as the start of the workday or during a lunch break—but depend on the availability of downtime. For instance, Julieta, the car dealership receptionist, comments that after her usual first visit in the morning, she leaves open her preferred news site on her computer monitor "but sometimes I don't even click on it once. It depends on the time I have" (personal communication, February 28, 2007). Similarly, Alba, a forty-seven-year-old lawyer, says that after her first visit, she looks at online news sites "once or twice per hour. But if I have a meeting, of course I can't look [at them]" (personal communication, February 13, 2007). As Josefina, a thirty-five-year-old writer, puts it, "The more leisure there is in my life, the more I log on" (personal communication, March 19, 2007).

These subsequent visits are often motivated by the need for a distraction or for more information after learning about an event. Josefina notes that during writing sessions "many times I take breaks . . . and look at the headlines on Clarín.com" (personal communication, March 19, 2007). Manuel, a twenty-seven-year-old employee in a computer repair shop, comments, "If I look again [at news sites, after the first visit], it is to search for something specific, to update the information on a sports game that is live on the site, to look for [information about] the movies that are being shown at theaters, or because I learned about a breaking news story. So I visit the site, look at [the specific issue that motivated the visit] and that's it. I don't reread everything else" (personal communication, March 30, 2007). Thus, the roles played by the availability of time, the need for distraction, and event occurrence (all, by definition, variable and unforeseen) in shaping the frequency and timing of these subsequent visits make them far less routine than the initial visits.

Subsequent visits diverge from the initial visits in that they are not comprehensive, methodical, long, or marked by the strong presence of print content. Instead, they are limited, disorganized, brief, and focused on breaking news or some other form of novel content. Visits are often limited to the top screen of the homepage to check the content that might be new since the last time the site was visited. Federico, a twenty-four-year-old economist whose preferred site is Infobae.com, comments that during these subsequent visits "in general I only read the top part [of the homepage]. Since I already visited the site that day, I look only at stories at the top because they are the updated ones" (personal communication, January 18, 2007). Fernando, a twenty-six-year-old film editor, mentions a similar practice in his routine reading of Clarín.com: "If I go from top to bottom at one point, I will see a story that I've already seen [that day], then I stop. . . . It's super-superfast" (personal communication, January 17, 2007).

Furthermore, subsequent visits that are motivated by learning about a breaking news story are often restricted to finding more information about it, with limited branching out to other stories. This is consistent with findings from an ethnography of news consumption commissioned by the Associated Press and conducted in India, the United Kingdom, and the United States: "Participants in the study said that they checked updates and headlines as a way to pass time and break boredom [while at work]. The news they most frequently accessed largely consisted of headlines and updates" (Associated Press, 2008, p. 40). Gerardo, a forty-eight-year-old engineer working for an automotive firm, says, "The first time [that I look at the homepage of a news site on any given day] is from top to bottom. I look at everything. . . . Then, I don't look [again] at everything in detail to know what news it has. If I were listening to the radio and they mentioned a story that interests me, then I would go [online] and specifically look for it" (personal communication, April 10, 2007). Interviewees report spending less time, clicking on fewer stories, and often looking at online news while doing something else during subsequent visits to an online news site. Alexis, the psychiatrist, puts matters in the following terms:

I always look at Clarín.com and Lanacion.com more than once a day . . . in particular the headlines and the breaking news stories, and I keep looking at them all the time. . . . I have never thought about this before [the interview,] but I now realize that I look [at these two sites] many times [and spend] very little time [with them during each visit] . . . between five and ten times a day. . . . And have you noticed the issue of having to do everything fast, of the whirlpool [of everyday life]? Well, I'm talking on the phone with my sister and I look at the Internet while I talk. And maybe I don't look at anything but I visit sites anyway.   (PERSONAL COMMUNICATION, DECEMBER 26, 2006)

These sequential and dynamic patterns that characterize first and subsequent visits are also tied to key spatial and temporal coordinates of news consumption.

Space and Time

Media scholarship has long discussed the *where* and *when* of news consumption (Bogart, 1989; Gauntlett & Hill, 1999; Lull, 1980; Webster & Phalen, 1997). The quintessential spatial location of news consumption has been the home. Silverstone forcefully makes this point for ordinary television viewing: "Television is a domestic medium. It is watched at home. Ignored at home. Discussed at home" (1994, p. 24). Dayan and Katz extend this notion to extraordinary viewing practices by stating that "media events *privilege the home*" (1992, p. 22, emphasis in original). Bogart also underscores the importance of the domestic space for the consumption of newspaper and radio news by noting that 80% of the reading of morning papers is done at home, 94% of the reading of evening newspapers is done at home, and 60% of all radio newscasts are listened to at home (1989, p. 153). The temporal patterning of news consumption throughout the week is also addressed in various studies of print and broadcast media. For instance, Sunday is the day most newspapers are read, and according to Bogart, the Saturday newspaper is read less than the Monday through Friday newspapers (1989, p. 79). For television, Gauntlett and Hill argue that "weekends generally are seen as a less-pressured time, when respondents felt able to watch programmes which they would not watch on their more time-conscious weekdays" (1999, p. 29). Furthermore, a recent survey conducted in six European countries revealed that the peak time for listening to the radio is between 6:00 and 9:00 AM and for watching television is between 7:00 and 11:00 PM (Online Publishers Association—Europe, 2007).

The studies conducted for this book suggest that there are strong spatial and temporal patterns of news consumption in the online environment and that they differ from those prevalent in traditional media. Forty-eight of the fifty interviews feature extensive discussions about whether online news consumption varies depending on whether it takes place in a home, an office space, or both and either only during the week or also during weekends. The distribution of these temporal and spatial coordinates is quite evenly divided. Of these forty-eight people, nineteen visit news sites at home, seventeen in the office, and twelve in both places. This amounts to 40%, 35%, and 25%, respectively, of this slightly reduced interview pool. In addition, twenty-two of these interviewees look at online news only during the week, and the remaining twenty-six look at it also during the weekend (or 46% and 54% of this pool, respectively).

The physical setting matters to those who consume news at the office, in particular those who work in an open space layout. For instance, Ana, a twenty-four-year-old clerical worker in an insurance company whose desk was located in this kind of layout, says, "My manager, who sits behind me in a cubicle, only sees my back. But even if I cover my computer monitor [with my body], it is possible to see what I'm doing. So I try not to look at news sites a lot. When she is not around, I look more" (personal communication, March 8, 2007). In contrast, Florencia, a thirty-one-year-old clerical worker in a health services firm, notes, "I don't have anybody behind me who can see what I'm doing. . . . There are offices where people are looking at what's on your screen. It's not my case. I have a lot of privacy. And in the office next door, too, they look at the Internet a lot" (personal communication, April 19, 2007).

In addition to the physical layout, consuming news in the office is also shaped by a certain sense of guilt that at least some interviewees express about doing something that could be perceived as personal or leisurely when they are supposed to be doing chores for which they are paid.[4] Natalia, a twenty-five-year-old human resources specialist, says that "I wouldn't stop answering the telephone because I'm looking at online news, but I don't like it that someone might be passing by and would see me reading the news" (personal communication, March 19, 2007). Silvia, a twenty-three-year-old accounting analyst, comments, "You don't go to the office to waste time; you go there to work. . . . And if you don't have anything . . . to do, well, then you look at online news. . . . It's an ethical matter" (personal communication, December 4, 2006). Juan Martín, a twenty-three-year-old economist in a multinational corporation, echoes Silvia's language: "There's the moral or ethical restriction that you aren't working if you are reading a news site. There isn't much beyond that" (personal communication, February 21, 2007). This sense of guilt does not prevent these and other interviewees from consuming online news in the office—almost all of them do so—but limits somewhat the time and attention devoted to it. In addition, it is worth noting that this feeling of guilt does not apply to several other interviewees, such as Fabiana or Julián mentioned above, who work in office environments where access to online news is regarded as normal. When Stella, the public opinion research firm employee, is asked whether visiting news sites at work is seen as negative in her office, she replies, "No. . . . My boss reads them [too] and even talks about the news with me" (personal communication, March 5, 2007).

Interviewees who regularly consume online news in an office space also mention the influence of privacy concerns. Pablo, a twenty-seven-year-old lawyer, says that he does not watch videos or listen to audio "because I'm in the office" (personal communication, February 21, 2007).[5] Ana, the insurance company employee, notes that when she visits news sites at home, she "looks at things that I know they don't let me look at in the office" (personal communication, March 18, 2007). As with the physical layout, these privacy concerns do not prevent people from visiting news sites, but at least in some cases, they seem to shape their practices. Diego, a thirty-five-year-old engineer in a food production company, summarizes the tension between norms and practices as follows: "There are certain written rules [about use of the Internet at work]. They basically protect [the firm] if there is some abuse and it has to take any [disciplinary] measures. There are some measures that are quite tough, and people use the Internet moderately so that they are not pursued. The measures are very strict, but everybody violates them moderately" (personal communication, April 13, 2007).

The consumption of online news in the office setting also has consequences outside the office. Consumers are less likely to look at online news when they return home during the week and when they are not in the office on weekends. Interviewees often associate online news with computers and computers with work. This association means that the ideational and emotional distance they often try to construct between work and home negatively affects their predisposition to look at news sites beyond the office setting.[6] For instance, Alejo, a forty-year-old self-employed computer specialist, says, "At home I have a computer in a room upstairs but I never see it. At home no news . . . because I work with computers. . . . I have a son and play with him [at home]. And I do this on purpose since I don't want to keep working. This is why I have an office, because I couldn't work at home" (personal communication, March 19, 2007). Ana's comments resonate with Alejo's: "When you're working with the computer all day, sometimes I get home and even though I don't have access to Messenger, Hotmail, Yahoo, or my email inbox at work . . . I get home and I don't want to have anything to do with the [computer]" (personal communication, March 8, 2007). Some interviewees who view online news sites in the office but not at home use their computers for other purposes when they are not in the office. These purposes are often seen as private or leisurely, such as answering personal email or researching a vacation trip. Valeria, a thirty-three-year-old administrative employee at an airline company, explicitly connects online news with work and personal email and other uses of the Internet with the domestic sphere:

Valeria: It is rare that I read online newspapers in the evening [after leaving the office during the workweek].
Interviewer: Do you use the computer for other things at home?
Valeria: Yes, in general to [navigate the] Internet, to search for some information that I need [to know], to do email, and nothing else. *I don't work with the computer at home.* (PERSONAL COMMUNICATION, APRIL 17, 2007, EMPHASIS ADDED)

Consuming online news in the office also negatively affects visits to these sites during the weekend. Of the seventeen people who look at online news in the office, only one also does so during the weekend (table 5.1). In contrast, of the nineteen interviewees who visit news sites at home, sixteen, or 84%, of this subsample also look at them during the weekend. A comparison of the proportion of interviewees who look at online news during the workweek and on the weekend versus only during the workweek yields a significant ($p < .01$) difference of seventy-eight percentage points between these two distinct types of online news consumers. Gastón, a thirty-three-year-old engineer working for a consulting firm, says that "we try not to turn the computer on during the weekends . . . because we use the computer during the week. Unless I have to work at home during the weekend, I try not to turn it on" (personal communication, April 4, 2007). Federico, a thirty-one-year-old psychiatrist, also expresses a preference for not surfing the Web during the weekends "because I associate it with work. I try to connect less during the weekends. . . .

Table 5.1.   Interactions between Spatial and Temporal Coordinates of Online News Consumption

	Location of online news consumption		
	Home (19 interviewees)	Office (17 interviewees)	Home and office (12 interviewees)
Days of the week of online news consumption			
Weekdays only*	16%	94%	25%
Weekdays and weekends*	84%	6%	75%

Note: Rows marked with an asterisk (*) indicate significant ($p < .01$) differences between home and office.

From Monday through Friday the computer is on. I'm waiting for clients to arrive and I log on. In contrast, at home I have to go to the computer, turn it on, . . . and I'm not interested [in doing so]. Thus, in general, I don't log on" (personal communication, December 28, 2006). Esteban, a thirty-five-year-old Web designer, says his consumption patterns are the same throughout the week "because I work on my own [at home] and I don't have a fixed schedule. Maybe I don't distinguish Saturday and Sunday [from the rest of the week]" (personal communication, January 16, 2007).

This comparison leads to people who consume online news at home, either exclusively or in addition to doing so at work. Only four of the nineteen people who do this exclusively at home work in an office. The majority work at home, and the remaining few are retired, unemployed, or full-time students. Several of these interviewees continue visiting news sites throughout the day. Irina, a thirty-nine-year-old owner of a small video production business who alternates between working at home and at an office space nearby, comments that "I look [at news sites] three times a day: in the morning, afternoon, and evening" (personal communication, February 20, 2007). Julieta, a twenty-one-year-old political science major, has a somewhat similar routine: "in the morning . . . and then noon, and afternoon again" (personal communication, March 19, 2007). Others, like Esteban, the Web designer, prefer to consume online news late at night: "Last night I went to sleep at 5:00 AM. I stayed up working until dawn. . . . I work the most at dawn. And I like that. . . . I read the [online] newspapers late. At around 2:30 or 3:00 AM I check to see if that day's *Clarín* and [sports daily] *Olé* are already up [on their sites]" (personal communication, January 16, 2007). Mónica, a fifty-six-year-old unemployed schoolteacher, also has nocturnal habits: "[I] generally [look at news sites] after 10:30 or 11:00 in the evening" (personal communication, March 21, 2007).

Of the twelve interviewees who look at online news both at home and in the office, ten work in an office, and the remaining two work both at home and in an office. Some of the people in this category visit news sites at home because they have little time to do so in the office in the midst of very hectic work schedules. Juan Martín, the economist, says that he reads online news "when I have a moment. But I don't often have time in the office. . . . So, when I get home [after 6:00 PM] I might read a couple of [online] newspapers. . . . The time to read [online] newspapers is more in the afternoon than during the day" (personal communication, February 21, 2007). Others, such as Fabiana, the public sector employee, mention looking at news sites at home in the evening to follow up on stories first encountered in the office during the day or to see if something new happened since leaving the office. The consumption of news sites at home is more circumscribed and shorter than in the office.

These quotations and the information presented in table 5.1 indicate that those who consume online news at home—either exclusively or along with consumption in the office—do so during more periods of the day and also during weekends. In part, this is because the association between computers and work is not so prevalent, and more generally, the boundaries between work and home are more porous than among those who consume online news only during the regular workday. Like the Web designer Esteban, the writer Josefina comments that "I try not to work on weekends, but if I have to write something [then], I do it. . . . I don't have [the workweek and the weekend] divided, which is also why it's good to have access to the Internet and online newspapers all the time" (personal communication, March 19, 2007). The less well-defined separation between the worlds, spaces, and artifacts of work and home also means that these interviewees feel less guilty about looking at news sites in the midst of their work routines, beyond the fact that many of them are self-employed and rarely have someone looking over their shoulders. The home setting also makes them less concerned about privacy matters.

As mentioned above, the spatial patterning of online news consumption is also related to a key temporal coordinate: the distinction between the workweek and the weekend. Interviews with consumers indicate a strong presence of the print content—especially on the first visit to an online news site—coupled with minimal use of the print artifact during the week. The situation is exactly the opposite during the weekends: a stronger presence of the print artifact but a comparatively weaker interest in the print content by those consuming online news. Amanda, a graphic designer in her thirties, sums up a pattern common among many interviewees: "Every day I get to the office and almost the first thing I do . . . is to look at *La Nación* and *Página/12* online, and then I look [on the Web] at [Spanish daily] *El País* and [French daily] *Le Monde*. . . . On Saturdays I remain outside the news system, and on Sundays I generally buy [a print] newspaper" (personal communication, March 22, 2007). Lorena, a Spanish-language teacher, expresses a similar separation between online and print in terms of workweek and weekend: "I read the print newspaper on Saturday and Sunday. I don't have a laptop . . . [and reading] lying down [on weekends] implies print. Plus, I have an affinity for print" (personal communication, March 2, 2007). Marcela, the advertising sector worker, concurs with Lorena: "I don't [visit news sites] on weekends. I like the activity of sitting down and reading the newspaper. . . . It's only during weekends that I have time to do this" (personal communication, January 29, 2007).

The greater use of the print artifact and the lesser consumption of print content from online news sites during the weekends among consumers of online news are also related to interest in news about live sports events, especially on Sundays. Stella, the public opinion research firm employee, says, "Yesterday afternoon [a Sunday], I looked at [online news] to see what had happened and I looked at soccer [news], nothing else" (personal communication, March 5, 2007). Natalia, the human resources employee, comments, "I read [online news] several times a day on Sundays, mostly for sports, [to learn about] scores of soccer games and those of other sports" (personal communication, March 19, 2007). Martín, the lawyer, concurs with Stella and Natalia, noting that during weekends "it's mostly sports. Because there is a lot of sports activity during the weekend, and [news sites] update all [the scores], I go to *Olé* and I hit 'refresh, refresh, refresh.' I must stay one hour and a half, two hours looking at *Olé*. Well, it's not that I'm looking at *Olé*, but I do other things, check my IM, and then I go back to *Olé*" (personal communication, February 26, 2007).

Table 5.2 summarizes an analysis of the five most popular content categories within the top ten most-clicked stories on Clarín.com, Lanacion .com, and Infobae.com (note that the top five categories vary slightly between news sites). In addition to identifying and ranking each category for each site, it also shows what percentage of those stories in the respective top ten most-clicked lists belong to each of these categories and the presence and absence of variance between the workweek and weekend. At least four patterns are noteworthy. First, taken together, these five

Table 5.2. Top Five Content Categories of the Most-Clicked Stories on Clarín.com, Lanacion.com, and Infobae.com

| | Clarín.com | | Lanacion.com | | Infobae.com | |
	Weekday (n = 500)	Weekend (n = 200)	Weekday (n = 500)	Weekend (n = 200)	Weekday (n = 500)	Weekend (n = 200)
Position						
First*	Sports: 25%	Sports: 54%	Sports: 26%	Sports: 40%	Sports: 30%	Sports: 42%
Second	Crime: 20%	EAC: 8%	Politics: 24%	Politics: 23%	EAC: 20%	EAC: 22%
Third	EAC: 15%	Foreign: 7%	EAC: 15%	STM: 11%	STM: 17%	STM: 10%
Fourth	Foreign: 8%	Crime: 6%	Foreign: 10%	Foreign: 8%	Crime: 7%	Crime: 4%
Fifth	Politics: 7%	Politics: 6%	Crime: 5%	EAC: 6%	Foreign: 5%	Foreign: 4%
Total first through fifth	75%	81%	80%	88%	79%	82%
Difference between first and fifth*	18%	48%	21%	34%	25%	38%

Note: Rows marked with an asterisk (*) indicate significant ($p < .01$) differences between the weekday and weekend results on each site. EAC = entertainment, arts, and culture. STM = science, technology, and medicine.

categories attract most of the attention on each of the sites; they account for at least three-quarters of all content on each of these sites during the workweek and on the weekend. Second, there is remarkable stability in the content preferences of the public across sites and between the workweek and weekend: nearly the same categories show up on each of the sites; the main differences are their place in the ranking and the proportion of attention they get. Third, a cursory look at this table reveals that sports are the top content category on all of these sites. But fourth—and most relevant for the issues discussed in this subsection—there is a significant difference in the prevalence of sports between the workweek and the weekend. During the week, sports stories make up 25%, 26%, and 30% of the most-clicked stories on Clarín.com, Lanacion.com, and Infobae.com, respectively. During the weekends, the proportions increase to 54%, 40%, and 42%, respectively. This yields significant ($p < .01$) differences of twenty-nine, fourteen, and twelve percentage points, respectively, between the week and the weekend. Another sign of the prevalence of sports during the weekend is that its distance from the fifth-ranked content category on each of these sites also widens from the week. It goes from 18%, 21%, and 25% on Clarín.com, Lanacion.com, and Infobae.com, respectively, during the week, to 48%, 34%, and 38% during the weekend. This amounts to significant ($p < .01$) differences of thirty, thirteen, and thirteen percentage points, respectively.

In addition to the desire for sports news (in particular, multiple visits to the homepage to check on game scores), many of those who visit online news sites during the weekend mention spending less time there than during the week because they prefer to undertake leisure activities outside their homes. Alba, the lawyer, says that she checks news sites "less [often than during the week] because I go out more and spend less time with the computer" (personal communication, February 13, 2007). Alexis, the psychiatrist, concurs: "Yesterday [a Sunday] I looked at online news only in the evening because I spent all day outside [my home]" (personal communication, December 26, 2006). But a handful of interviewees mention spending more, not less, time reading online news during the weekend, in part because it is the only time during the week that they have significant available downtime. For instance, Ana, the insurance company clerical worker, says, "I wake up early . . . turn on the computer, [and] sit [by the desk] with my coffee, my biscuits . . . and while I listen to music, I begin to read [online] newspapers, do Google searches, [and] check my email. At home I'm more relaxed [than in the office]" (personal communication, March 8, 2007) Thus, whether people spend less or more time visiting news sites during the weekend, their consumption experiences differ from those of the workweek.

Sociability

Studies of news consumption habits often stress the extent to which they are ingrained in the relational structures of everyday life (Bausinger, 1984; Bogart, 1955, 1989; Chan & Goldthorpe, 2007; Jensen, 1990; V. B. Martin, 2008; Palmgreen, Wenner, & Rayburn, 1980; Robinson & Levy, 1986). In her study of how people process the news, Graber finds that when "a topic had become the focus of attention for conversation, among their friends and associates, when it seemed to arouse a lot of public controversy, or when one of their contacts persisted in mentioning the topic, [consumers] were apt to search for relevant information" (1984, p. 83). Similarly, scholarship on communication technology shows that new artifacts are often used in a way that reinforces existing social networks (Baym, Zhang, & Lin, 2004; Hampton, 2007; Hampton & Wellman, 2003; Kline, 2000; Ling, 2008). Thus, in his study of the adoption of the telephone, Fischer argues that "Americans apparently used home telephones to widen and deepen existing social patterns rather than to alter them" (1992, p. 262).

Patterns of social relations also shape the consumption of online news at work and in ways that resonate with the findings from these studies on news and communication technology. This sociability is almost entirely offline in a dual sense. First, these relationships are always layered on top of preexisting ties with coworkers, family members, or friends rather than being new, online-only interactions. In other words, no interviewee says that she discusses the news with people encountered in chat rooms, blogs, or other virtual spaces. Luis Ignacio, the culture industry entrepreneur, bluntly exclaims, "Virtual friends? No!" (personal communication, December 13, 2006). Second, interviewees routinely report that interactions take place primarily face-to-face and only secondarily via online communications, such as by sending story files or links via electronic mail. Furthermore, some interviewees note that they do not send stories electronically at all, in part due to the perceived restrictions of the office environment. Valeria, the airline company employee, says, "I don't [send stories by electronic mail] . . . because maybe you send a story to someone and they think that you're wasting time. If I see something that seems interesting I print it and talk about it [with coworkers]. Or I leave it [on a table] in case someone might want to read it" (personal communication, April 17, 2007).

Among those who send news stories electronically, many report that the content of these stories tends to be skewed toward the entertaining or the bizarre. Julieta, a political science major who moved to Buenos Aires from a small town in a nearby province, comments that "the last story I sent [electronically] was that gossip had been penalized in a city in Colombia. I sent it to everybody in my hometown so that they would be afraid. It was a joke" (personal communication, March 19, 2007). Along similar lines, José, a twenty-year-old employee of a bookstore, says, "The other day Lanacion.com published a story that the French people wanted to have mandatory naps, so I sent it to my manager. [And] my friend sent me a photograph of [then vice president Daniel] Scioli [who uses a prosthetic arm after losing his biological one in an accident] without his arm. He said to me . . . 'How come he is photographed without his arm?' 'I don't know, he might be looking for compassion,' I said. And we laughed for a while" (personal communication, February 6, 2007).

Content differences appear to mark the conversations among coworkers compared with those with family members and friends. Two features characterize the discussion of news in the office space: an avoidance of sensitive political or economic topics[7] and an emphasis on light topics or stories relevant to work. Juan Martín, the economist, makes reference to the first pattern when he states that "the coworker who sits next to me . . . every time he looks at Lanacion.com [he] says, 'Look at what happened in Thailand [or the] earthquake in Indonesia' or things like that, but [stories about] politics or national economics—never" (personal communication, February 21, 2007). Florencia, the health services firm employee, refers to the self-conscious strategies used in her office space to avoid politically sensitive topics: "We're two people in their thirties and a person who's in her fifties and very right wing. . . . She comes from a military family, so we almost never talk about political issues because if we say, 'I don't agree with this thing that the government has done,' she replies, 'Yes, until the tanks are not on the street . . .' So we avoid [these topics]" (personal communication, April 19, 2007).[8] Pablo, the lawyer, notes, "At work we talk about funny stories. We send them by email and laugh. But we don't do like in a coffee place where you talk about what's going on [in the world], because we are in an environment that is not appropriate for that" (personal communication, February 21, 2007).

Pablo's remarks resonate with those of José and Fabiana and underscore the preference for light topics in workplace conversations about online news. Fernando, the film editor, says that at his workplace they generally talk about "something having to do with entertainment. Someone was found drunk in so-and-so place, or someone else got divorced. . . .

It's always silly stuff. Yes, these are the topics that generate the most debate" (personal communication, January 17, 2007). Julián, the accounting firm employee, comments on the prevalence of sports stories, another light topic (although one that sometimes stirs passionate arguments), in the common conversations about news in his workplace: "We talk . . . mainly about sports. 'Now [soccer team] Boca [Juniors] is going to sell this player,' and then a discussion arises. . . . We talk about it while we're doing something that is not very demanding" (personal communication, January 4, 2007).[9]

Work-related stories are also often part of social exchanges among coworkers. Laura, the marketing specialist, says, "If Unilever has a new online portal . . . I tell the account manager, 'Take a look at this, it may interest you'" (personal communication, December 1, 2006). Vanina, a forty-year-old teacher, shares an anecdote that illustrates the presence of this kind of content in news-related social exchanges: "The other day there was a story—I don't remember if it was on Lanacion.com or Clarín .com—that said that [Francesco] Tonucci, the Italian pedagogue, had stated that children had to participate more in school management. . . . It was interesting, so I sent it to coworkers and we talked about it. Because two people sent the story at the same time, minutes apart from each other, we discussed it a lot" (personal communication, February 22, 2007).

Social relations that concern online news and that take place with family and friends appear to be more oriented toward personal matters and more tolerant of contentious arguments over public affairs subjects. Mónica, the unemployed teacher, says, "I have a friend who lives in Paris and is from [the northeastern city of] Paraná, . . . so when there was all the [political] mess of the highway pickets in [the nearby city of] Gualeguaychú,[10] I [sent emails saying,] 'How come you aren't aware of what's going on? . . . Start looking at [online] newspapers . . . and familiarize yourself!" (personal communication, March 21, 2007). Cecilia, a twenty-eight-year-old municipal government employee, says that she talks about online news "with my friends, my boyfriend, [and] my family. . . . With my friends we devoted many encounters to the [Nora] Dalmasso case. . . . I also have a friend who is an assistant of a congresswoman, and sometimes we talk about news related to congressional bills—for instance, when there was discussion about an abortion for a mentally disabled girl who had been raped. . . . Or sometimes I talk about politics with my boyfriend" (personal communication, March 20, 2007).

There appears to be a reciprocal relationship between sociability and online news consumption: social interactions affect consumption, and consumption shapes these interactions. This reciprocal relationship happens before and after a specific news-related social exchange takes place. On the one hand, for the sake of participating in ongoing conversations, people sometimes pay more attention to certain news stories than they would otherwise. In other words, the knowledge that certain news-related conversations are likely to take place accentuates the consumption of relevant stories in anticipation of the actual occurrence of those conversations. For instance, Florencia, the health care administrative worker, says that in her office "they talk about the [Carlos] Carrascosa case [a high-profile crime story], so one reads about it in part to have something to talk about" (personal communication, April 19, 2007). On the other hand, if during a social encounter a person learns for the first time about a particular story, she is prompted to visit a news site to learn more information about it. According to Julieta, the car dealership receptionist, "If [interlocutors] are talking [about a piece of news] and I don't know about it, rest assured that, as soon as possible, I log on to see what they're talking about" (personal communication, February 28, 2007). Silvia, the accounting firm employee, agrees with Julieta: "You went to have lunch [with coworkers], and they told you something you didn't know. So when you went back [to the office,] you looked at it" (personal communication, December 4, 2006). Thus, either *ex ante* or *ex post*, sociability tends to be consequential for online news consumption.

Concluding Remarks

This chapter has examined the consumption of online news at work. Several issues stand out. This consumption is a normal aspect of the daily routines of many workers. It contributes to a displacement of the news consumption habit from traditional to digital media among those who already have that habit and fosters the emergence of such a habit among those who did not have it. Furthermore, the sequence and dynamics of online news consumption at work are marked by the prevalence of the "readable Web." People are far more focused on obtaining information from news sites than on taking advantage of the "writable Web" through participation in blogs, forums, and other commentary spaces. (Further evidence of this will be presented in the following chapter.) This reading stance exhibits a dominance of non–public affairs content, a substantial interest in print news during consumption that lasts until the early afternoon, and the key role of the content available on the homepage. The relative importance of the homepage is also evident in that people do not often click on stories, especially during subsequent visits. When they do click on stories, they do so on relatively few and tend not to read them thoroughly. This importance of the homepage and its main stories reinforces the adequacy at the consumption end of the strategy for the content analysis of online news products pursued in chapter 4.

This portrait of consuming online news at work shows that spatial and temporal coordinates as well as sociability patterns also shaped the practices and experiences of interviewees. People who read the news online in an office setting are more likely to feel somewhat guilty about doing so when they are supposed to be working and are more concerned about privacy issues. They are also less predisposed to look at news sites at home during the week and on the weekend—unless they work during the weekend. Moreover, consumption during the weekend is marked by an even stronger interest in non–public affairs content and a lower interest in the content of the print newspaper coupled with a higher consumption of the actual print artifact. Finally, preexisting social relations shape and are shaped by online news consumption. Conversations that take place in the workplace tend to avoid contentious topics often present in public affairs stories. Workplace conversations tend to gravitate toward entertaining news items and those with relevance to work-related matters.

This depiction of online news consumption at work reveals a tension between continuity and discontinuity in its comparison with news consumption in traditional media. First, and concerning issues of sequence and dynamics, the routine configuration of consumption habits, the multiple visits during the day, and the contours of the first visit resonate with watching news on television and, especially, reading it on the pages of a print newspaper. But the divide between the first and subsequent visits and the peculiar character of the latter differ markedly from the typical patterns of reading print news or even the channel-surfing practices of watching broadcast news.

Second, the discontinuity is most visible in relation to the spatial and temporal coordinates of news consumption. The office space emerges as a prime locus of news consumption for a significant proportion of those in the workforce. This shifts the home from the dominant position it held in the past as the place where people get the news. The time of work also becomes the time of getting the news. It thus displaces the prevalence that the periods before and after work once had in this regard. Furthermore, these new temporal coordinates affect the balance between the workweek and the weekend in terms of time spent consuming news. Whereas print newspapers were and still are read mostly during the weekend, the pattern becomes inverted for online news sites, because they are most often consumed during the workweek.

Third, matters of continuity are strongest when it comes to patterns of sociability. As with print and broadcast media, news consumption is embedded in existing social relations. Because of the norms that govern social interaction in the workplaces of most interviewees, the only notable discontinuity is a tendency to focus conversation about the news on non–public affairs subjects. In comparison, there is a higher level of openness toward discussing public affairs stories in conversations with friends and family members.

This analysis reveals that the news-at-work phenomenon is characterized by the emergence of novel features of online consumption (subsequent visits, increased importance of homepage content, spatial and temporal relocation, and reduced attention to public affairs subjects) within the context of traits that have long marked traditional media consumption (routine configuration of the first visit, sustained use of print on Sunday, and continued relevance of existing social networks). It is too soon, however, to tell whether this is a transient phase or a more durable trend. The news-at-work phenomenon is relatively recent and has not affected the youngest generation of online users who have not yet entered the workforce. This study has not examined the online news consumption habits of people under the age of eighteen. Therefore, it is not possible to determine whether these younger people might develop radically different consumption habits during their adolescence and early adulthood that might shape how they obtain the news online at work later in their lives. If such an effect of the "digital natives" existed, it would likely tilt the balance in favor of discontinuity with the consumption of traditional media.

Beyond the specifics of online news consumption, the account presented in this chapter calls into question taken-for-granted assumptions that are widespread in scholarship about work and media. On the one hand, organizational studies analyze how media and information technologies are used in the workplace (Orlikowski, 1992, 2000; Rice & Gattiker, 2001; Sproull & Kiesler, 1991; Yates, 1989). These studies generate valuable contributions to understanding the intersection between communication, materiality, and labor by making visible the instrumental uses of these technologies in work settings. However, this dominant focus makes less visible the range of leisurely uses of these technologies and their consequences for the social fabric of work. On the other hand, as stated above, communication scholarship has all but naturalized the home setting as the place where media are consumed and has focused on leisure as the raison d'être for this consumption. This stance obscures other settings, such as the office or the home as a place of paid labor, where news is also consumed.

These assumptions and the division of academic labor tied to them resonate with what Mills (1951) calls the "big split" that followed industrialization and that divided work from nonwork practices and meanings. According to Nippert-Eng, "The normative expectations of a segmented home and work experience have resulted from the separation of the values, activities, social functions, and people of home and work into separate spatio-temporal locations" (1995, p. 18). This division has reverberated across the social sciences and engendered, in V. Zelizer's (2005a) apt formulation, a "hostile worlds" view that separates scholarship on the arenas of production and economic rationality from that of consumption and leisure logic.[11] This division has not always been able to fully characterize either social world. This becomes evident in studies that analyze various challenges to their stark distinctions in phenomena as varied as the presence of music in the workplace (Bull, 2007; Korczynski, 2003, 2007), the use of media and technology during household labor (Cowan, 1983; Spigel, 1992), the culture of work contractors (Barley & Kunda, 2004), the dynamics of intimacy in economic life (V. Zelizer, 2005b, 2009), and the role of side production in factories (Anteby, 2008).

My analysis of the consumption of online news builds on these and other related studies to suggest the need to turn the dominant characterizations of work and home and instrumental and leisure uses of technology and media from *givens* into *outcomes* of social inquiry. In the emerging phenomenon of news at work, the office is not a milieu devoid of non-instrumental uses of information technologies, nor is the leisurely home environment the only or even dominant context in which news consumption takes place. The recent and ongoing transformations in the social worlds of work and the media cannot afford to make sense of the contemporary environment by using taken-for-granted assumptions or a division of academic labor that already had limitations in the past but has become remarkably dated.

Finally, this account of the general practices, interpretations, and experiences associated with the consumption of online news at the time and place of work provides background that is essential for understanding the more specific dynamics associated with consuming an increasingly less diverse supply of content, which is the subject of the next chapter.

SIX

The Consumption of Increasingly Less Diverse News Content

February 22, 2007, is a day packed with interviews for this book, and some help crystallize key insights that have been building for months. The opening of chapter 4 refers to one of these interviews, with *Clarín*'s Alberto Amato. The interview takes place immediately after a conversation with his editor on the national desk, Fernando González. At one point González mentions some issues related to the newspaper's readers. I take advantage of his remarks to ask whether he pays any attention to how the print stories are consumed on Clarín.com. He grabs a piece of paper and says:

This is my news budget for the day, and I always write it on the back of the ranking that lists the top twenty most-read stories on Clarín.com [that day]. So I know from the edition of today's paper . . . that my front-page story [referring to the top story by the national desk] ranked twelfth. It's very difficult for us to place [a story in the ranking] . . . because people are not interested. So you compete against— [He interrupts himself and looks at that day's rankings.] Now everybody is sorry for Britney Spears. [There's a story on] cheese and country bread [in the weekly cooking section], and it's not easy. [He reads the following headline aloud:] "[Tennis player Guillermo] Cañas moves [the public] nonstop." If I had a politician who moved [the public] nonstop, it would be easier for me! **(PERSONAL COMMUNICATION, FEBRUARY 22, 2007)**

The day began with a breakfast meeting with Vanina, the school-teacher, in a coffee shop located at the corner of Hidalgo and Díaz Velez, just blocks away from Parque Centenario in the Caballito neighborhood. There, while we indulge in *medialunas* and *cortados,* Vanina, an avid consumer of online news who routinely visits a number of sites, speaks extensively about her impression that Clarín.com and Lanacion.com often carried very similar stories. Talking about Clarín.com, she says, "If there is any difference with Lanacion.com, I couldn't explain it. . . . I don't see a change [from one site to the other] in what is the first presentation [of the news]. As a reader, I don't see . . . a substantial difference." As the conversation unfolds, I ask Vanina what she thinks and feels about the increasingly similar news stories offered by the leading media. "It gives me stomach pain because there is that sense of [something] monopolistic, that there are two [news organizations] telling you the same story. . . . It gives me a feeling of claustrophobia . . . of confinement." As her dislike of this state of affairs becomes evident, I then ask whether she thinks things could change and, if so, how:

> The technological conditions could allow it, but I don't know about the economic and political ones. . . . Doesn't anybody realize that they could take advantage of the Internet much more [than they currently do]? . . . There is something [potentially novel] in the blogs, but it's a very elitist thing for a very small [*mínimo*] group that accesses them. What strength does [the blogosphere] have [to present an alternative]? [Later on, talking about the mainstream media:] It all seems a hank of wool that is the same for everybody. Then, you get everything from the same wool.
> (PERSONAL COMMUNICATION, FEBRUARY 22, 2007)

Taken together, the excerpts from these two interviews motivate four interrelated sets of questions that cut across the dynamics of consuming homogenized news. First, to what extent are journalists aware of how online news is consumed, and how does this awareness affect their work? Second, is the consumption of online news more or less convergent than its supply? In other words, are the story selection patterns of consumers and journalists equally or differently homogenized? Third, as was evident in Vanina's case, the lack of diversity in editorial offerings can trigger powerful reactions from the public. Thus, how do people experience the consumption of an increasingly similar supply of news content? Fourth, do other consumers share Vanina's dislike for homogenized news and why? If they agree with Vanina, what can be done to change this situation in an era supposedly marked by the seemingly endless frontier of peer-to-peer cultural production? How much do they try to change this state of affairs?

My analysis will show that journalists are more cognizant of consumer preferences than in the past. This increased knowledge heightens pre-existing tensions between editorial relevance and consumer taste. Despite these tensions, journalists still tilt the balance in favor of editorial relevance. I will then show that there is a lower level of similarity in consumer story choice than in story selection among journalists. I will also demonstrate that journalists' choices concentrate on public affairs topics but consumers' choices focus on non–public affairs subjects. These differences indicate that consumers enact a significant level of agency in their appropriation of media content. Next, I will show that consumers have a negative evaluation of news homogenization but feel relatively powerless to change it. However, their engagement with news-oriented, user-authored content spaces is limited despite this negative evaluation. These results signal the enactment of a lower level of agency associated with changing the news than with consuming the stories supplied by the media, thus suggesting dimmed prospects for consumer-driven social reform. A spiral of sameness has emerged in which journalists and consumers are part of a game to which they actively contribute through their everyday practices even though they dislike it and feel powerless to change it. Thus, the paradox of more information but less news is further stabilized.

Journalists' Knowledge about Consumers' Choices and How It Affects the News

In his celebrated study of news work, Gans (1980) shows that journalists tend to exhibit a marked disregard for the public's preferences as they undertake their tasks.[1] This lack of attention to the audience in daily journalistic practice was quite strong during most of the twentieth century and resulted from three concurrent factors. First, the monopoly or oligopoly position occupied by most mainstream news organizations facilitated the dissemination of news that people "needed" rather than news that they "wanted" (paraphrasing Mindich 2005) because advertisers had little choice but to come to these organizations to reach the public. Second, the prevalence of occupational values characterized by a strong public service orientation favored coverage of public affairs stories. A marked separation between the editorial and commercial sides of the enterprise at most reputable media also made this possible. Third, the tools available for researching the public's behavior, such as circulation statistics, ratings, surveys, and focus groups, yielded aggregate and indirect information. In most cases, this information was too abstract to gauge actual interest in specific stories and exerted a rather diffuse and not highly effective pressure on journalists.

However, all these factors have experienced significant changes during the past few decades. This trend started in the 1980s and has greatly accelerated in recent years. The industry has become increasingly competitive, which has resulted in more choices for consumers (Prior, 2007). In turn, this has put greater pressure on organizations to deliver products with high levels of market penetration. The industry has also experienced increased permeability to market pressures, an erosion of the wall separating the editorial and commercial sides of the news enterprise, and a greater orientation toward the public's perceived preferences and behaviors (E. Cohen, 2002; Klinenberg, 2005; McManus, 1994; Sumpter, 2000; Underwood, 1993). Finally, the technologies available for knowing these preferences and behaviors have become more sophisticated, especially in the case of online media. These technologies yield information that is disaggregated at the story level. They show the number of times each story has been clicked on and also potentially useful information, such as the average time consumers spent on each story, and the stories visited immediately before and after (Boczkowski & Peer, in press; MacGregor, 2007; Thorson, 2007).

These changes amount to a major transformation in the social and technological environment of the public's visibility to the news industry. This transformation is the other side of the observability coin examined in chapter 3. Whereas this latter has to do with the production sphere, the former is related to the visibility of the domain of consumption. But as stated in chapter 3, whether and how this transformation in the social and technological environment of news work is consequential depends on situated patterns of practice. The ethnographic studies of news production conducted for this book suggest that print and online journalists realize some of these transformations in their daily work, but they do so with noteworthy differences.

In the print newsroom, there is no uniformity regarding the attention given to the consumption data of their respective online counterparts. Some journalists look at the data routinely, but others do not. This division is somewhat correlated with position in the organizational hierarchy: most editors mention monitoring the data, but this habit is less prevalent among reporters. Furthermore, the discussion of these figures and other sources of information about that day's morning edition is part of the afternoon editorial meeting at both *La Nación* and *Clarín*. These figures are assessed with a focus on the performance of print stories among Internet consumers. Fernando Rodríguez, metro editor at *La Nación*, maintains, "More than anything I check . . . the repercussions of our [editorial] bet" (personal communication, March 20, 2007). Julio Blanck, coeditor-in-chief at *Clarín*, says, "With [coeditor-in-chief Daniel] Fernández Canedo, what we sometimes do, [and] I do it almost always [by myself], is to check how many of the top twenty most read [stories on Clarín.com] were on the newspaper front page [that morning]." He adds, "It is to see if the front-page selection criteria have [anything] to do with the interest of the public or with a logic of ours that speaks of the public's existence and negates it in practice" (personal communication, December 14, 2006).

Journalists at both print newspapers commonly check these statistics once a day. At *Clarín*'s newsroom, for instance, printouts with the top twenty stories on Clarín.com circulate shortly after noon, and many editors and reporters consult this source. This timing is because journalists are aware that print stories typically get more exposure in the morning hours, and the interest of online consumers then shifts to newer content—an issue explored in chapter 5. The daily frequency is related to an ambivalence about knowing this information. Asked why he looks at online usage data only once a day, Daniel Fernández Canedo, coeditor-in-chief at *Clarín*, replies as follows:

First, because it seems to me that we still don't want to see that [information]. Second—and this is a personal opinion—because I believe that we, print journalists, have a great pride [*soberbia*] in our power [to control] the news and the . . . production of news. We still believe that we can [do our job] without looking at those readers on the Internet. We don't want them to drive us. Between driving and being driven, we choose to drive [*Entre manejar y ser manejados, elegimos manejar*]. I'm not saying that it's good, but . . . (PERSONAL COMMUNICATION, DECEMBER 14, 2006)

In contrast to their print peers, the monitoring of site usage is more uniformly prevalent and more frequent among online journalists. That is, reporters as well as editors look at these figures, and they do so several times during the day. This was evident throughout the observation phase of the ethnography of news production at Clarín.com. It is also repeatedly mentioned in interviews with staffers at this site and at Lanacion.com. A reporter in the Conexiones unit of Clarín.com says that she monitors the information on the most-clicked stories on her site "all the time . . .

several times a day" (personal communication, December 13, 2005). A colleague in the Ultimo Momento unit does so about "every hour and a half" (personal communication, July 28, 2005). Lanacion.com's sports editor Ariel Tiferes mentions looking at this information about his site "a whole lot. . . . Our system updates the information hourly. I check it every time it updates" (personal communication, December 14, 2006). Lanacion.com makes this information publicly available to consumers on the homepage and at the bottom of each story. This editorial and design feature also reinforces the visibility of this information within the newsroom. In the words of one of the site's staffers, "[I look at it] a lot because it is at the bottom of the stories I write. So I see it all day" (personal communication, December 18, 2006).

Despite the differences between print and online journalists in their realization of the increased visibility of online consumers, there is a strong convergence of opinion in terms of what they learn about the factors that shape online news consumption. As with news disseminated in other media, most journalists agree that the main factor has to do with content focus. Non–public affairs stories—in particular sports, crime, and celebrity subjects—are substantively more popular than public affairs news among online news consumers. Clarín.com's Conexiones television writer Guadalupe Diego says, "Sports, scandals, sex . . . are topics that everybody [clicks] to read" (personal communication, December 1, 2005). Furthermore, interviewees stress that stories that combine two or more of these topics are strong favorites among the public. Lanacion. com's sportswriter Alejo Vetere gives the example of a story about the romance between soccer player Fabián Cubero and top model Nicole Neuman: "She left her husband after a photo shoot for *Hombre* magazine [in which Cubero also participated]. People followed this topic insatiably. So if you published any statements by Cubero, you knew that [the story] was going to do [well]" (personal communication, December 19, 2006).

These consumer preferences are not news to seasoned journalists. The novelty resides in the reduced ability to ignore them in their everyday work practices. That is, in the past it was easier for journalists to avoid regular exposure to figures about consumer behavior, but this avoidance has become more difficult in the contemporary setting. *Clarín's* Julio Blanck says, "You can't pretend that you don't know what's going on" (personal communication, December 14, 2006). This comment by Blanck echoes the statements by Fernando González presented above. They also point to one of the major consequences of this increased visibility of consumption preferences in daily editorial practice, in particular for those who produce public affairs content: it intensifies a preexisting tension between the logic of the occupation and the logic of the market. The first underscores the greater importance of stories about politics, economics, and international affairs, whereas the latter privileges the more popular topics of sports, entertainment, and crime. This tension surfaces in several interviews with journalists, such as the one conducted with *La Nación*'s Inés Capdevila:

Interviewer: Do you feel this crossroads between the occupational mandate [*el deber ser*] and the pressure from the market more now than when you came back [from your graduate studies at the University of Missouri in 2001]?
Capdevila: Yes, notably more.   (PERSONAL COMMUNICATION, MARCH 21, 2007)

Journalists live this tension in a way that combines an overall feeling of frustration with a certain desire to turn it into a learning opportunity. For Julio Blanck, "The first [thing] you feel . . . is a challenge. Most of the time you feel impotence for not knowing [how] to solve it, or not so well as you would like. . . . it's in each one [of us] what you do between the challenge and the recurrent impotence to find an effective solution the next day. You can remain closed [*te podés cerrar*] and tell yourself that people don't understand anything. Or you can say, 'If I say something and people don't understand me, then some blame must fall on me'" (personal communication, December 14, 2006).

A journalist at Lanacion.com expresses these themes of increased market pressures accompanying greater visibility of consumers, a feeling of frustration, and a desire to learn from this situation as follows:

I'm here banging my head [against the wall] to see if I can explain to you that Uruguay [attacked] Argentina in the [International] Courts at The Hague, and the truth is that people are not interested [in the story]. So it gives me a [certain sense of] disappointment or frustration. But on the other hand, it seems that it also forces me—and this is a good exercise—to try to make my themes closer . . . to issues that can be really important to people. . . . I don't reject the exercise, but it bothers me that this criterion [referring to the popularity of online stories] matters.
(PERSONAL COMMUNICATION, DECEMBER 18, 2006)

Journalists arrive at a sort of compromise to solve this tension between the competing logics of the occupation and the market that has intensified with the increased visibility of online news consumption patterns. This solution reinforces the core occupational values but opens some peripheral elements to change. A Conexiones staffer at Clarín.com stresses the maintenance of core values by saying, "If I were driven by what people want, I would be writing about sex and celebrities, and I'm not interested in these topics" (personal communication, October 20, 2005). Julio Blanck comments, "I don't believe . . . we have to give people what they ask for, because there is also . . . an editorial stance: *Clarín* stands here and tells you a given topic in this way" (personal communication, December 14, 2006). But this maintenance of core values is accompanied by signs of modification in the construction of stories, at least in the case of online news. For instance, an editor on the national desk at Clarín.com comments on "the need to search for new models of writing headlines. . . . It is important to write good headlines . . . with a great hook [*mucho gancho*] . . . because the national news needs that . . . for the Internet reader" (personal communication, July 20, 2005). Lanacion.com's Ariel Tiferes says, "Repercussions in [foreign] media [of a piece of news having to do with Argentina] are a [type of] story that we hate [to do] at this point . . . but people always click on [this type of story] . . . so, well, we're forced to a certain extent [to publish it]" (personal communication, December 14, 2006).

The analysis of news work presented in chapters 2 and 3 showed that journalists often make editorial and technological decisions based on the representations they have of their public. These representations contribute to shape, borrowing from Hall (1980), the encoding of the news in particular ways.[2] The account presented in this section adds a critical layer to make sense of the role that these representations play in the dynamics of imitation. It shows that many journalists have taken advantage of the new conditions of audience visibility to develop a more fine-grained understanding of the public's decoding of the news—at least in terms of what stories consumers choose from the overall editorial offering. Increased awareness of the public's preferences is an element of the everyday routines of journalists. Furthermore, this awareness also highlights in journalistic consciousness the character and size of a gap between the core news product supplied by the organizations studied and the dominant decoding practices of their publics as represented by their story selection patterns. The awareness of this gap means that the journalistic encoding of the news in ways that follow traditional occupational values—including those that contribute to the monitoring and imitation dynamics analyzed in chapters 2 and 3—tends to be done while cognizant of the divergent decoding behavior and takes place in spite of it. The next section presents evidence of how wide and deep this gap is.

Comparing Journalists' and Consumers' Online News Choices

Building on the findings presented in chapter 5, this section compares the online news choices of journalists and consumers on Clarín.com, Lanacion .com, and Infobae.com. More precisely, it compares these choices across sites and within each site. It draws on findings from two studies introduced in chapter 1. The first study concerns journalists' choices and uses data collected about the stories on the first screen of these sites' homepages during the autumn of 2005. The second study is about consumers' choices and uses information about the most-clicked stories on each of these sites and a control group of stories published on their respective homepages during the autumn of 2006.[3] Because the first study collected data only from Monday through Friday, the analysis in this section does not consider the second study's data collected on weekends.

The comparison across sites examines the stories that have content overlap in the journalists' and consumers' data sets. Of the 1,620 stories in the journalists' data set, 1,183 are hard news, and 619 of these hard-news stories have content overlap. Of the 1,500 stories[4] contained in the data set of consumers' most-clicked stories, 886 are hard news, and 316 of these have content overlap. Because all but 3 of the stories with content overlap in the journalists' data set are hard news, the analysis of the consumers' data set also focuses exclusively on this news. As with the analysis presented in chapter 4, the population of hard-news stories is used as the denominator in calculations of the proportion of stories with content overlap.[5] It is worth noticing that the 316 stories with content overlap not only represent the stories that were popular among consumers on at least two of the three sites but also appear to be stories in which consumers are particularly interested. Their average ranking is 4.58, in contrast to 5.94 for hard-news stories without content overlap.

Table 6.1 summarizes the three main findings that emerge from the comparison of the convergent online news choices made by consumers and journalists. First, the level of content overlap is much lower for consumers than for journalists. That is, whereas 36% of consumers' choices converge across more than one site, this value rises to 52% in the case of journalists. This yields a significant ($p < .01$) difference of sixteen percentage points between the level of convergent choices of consumers and journalists. The second and third key findings are related to the important differences in the thematic distribution and level of concentration within the respective convergent choices. Regarding the former, only 31% of the hard-news stories with content overlap that make it to the top ten most-clicked stories are about public affairs, but 58% of journalists'

Table 6.1.   Comparison of the Top Convergent Online News Choices of Journalists and Consumers, Hard News Only

	Consumers' choices: top ten most-clicked stories	Journalists' choices: top stories of the day
Content overlap		
Yes*	36% (316)	52% (619)
No*	64% (570)	48% (564)
Content focus (stories with overlap)		
Public affairs*	31% (97)	58% (357)
Non–public affairs*	69% (219)	42% (262)
Concentration level (stories with overlap)		
Dyads*	66% (208)	44% (274)
Triads*	34% (108)	56% (345)

Note: Rows marked with an asterisk (*) indicate significant ($p < .01$) differences between consumers' choices and journalists' choices.

choices of the top stories of the day have this kind of content—yielding a significant ($p < .01$) difference of twenty-seven percentage points. Finally, the level of concentration of the most popular convergent news choices is far lower among consumers than among journalists. Whereas only 34% of these choices involve the three sites in the case of consumers, this figure rises to 56% in the case of journalists, which amounts to a significant ($p < .01$) difference of twenty-two percentage points.[6]

An examination of the most-clicked stories that occupy the first position in the ranking of all the sites in which there is content overlap reveals the thematic composition of the stories that most strongly capture the public's imagination. There are three triads and four dyads of stories of this kind. All address non–public affairs subjects. The triads of stories are about the following three events: the stingray attack that caused the death of Australian naturalist and television personality Steve Irwin, published on September 5, 2006; the first appearance on television of Austrian adolescent Natascha Kampusch after being freed from her eight-year captivity, published on September 6, 2006; and the announcement by Argentine soccer star Juan Román Riquelme that he would no longer play for the national team, published on September 13, 2006. In addition, there are two pairs of stories published on Clarín.com and Lanacion .com that occupy the top place in their respective rankings. The first pair of stories is about news of the death of Steve Irwin, published on September 4, 2006. The second pair is about record-high temperatures in the city of Buenos Aires on the day the stories were published, October 24, 2006. Finally, there are also two dyads of top-ranked stories shared by Clarín.com and Infobae.com, and both deal with soccer. The first pair, published on July 31, 2006, concerns statements made about former Argentine player Diego Armando Maradona. The second chronicles a match between the Argentine team Boca Juniors and the Uruguayan team Nacional de Montevideo, published on October 12, 2006. A cursory glance at this list underscores the strong dominance of content categories such as sports, celebrity, and crime in the convergent choices of consumers.

This conspicuous presence of non–public affairs stories in the most prominent convergent choices of consumers is consistent with the data about general patterns of consumer choice presented in the previous chapter. Furthermore, it signals a chasm between the convergent choices of consumers and the predominant thematic choices of journalists within each of these sites, which were heavily oriented toward public affairs stories. The magnitude of this chasm can be appreciated by contrasting consumers' top ten most-clicked stories with two types of story choices by journalists. The top journalistic choices collected in the 2005 study (the stories that journalists deemed most newsworthy and placed at the top of the screen on their respective sites) and the editorial offerings represented by the control group collected in the 2006 study (the stories that journalists considered newsworthy enough to merit inclusion on their respective homepages but not necessarily placement at the top of the screen).

This analysis, focused on hard news only, reveals the existence of sizable and significant thematic differences between the choices of consumers and both types of journalistic choice on all three sites (table 6.2). Whereas only 24% of the top ten most-clicked stories on Clarín.com are about public affairs news, 51% of the top journalistic choices and 38% of the overall homepage editorial supply are about this type of news. This yields significant ($p < .01$) differences of twenty-seven and fourteen percentage points, respectively. On Lanacion.com, even though nearly half—43%—of the most-clicked stories concern public affairs matters, this figure rises to 62% of the top journalistic choices and to 56% of the thematic composition of the homepage. This results in significant ($p < .01$) differences of nineteen and thirteen percentage points, respectively. Finally, the differences in the thematic preferences of consumers and journalists widen considerably at Infobae.com. Only one-quarter of the consumers' choices are about public affairs news, but 67% of the top journalistic choices and 66% of the homepage editorial supply are about this type of content, for significant ($p < .01$) differences of forty-two and forty-one percentage points, respectively.

Table 6.2.   Comparison of the Public Affairs and Non–Public Affairs Choices of Journalists and Consumers, Hard News Only

	Consumers' choices: top ten most-clicked stories	Journalists' choices: top stories of the day (2005 study)	Journalists' choices: control group (2006 study)
Clarín.com			
Public affairs*	24% (72)	51% (181)	38% (90)
Non–public affairs*	76% (230)	49% (174)	62% (149)
Lanacion.com			
Public affairs*	43% (153)	62% (240)	56% (97)
Non–public affairs*	57% (205)	38% (149)	44% (77)
Infobae.com			
Public affairs*	25% (57)	67% (296)	66% (127)
Non–public affairs*	75% (169)	33% (143)	34% (65)

Note: Rows marked with an asterisk (*) indicate significant ($p < .01$) differences between consumers' choices and both journalists' choices categories: top stories of the day and control group.

Two issues emerge from this comparison of the online news choices of consumers and journalists within each of these three sites. First, the thematic gap in the respective choices of these groups on Clarín.com and Lanacion.com narrows from the top stories of the day placed at the top of the computer screen to the overall editorial supply published across the homepage. Because the top stories are the main part of the editorial supply by which journalists aim to set the agenda, their greater failure to capture the consumers' interest might signal a diminished ability of these two news organizations to exert influence on the general audience about public affairs subjects.[7] (This issue will be discussed again in the concluding chapter.) The size of the gap at Infobae.com further reinforces the need to consider this point.

A second issue concerns the role of Lanacion.com, the online site of Argentina's quality news organization, in disseminating news about public affairs. As in many countries, consumers of this kind of outlet tend to be more interested in public affairs than the average consumer. Contrasting the choices of consumers on Lanacion.com with those on Clarín.com and Infobae.com indicates that this was the case in the present data set. However, even on the quality online news site there is a considerable thematic gap between the supply and demand of news.

The dominance of non–public affairs stories in the convergent consumer choices is consistent with findings about general news choices presented in chapter 5. The analysis of the top content categories in the most-clicked stories revealed the prevalence of sports news across sites, during the week and on the weekend. Furthermore, those who consumed online news in an office setting noted the preference for "lighter," non–public affairs topics over the "heavier," public affairs ones. They also stressed that non–public affairs stories provided better fodder for conversations with coworkers than the often more contentious and sensitive topics presented in public affairs news.

In addition to being consistent with the relevant dynamics of the news-at-work phenomenon, the results presented in this section can also be interpreted from the vantage points of production and consumption. Each mode of interpretation is discussed.

The content analysis findings summarized in tables 6.1 and 6.2 converge with the results from the ethnographic studies of news production presented in the previous section. Online journalists are increasingly aware of the news choices made by consumers of their sites. They experience a tension between the overall preferences revealed by these choices and dominant occupational values, yet they tend to stick to these values in the face of dissonant consumer preferences. That the logic of the occupation prevails over the logic of the market underscores the notion, introduced in chapter 4, that in the context of the present study the dynamics of imitation prevail over the forces of product differentiation, in this case, those driven by demand-side factors that are consequential in other media contexts (B. Anand, Di Tella, & Galetovic, 2007; Gentzkow & Shapiro, 2006, 2007; Mullainathan & Shleifer, 2005).

The account of the homogenization of news content presented in chapters 3 and 4 is built on the idea that it results from how journalists have reacted to changes in the production sphere. In principle, a plausible alternative or complementary explanation is that journalists have actually reacted to perceived changes in the nature of consumption. However, the large gap between the online news choices of journalists and consumers in terms of the proportion of stories with overlap and their divergent thematic distribution and level of concentration enable the analysis to rule out this alternative or complementary explanation. Had changing consumer preferences been a major driver of the observed variance, the choices of online consumers would have been more (not less) convergent than those of journalists. In addition, the convergent stories would have clustered more (not less) on public affairs topics. Although the studies that form the basis of this section gathered data at one point in time, the size of the gaps between the choices of online journalists and consumers, the consistency between these choices and the ethnographic evidence on their respective production and consumption routines, and the longitudinal evolution of the print samples toward more (not less) similarity in story selection suggest that the above-mentioned alternative or complementary explanation is not applicable to the present case. In the concluding section I will further elaborate this issue and the role of consumption in accounts of imitation.

Looking at the results from the vantage point of consumption sheds light on how agency dynamics shape the appropriation of homogenized news. Agency has been a critical element of accounts of consumption of media texts (Ang, 1989; Hall, 1980; Katz, Blumler, & Gurevitch, 1974; Lull, 1980; Radway, 1991), technological artifacts (S. Douglas, 1988; M. Martin, 1991; Marvin, 1988; Oudshoorn & Pinch, 2003), and economic goods (Bourdieu, 1984; Douglas & Isherwood, 1979; Sahlins, 1976; V. Zelizer, 2005a; Zukin & Smith Maguire, 2004). There are differences in how these three kinds of accounts approach agency in consumption. But they converge in signaling that consumer practices (in addition to being influenced by production dynamics) are also fundamentally affected by variations in factors such as class, ethnicity, relational networks, and the situational context. A popular line of argument in studies of media texts and technological artifacts is that often people consume differently from what producers supply them (Feenberg, 1992; Fischer, 1988; Kline, 2000; Liebes & Katz, 1990; Morley, 1992; Silverstone & Haddon, 1996). That is, consumers frequently deviate from the preferred reading and uses embedded in texts and artifacts. Instead, they gravitate toward different forms of negotiated and oppositional readings, creative uses, resistance positions, and even nonuse of artifacts.

The analysis in this section shows that this was the case. Readers enacted a high level of agency in their selection of the most popular stories within and across the sites, as indicated by the divergence in the volume of overlap and thematic distribution of their choices from those of journalists. Thus, at the level of choice, consumers were not passive recipients of a highly uniform news product. On the contrary, they actively selected to consume a different content mix than that privileged by journalists. This gap between the choices of journalists and consumers has been noted in studies of the news in various media (Bird, 2003; Couldry & Markham, 2008; Hagen, 1994; Jensen, 1990). In the introduction to Hughes's *News and the Human Interest Story*, Park states: "It is a curious fact—one of those facts about human nature that philosophers were wont to observe and record before the study of human nature became systematic and scientific—that the things which most of us would like to publish are not the things that most of us want to read. We may be eager to get into print what is, or seems to be, edifying, but we want to read what is interesting" (Park, 1981 [1940], n.p.).

The novelty of the analysis in this section resides in its ability to more precisely measure the size and thematic distribution of this gap. More important, the relevance of the analysis for the main objective of this chapter is the clear indication that people are not passive recipients of homogenized news but exercise a considerable degree of latitude in how they choose to consume the products supplied by media organizations. This finding constitutes an important step toward understanding the dynamics and consequences of consuming homogenized news. But because the evidence presented in this section is "merely supply and consumption figures, not figures registering the effect of mass media" (Lazarsfeld & Merton, 1948, p. 99), the next two sections continue the analytical process by delving deeper into the experience of consuming increasingly similar news.

The Experience of Consuming Homogenized News

Most consumers visit a variety of sites in a routine fashion—as was evident in chapter 5. Twenty of the fifty interviewees read more than one online news site regularly every day. Although the remaining thirty interviewees have a preferred news site, many supplement its content by looking at a few other sites with notable frequency. For instance, when readers of Lanacion.com want to learn more about breaking news, they often visit Clarín.com or Infobae.com because these sites are known to be faster at updating news than the former. Tristán, a thirty-four-year-old software consultant, says, "The first visit of the day is to Lanacion.com. Then, if I have to look at a breaking news story, I look at Infobae.com" (personal communication, March 31, 2007). Pablo, the lawyer, comments, "I always begin [the day] with Lanacion.com, and then as the day unfolds I keep reading Clarín.com because it's the fastest to update [its coverage]" (personal communication, February 21, 2007).

Because they regularly visit various sites or supplement a preferred site with frequent visits to others, more than half of the interviewees are in a good position to compare the news offered at these sites. When asked to compare the sites, the overwhelmingly dominant response is that "the news is the same; the framing is different." Pablo, the lawyer, states, "If you go to an [online] newspaper [site], it is like going to all [of the others]. . . . The [main] headlines of the day and the news in general are the same. Now, how they are [framed]—that differs" (personal communication, February 21, 2007). Natalia, the college student, agrees with Pablo, "The most important news [is published in] all newspapers. . . . But I notice the difference in the order, the importance that some give to a story, while others do not" (personal communication, December 18, 2006).

Several interviewees mention that the homogeneity of story selection extends to the broader media landscape. For instance, according to Manuel, the computer technician, "Everybody has the same news and that makes it boring, monotonous, with no variety. Buying a newspaper ends up being like buying any other one" (personal communication, March 29, 2007). Sebastián, the screenwriter, comments that before having broadband at home he used to watch a lot of news on television on several channels: "The same stories [were shown] in all the editions, in the morning and in the evening. . . . I think the same happens on the Internet. There are a few stories, and they are all the same" (personal communication, January 15, 2007). Norberto, a sixty-two-year-old accountant who devotes significant amounts of time to the news since retiring from his job, expresses frustration at cross-media patterns of content similarity: "The media . . . take a lot of advantage of the other's harvest [*la cosecha ajena*]. . . . During the day I listen to radio programs . . . and they . . . comment on the news that they read in the newspaper just like I do" (personal communication, January 19, 2007).

Because the common perception is that outlets differ mostly in how they frame the news, many consumers convey a sense of interpretive savvy in their reading of specific stories as well as their appropriation of a particular outlet. Interviews are full of instances in which people elaborate on how the same story is treated differently in various outlets or how these outlets construct their stories more generally. This is not to say that people's actual interpretations are good or bad or right or wrong but that, overall, people exhibit a sense of sophistication as readers of news texts. Bringing to mind the commercials that test the ability of blindfolded people to distinguish among different soda drinks, Fabiana, the public sector employee, confidently asserts, "If you give me two articles and don't tell me where they come from, I will tell you which one is from [*La*] *Nación* and which one from *Clarín*" (personal communication, February 20, 2007). Sebastián, the screenwriter, notes that he looks for the same stories in various outlets "to understand how each one plays [its game]. It's for information more on the stance that each one takes to tell you the news than on the news itself" (personal communication, January 15, 2007).

In light of the intensity of people's interpretive practices, it is not surprising to find that they have a number of explanations for the dominant belief that the news is the same but its framing differs across outlets. Four reasons mark accounts of the homogeneity in the selection of stories: the main stories must be carried by all outlets; all consumers want the same stories; most sites draw on the same source materials; and sites routinely monitor their competitors and replicate the content of their stories.

Laura, the marketing specialist, talks about the idea that some news imposes its presence across sites by its own weight: "You have a news mass [*una masa de noticias*] that is inevitable [to publish]. The president of Mexico took office today, and with the exception of some newspapers that cater to a very special public, all of the others are going to publish the story" (personal communication, December 1, 2006). Several interviewees agree with Laura's assessment, but they also note that this accounts for only a small fraction of the daily supply of news. Some attribute the similarity of other, less important stories to a perceived lack of diversity in consumer taste. Julián, the accounting firm employee, says that the news stories "that sell are all the same" (personal communication, January 4, 2007). Natalia, the college student, echoes him: "If the three newspapers publish the same [stories], it is because those are the news that people read or the ones that interest them the most" (personal communication, December 18, 2006).

The third and fourth common explanations concern two production dynamics: the reliance on wire service copy and the perceived deliberate imitation across sites. Alba, the lawyer, matter-of-factly states, "Obviously, if it's the same wire [copy], they will publish the same" (personal communication, February 13, 2007). Valeria, the airline company worker, offers, "Looking at [the news production process] from the outside and without knowing how it actually happens . . . it seems that all [the sites] get the information from the same news agencies, and there is very little research that they do on their own. Therefore, if they get the information from the same place, it is very difficult for it to have different content" (personal communication, April 17, 2007).

Some interviewees infer significant monitoring and imitation across outlets. Fernando, the film editor, says, "I believe that [the new national daily] *Perfil* and *Clarín* are looking at each other all the time" (personal communication, January 17, 2007). Juan Martín, the economist, offers the following elaboration on the consequences of monitoring:

Sometimes so much information un-informs [*des-informa*] you. In the sense that if all the [online] newspapers rely on the same information and this happens at great speed—I'm thinking out loud, [but] maybe this doesn't generate much incentive to undertake [independent] research because [the journalists] know that they always have this externality that soon after they publish a story their competitor discovers it and publishes it too. **(PERSONAL COMMUNICATION, FEBRUARY 21, 2007)**

In addition to these notions about the homogeneity of story selection, two ideas dominate consumers' accounts of why different outlets diverge in their framing of the same stories. One is the need to cater to their different publics, and the other is the influence of political and economic interests on the media.

Reflecting about the differences in news construction between *Clarín* and *La Nación*—both in print and online—Fernanda, a twenty-two-year-old college student, says, "Every newspaper treats their news and topics to satisfy their [respective] publics" (personal communication, February 8, 2007). Quite often these publics are defined by class markers. Fabiana, the public sector employee, notes that "*Clarín* is more of the people . . . and *Nación* is of a certain elite class" (personal communication, February 20, 2007).

More common are explanations that attribute the differences in the framing of news across outlets to the perceived divergent political or economic interests of the corporations that own these media. According to Ana, the insurance company employee, the various outlets "distinguish themselves by how they write, because they clearly have an ideology" (personal communication, March 8, 2007). Furthermore, consumers who stress this type of influence often do so in a way that expresses skepticism about the news organizations involved. Luis, the culture industry entrepreneur, says:

Here [in Argentina] everything varies in relation to politics [and] business. So this is a factor that has made me doubt *Clarín* for a number of years. [Grupo Clarín] is such a huge business, they are so interdependent with the government, that I always see the news as . . . being filtered. In *La Nación,* there's some of the same but on another [scale] since they are not so involved in the economic status quo. It's a newspaper, a building; it might have some [additional] business, but it's not an enormous media group. **(PERSONAL COMMUNICATION, DECEMBER 13, 2006)**

Interviewees were probed about their reactions to the homogenization of news. Those who expressed a perception of this phenomenon were asked whether they liked it and what feelings it provoked. Those who did not share this perception were invited to imagine a scenario five years into the future in which the news supplied by various outlets became increasingly similar. Then they were asked whether they liked this scenario and how they felt about it.

Regardless of whether they already perceive the presence of this phenomenon or imagined it in the future, most consumers react negatively to the loss of content diversity. Esteban, the Web designer, says that in the current environment "everything becomes homogenized [whereas] the ideal thing is that each one retains its profile" (personal communication, January 16, 2007). Lorena, the teacher of Spanish as a second language, reflects that "it's always better to have difference. The single, monolithic voice—no!" (personal communication, March 2, 2007). Gerardo, the engineer, concurs with Esteban and Lorena: "I don't like the homogeneity [of things]; it tends to make everything uniform, alike. It seems boring to me" (personal communication, April 10, 2007).

This dominant reaction of dislike is tied to an overwhelmingly negative affect. Some, like Vanina, the teacher quoted at the beginning of this chapter, express their feelings rather viscerally. Others, like Alexis, the psychiatrist, talk about their emotions in a distant and intellectualized way: "It provokes a very moderate irritation in a context . . . in which we can't trust anybody or anything anymore, in which everything has some sort of interest [behind it], and nothing is as genuine as what it seems. . . . Then, I say, 'Well, it's what we have' [es lo que hay]" (personal communication, December 26, 2007).

The main exception to this dominant reaction of dislike and negative affect comes from a handful of the youngest interviewees—those in their twenties. They expressed a mix of indifference and cynicism.[8] Laura, a twenty-seven-year-old philosophy major and part-time teacher who is well aware of the homogenization of news, says, "If I like the [editorial] line of the newspapers, then it doesn't matter to me. I don't need opposition. . . . And I'm saying this very honestly, in a supernarcissistic fashion" (personal communication, March 20, 2007). When Silvia, the accounting analyst, is asked to imagine the future scenario, she answers, with a distant tone, "It doesn't bother me. . . . I'm not interested in the fights among them [referring to the media]" (personal communication, December 4, 2006). Guido, a twenty-six-year-old literature student, reflects on the future scenario in this way: "I would accept a complaint only from someone who read at least five newspapers. If you read only one, then why does it bother you? . . . It seems an easy discourse to me. . . . I don't think it's anything dramatic. We lived in an idyllic world and now it's destroyed" (personal communication, February 21, 2007).

When asked whether anything can be done to alter a situation—perceived or imagined—of a high level of content homogeneity, some interviewees stress changes in their behavior and others in the actions of the media industry. Those who focus on the self tend to underscore the importance of reading multiple sources and critically contrasting coverage of the same events. Natalia, the college student, frames this alternative as follows: "It's good to see the same news [story] in different media and try to analyze what the reality is . . . [but] it's something half complicated [and] half utopian. . . . You need time and access to the Web, because not everybody has it. And you aren't going to buy four newspapers because they are increasingly more expensive [than before]" (personal communication, December 18, 2006). Most of the consumers who talk about solutions initiated by the media industry say that the best chance would come from the emergence of a new site or publication with an agenda and behavior different "from the rest." For Ana, the clerical employee at an insurance agency, "A form of avoiding [content homogenization] would be that a new medium emerges some day." Asked how likely this would be, Ana replies, "The truth is that I see that as quite complicated" (personal communication, March 8, 2007).

Echoing Natalia and Ana, most consumers converge in signaling the low probability of an alteration in the landscape of homogenized news, regardless of whether they focus on changes in their own behavior or in that of the industry. Manuel, the computer technician, concurs with Natalia and Ana: "I don't know if I lost the utopias of my adolescence, but you can't go against this, it's very difficult" (personal communication, March 29, 2007). This perception of a low probability of change is often tied to comments that convey a sense of disappointment about the possibility of positive social transformations in the context of Argentina's recent history. As described in chapter 1, the failed neoliberal reforms of the 1990s and the economic and political crisis that erupted in 2001 were the culmination of decades of growing deterioration in the strength, quality, and stability of the country's political and economic institutions (Levitsky & Murillo, 2005c, 2009):

Institutional weakness became a dominant feature of twentieth-century Argentine politics: Whenever the political or economic rules of the game were perceived to harm the short-term interests of those in power, they were circumvented, manipulated, or changed. The political and economic consequences of this institutional instability were a Hobbesian world of high uncertainty, narrow time horizons, and low trust and cooperation. (LEVITSKY, 2005, P. 72)

In addition to undermining the country's political and economic spheres, this historical intensification of a pattern of institutional weakness has also had powerful consequences for the cultural fabric of society. Studies of the period that followed the crisis of 2001 and 2002 show its impact on the relational, ideational, and affective dimensions of everyday life (Armony & Armony, 2005; Borland & Sutton, 2007; Grimson & Kessler, 2005; Lakoff, 2005; Sutton, 2007; Svampa, 2005; Whitson, 2007). The consequences that are more directly relevant for this study have to do with a pronounced skepticism about the likelihood of positive social change, a feeling of powerlessness regarding the alteration of social structures—especially those that are marked by powerful political or economic interests—and a resulting sense of alienation from public participation.[9] For Armony and Armony, "The combination of fragmentation in society with increased cynicism about the virtues of politics and the role of the law reinforced a sense of anomie and disorientation" (2005, p. 34). Thus, when asked about the possibility that the homogeneity of content might decrease in the future, Irina, the owner of a family video production business who dislikes the current state of affairs with online news, expresses a strong sentiment of pessimism linked to the post-2001 crisis: "Reality is tough . . . one doesn't want to realize that, like in 2002. . . . This is the anesthesia of reality [*la anestesia de la realidad*]" (personal communication, February 20, 2007). Irina's comments amplify ideas and sentiments expressed by Alexis, Manuel, and Ana, among others.

This sense of pessimism is aggravated by the notion that many interviewees have about the political interests that shape the media agenda. To most people, politics is something that powerful actors do to increase their power. The regular folk are not only excluded from this process but are also disempowered by it. Auyero (2007) concludes from his conversations with victims and victimizers of the lootings that triggered the onset of the 2001 crisis: "'Politics' (as in the expression 'it's all about politics') connotes something profoundly disempowering for them ('What can we do?'). When speaking about politics, they refer to something coming from above, something beyond their control—sometimes they hint at a sort of conspiracy, but most of the time they use the language of politics to talk about how impotent and vulnerable they feel" (2007, p. 148).

Echoing Auyero's conclusions, Julieta, the receptionist at a car dealership, reflects on the reverberations of the post-1990s period: "I remember a Sunday at the kitchen table and we talked about politics. Today we don't. It seems to me that this is because the nineties wiped everything out: ideologies, ideals, [and] interests. It's very rare to hear a guy of my age talk about politics. If he talks about politics, you should ask him if he is a militant [in a political party]. The person who is not a militant doesn't talk about politics" (personal communication, February 28, 2007).

The skepticism about the likelihood of positive social change and the sense of powerlessness to alter matters that are perceived to be tied to powerful political and economic interests contributes to a sense of alienation from collective participation.[10] As will be shown in the next section, although many interviewees dislike the current state of affairs, few take advantage of online spaces of peer-to-peer cultural production, such as blogs and forums, to alter it by reporting stories not published by the media or sharing their views on media-written stories. This is consistent with findings presented in chapter 5 about the dominance of an "intake" stance of online news consumption that privileges the readable Web over the production-oriented capabilities of the writable Web. Furthermore, even the reading of postings by fellow consumers is quite limited.

The analysis presented in this section has shown that the consumption of homogenized news is marked by negative evaluation and affect on the part of consumers. Furthermore, this evaluation and affect are accompanied by a sense of powerlessness with respect to their ability to change the state of affairs, a feeling of skepticism about the likelihood of this change—regardless of the change agent—and a stance of alienation from social participation. There is an important parallel with a perception that many journalists expressed about the rising homogeneity of news, as noted in chapter 3. They expressed dislike for the state of affairs and a feeling of powerlessness—"because this is how things are now." Furthermore, the relatively low level of agency conveyed in this portrait of consumer experience presents a stark contrast to the high level of agency enacted in the selection of what stories to consume. This is because there are two dimensions of agency at play. One has to do with consumption choices that remain largely an individual form of social action, even though, as was shown in chapter 5, they shape and are shaped by interaction dynamics. The other has to do with practices that shift the register from consumption to production—from taking what is given to giving what others might take—and are therefore oriented toward participatory actions that directly aim to alter the collective sphere. To better understand the dynamics and consequences of these two forms of agency, in the next section I examine consumers' divergent appropriation of two kinds of interactive applications that have become increasingly popular in news sites: polls, on the one hand, and blogs, forums, and commentary spaces, on the other.

Agency in Consumption between Choice and Participation

Interactivity has long been considered a hallmark of online news (Allan, 2006; Boczkowski, 2002; Deuze, 2003; Mitchelstein & Boczkowski, 2009; Pavlik, 2001). Two of the most pervasive manifestations of interactivity are the ability of consumers to vote in polls covering subjects of the most varied kind and the opportunity to provide their opinions and stories in blogs, forums, and other commentary spaces. Because different expressions of these two kinds of interactive applications were quite prevalent among the top online news sites in Argentina during the period when interviews with consumers were conducted, these interviews included questions about what people did with and thought about them. A summary follows of the main findings that are pertinent to understanding the dynamics of agency as they affect the consumption of homogenized news.

Polls

About half of the interviewees say that they vote in polls provided by online newspapers and pay attention to their results. Some do it very often; others less so. Regardless of how frequently they engage with polls, those who do so associate their practice with a positive affect marked by playfulness. For instance, Federico, the psychiatrist, comments that he routinely looks at polls "because it's fun to see the results" (personal communication, December 28, 2006). Interviewees give three main reasons for their participation in online polls: assistance with navigating the social world, the chance to express their opinions, and access to content that could be used in offline social interactions.

Most consumers who monitor online polls and participate in them say they do so because the information they gather helps them to understand their fellow online consumers and calibrate their own take on issues vis-à-vis other consumers. Fernando, the film editor, says, "It interests me to know [what] the majority of the people think [about a topic]" (personal communication, January 17, 2007). Vanina, the teacher, comments, "I love the game of saying . . . 'in this question the majority is going to give [answer X].' It's a form of seeing . . . what the other readers of the newspaper think . . . and in general I'm not surprised [by people's answers]" (personal communication, February 22, 2007).

Another common reason mentioned by interviewees is that polls enable them to voice their opinion on topics that matter to them. Gerardo, the electrical engineer, notes that "I like to know that my opinion counts, and knowing the trends [expressed in the results] also interests me" (personal communication, April 10, 2007).

The third motive is tied to the common practice of using poll results as triggers for conversations with coworkers (when at work) or friends (during leisure time). When asked why he likes to know the results of online polls, Martín, the lawyer, answers, "To comment about them later. You get together with [a friend] and say, 'I see that the majority of people think so and so about issue X'" (personal communication, February 26, 2007).

Those who do not vote or pay attention to polls give two reasons for their lack of interest. Several interviewees mention a concern about the privacy of information in the online environment. Irina, the owner of a video production business, says, "I don't like to give my information on the Web, so I'm not interested in being asked to participate in [polls]" (personal communication, February 20, 2007). The second reason has to do with the perception of a low level of quality in the technical aspects of the polls—such as sampling and question formulation—and the ulterior motives behind them. Tristán, the software consultant, addresses the first point by saying that he does not participate in polls "because . . . they don't draw on a representative sample" (personal communication, March 31, 2007). Manuel, the computer technician, touches on the second by noting, "I distrust [polls and their uses] a lot" (personal communication, March 29, 2007).

Blogs, Forums, and Other Commentary Spaces

The vast majority of the interviewees say that they do not read any blogs, forums, and comments appended to news stories. Furthermore, the level of activity involved in contributing content to any of these user-authored options in online news sites is even lower than merely reading the content. In addition to this low level of engagement with these forms of online participation, the affect associated with them is strongly negative. In contrast to the playfulness often tied to polls, many consider blogs, forums, and commentary spaces "boring." Federico, the psychiatrist who thinks that polls are "fun," gives the following answer when asked about online participation in newspaper sites: "I don't participate in any forum or anything like that because I get bored" (personal communication, December 28, 2006). Beyond this negative affect, interviewees give four reasons for their limited use of this kind of interactive option of the online environment: lack of time, perceived low quality of discourse, little interest in online sociability, and privacy concerns.

Having limited time to devote to online participation is the reason most often mentioned by interviewees when asked why they do not consume blogs and forums or contribute content to them. Luis, the culture industry entrepreneur, says that he is not "very active in . . . community activities [online]. . . . I have a very heavy workload, and therefore, I feel that [these activities] distract me" (personal communication, December 13, 2006). Natalia, a college student who also has a job, ties this limited time availability to consuming online news at the time and place of work: "I'm not one for participating mostly because I try to take advantage of . . . my time here in the office to keep abreast of the news that is related to my job. And I try not to visit or become interested in any kind of site that might give the impression that I'm wasting my time at work" (personal communication, March 19, 2007).

Interviewees add that when they read the content of blogs and forums, they find the quality of the exchanges to be quite poor. They are appalled by the recurrence of profanity and put off by the predominant lack of dialogue among participants and the pervasive presence of contributors who voice their opinions in a monologue fashion. In the experience of Luis, a sixty-seven-year-old retiree: "Even though I don't participate [in blogs or forums], I can still see what others say and what the replies to their statements are. Lots of people take advantage of the situation to say stupid things [*gansadas*]. . . . If I express my opinion, I'm not interested in discussing whether I am right or not right with people I don't know. I do discuss these things a lot with friends of mine" (personal communication, February 6, 2007).

The remarks by Luis also point to the third reason often mentioned by interviewees, which resonates with a general pattern of online news consumption, described in chapter 5, having to do with a lack of interest in online sociability. Consumers perceive blogs and forums to be relational environments, and as analyzed in the previous chapter, they prefer offline to online social interactions. Even when interactions are about news discovered online, they tend to take place offline with colleagues at work or with family and friends outside work. In the words of Natalia, the clerical employee, "I like to give my opinion [about things] personally. I can't get used to opinion forums on the Internet" (personal communication, December 18, 2006).

Privacy concerns, another issue analyzed in chapter 5, also deter people from posting comments on blogs and forums. Lorena, the teacher of Spanish as a second language, says that she has "a paranoid suspicion that the media that furnish blogs [for consumers] in some way also extract certain information about personal consumption patterns" (personal communication, March 2, 2007). Tristán, the software consultant, mentions that he does not contribute to user-authored online spaces because he is "afraid that some day they [the sites] might sell the data base . . . of those who wrote" (personal communication, March 31, 2007).

There are two exceptions to this predominant lack of interest in blogs and forums. The first and most prevalent is that some of the same interviewees who say they do not read blogs of news sites visit other kinds of blogs. Quite often, the visited blogs are those of friends or those recommended by friends. When asked why they read such blogs but not those published by mainstream media, some interviewees, such as Irina, stress that the latter "don't inspire confidence" (personal communication, February 20, 2007), and others, such as Laura, say that they "don't respect the blog format" because mainstream media blogs do such things as filter comments (personal communication, March 20, 2007). The other exception is represented by a handful of interviewees such as Vanina, the teacher, and Cecilia, the cyber café employee, both of whom report that they fairly regularly spend time reading blogs and forums of news sites. They agree with many of the other interviewees in acknowledging some of the problems with the time this activity requires and the low level of quality on many of the posts. However, unlike most of these other interviewees, Vanina and Cecilia say that the content of blogs and forums adds to their understanding of social reactions to the news. According to Cecilia:

I like to see what [readers] think. . . . Sometimes . . . it makes me sick how there are people who say, "You are all idiots [*boludos*]" or post a comment looking for a fight [*buscar quilombo*]. But I don't interact with anybody [and] don't reply . . . because they are going to answer back and . . . will want to be right and I will want the same. But I like to read the comments because it's through them that I realize how society is and how people think. **(PERSONAL COMMUNICATION, JANUARY 24, 2007)**

The above examples highlight the infrequent engagement of interviewees with blogs, forums, and commentary spaces. When interviewees do engage, they adopt a consumer position consistent with the intake stance that often marks online news consumption: that is, they read rather than contribute content. In other words, even when people incorporate user-authored content into their appropriation routines of news sites, they treat the spaces that house that content as part of the readable Web, leaving its much-touted writable potential largely unrealized.

The comparative analysis of consumers' engagement with two kinds of interactive applications shows that the involvement and affect associated with polls is somewhat positive and that the uptake of blogs, forums, and other commentary spaces is minimal, and the affect tied to them quite negative. Although both kinds of applications imply a participatory form of agency, their respective appropriation differs. Voting in interactive polls is a close-ended, low-effort, and low-noise type of activity. Creating publicly available content in the form of a news story or a comment on an already-existing story is a more open-ended, higher-effort, and higher-noise endeavor. Thus, even in the case of online opportunities whose realization requires a form of participatory agency, consumers are more receptive to one—polling—that is largely based on a closed choice mechanism than to blogs, forums, and commentary spaces that require the type of involvement that marks conversational dynamics in large collective settings.

The difference in the appropriation of these two forms of interactivity provides a window into the character of participatory agency in online news environments that is crucial for making sense of the consumption of increasingly similar content. Scholarship on media texts and artifacts accounts for the emergence of situations in which readers co-construct content and users become agents of technological change (Douglas, 1988; Jenkins, 1992; Pinch & Trocco, 2002; Suchman, 2000; Yates, 2005). More directly relevant for the purposes of this book, studies of online news on the Web in particular, and new media in general, shed light on the processes that enable successful cases of user-authored content and the larger social consequences these cases might have (Benkler, 2006; Boczkowski, 2004; Gillmor, 2004; Jenkins, 2006; Sunstein, 2006). However, despite the high hopes associated with the possibility that these successful cases might generalize across the social body, recent research yields three sets of findings that deflate these hopes. First, bloggers and citizen journalists rely heavily on journalists for information (G. L. Daniels, 2006; Deuze, Bruns, & Neuberger, 2007; Haas, 2005; Lowrey, 2006; Reese, Rutigliano, Hyun, & Jeong, 2007). Second, during normal times there is very limited interest among members of the public in contributing news content to online news sites (Couldry, Livingstone, & Markham, 2006; Hujanen & Pietikainen, 2004; Pew, 2008b; Thurman, 2008; Ye & Li, 2006). Third, most blogs do not feature news content but resemble the personal-journal format (Herring, Scheidt, Bonus, & Wright, 2005; Lowrey & Latta, 2008; Papacharissi, 2007; Ornebring, 2008; Trammell, Tarkowski, & Sapp, 2006).

The analysis presented in this section is consistent with the image that emerges from these studies about the limited vitality of user-authored news. It adds to the findings of these studies by exploring some of the factors that contribute to this limited vitality in the present case and that might apply in other settings. Two main factors shaped the low level of enactment of participatory agency among the majority of the interviewees. One was the influence of local conditions associated with getting online news at work. These included the prevalence of a reading stance, the relatively little time available to consumers in the midst of their busy work routines, their concerns about privacy, and their preference for offline sociability. These conditions were analyzed in chapter 5. Second was the presence of a broader institutional context that, as argued in the previous section, people experienced as conducive to a sense of powerlessness, feelings of skepticism, and an alienation from the world of collective action when it came to the news. In this context, consumers become savvy readers of the news to learn about new developments that might impact their lives, but they have diminished expectations about their ability to foster positive social change. These local conditions and broader institutional features contributed to a low level of enactment of participatory agency among most consumers, even when confronted with a state of affairs that they disliked and that triggered markedly negative affect. Retreat, not reform, became the name of the game.

Concluding Remarks

The analysis presented in this chapter shows three patterns that mark the consumption of homogenized news.[11] First, there is a difference between the stories consumers most frequently choose to read and the top stories provided to them by journalists. This difference is expressed by a lower level of content overlap among the stories chosen by consumers than among those provided by journalists. It is also expressed by the divergent story selection thematic patterns between the two groups. Second, most consumers dislike homogenized news and associate their consumption with a negative affect. Third, this state of affairs tends not to trigger participatory efforts toward social change. (I will address the implications of the coupling of a dislike for news homogenization with a feeling of powerlessness to alter it, on the part of both journalists and consumers, in chapter 7.) Taken together, these three patterns create a complex set of dynamics for consumers by pulling them in opposite directions. Although the divergence between consumer and journalistic preferences and the negative assessment of homogenized news among consumers could lead to increased consumer-driven social processes, the stance of retreat that dominates consumer sentiment about participatory collective action suggests that this is far from the case. Conversely, this stance could indicate that consumers' choices are in line with those of journalists or that their evaluation of the situation is positive, or both. However, the behaviors and experiences of consumers suggest that this is not the case either.

To understand the coexistence of these complex dynamics shaping the consumption of homogenized news, it is important to highlight that two forms of agency are at play. On the one hand, the topics that journalists and consumers most value do not always converge. This divergence is not new. What is new in the present situation, however, is the interaction between technologies of knowledge that journalists can use to make the public's behavior more visible to them and a more competitive market that raises the cost of ignoring the public's preferences. Yet participating is not the same as choosing. The interaction between the local and institutional factors elucidated in the two previous sections accounts for the enactment of a much lower level of agency by consumers when taking advantage of the writable Web than when selecting from the content available on its readable counterpart. Thus, understanding the consumption side of imitation is inextricably tied to making sense of the forms of agency that mark the behaviors and experience of consumers.

The account presented in this chapter helps to theorize issues of agency and the role of consumption in imitation. The chapter contributes to a more textured depiction of consumer agency than the blanket assumption of activity that pervades most of the literature. In his overview of media consumption scholarship, Webster maintains, "Audience activity is a slippery concept" (1998, p. 202). The present account helps to make the notion of agency less slippery by unpacking the concurrent presence of two forms of agency, with two sets of determinants, that pull the various actors involved in somewhat-conflicting directions.

More central to this book's main conceptual topic is that this account also sheds light on the role of consumption in the dynamics and consequences of imitation. I show that consumption patterns were instrumental in setting in motion the processes that eventually led to a growth of imitation in production and similarity in the resulting products. As shown in chapter 2, journalists reacted to their discovery that a substantive fraction of the consumption of online news happened at the time and place of work by increasing the volume and frequency of publication, especially for hard news. In light of the production dynamics explored in chapter 3, these changes in online news triggered a cascade of unintended consequences. These consequences included an intensification of monitoring and an expansion of imitation that cut across the online-print divide and varied primarily by type of content and secondarily by medium. These consequences were shaped by a combination of situational and structural factors in news production. Together with the findings presented in chapters 4 and 5, the account offered in this chapter suggests that although consumption patterns laid the groundwork for an increase in similarity in news products, they have played no major direct role in determining the high rate of similarity and do not appear to challenge the status quo by triggering consumer-driven reform. That is, the analysis of (*a*) the divergent thematic news preferences and overlap levels in the respective news choices of journalists and consumers, (*b*) journalists' awareness of this divergence and their decision to stick with traditional editorial values to reaffirm their occupational jurisdiction, and (*c*) consumers' dislike of a homogenized news supply indicates that imitation appears to be substantially more dependent on processes and mechanisms that pertain to the sphere of production than of consumption. This finding is in line with the dominant notion that production forces are fundamental in the dynamics of imitation but adds the role that consumption plays in triggering the emergence of these dynamics.

Understanding consumption also enables an assessment of the cultural and political consequences of imitation that is anchored in the everyday behavior and experience of consumers. This assessment can reconcile what is normatively desirable with what is socially likely in light of dominant patterns of online news consumption. A detailed account of these consequences is at the heart of the next and final chapter of this book.

SEVEN

The Work of News in an Age of Information Abundance

Three meanings are associated with the first part of this book's title, *News at Work*. The first refers to the workplace as the main spatial and temporal locus of online news consumption for a large segment of the population. The second meaning points to a key rationale for the research design of the book: the examination of the work that goes into producing and consuming news stories. These two meanings are central to understanding imitation. The first focuses on salient contextual circumstances associated with the expansion of imitation in the journalistic field; the second enables the analysis to follow this expansion from the newsrooms where journalists labor to the workspaces where consumers appropriate the news. These first two meanings of the book's title are at the core of chapters 2–6. I will discuss what has been learned about them in the first half of this closing chapter. The next section concerns the main findings from the empirical examination of the production, products, and consumption of news and is followed by a section that reflects on these findings to develop theory about the dynamics of imitation.

A third meaning of the title *News at Work* refers to the cultural and political work that the news performs in society. This meaning has received less attention than the first two in the preceding chapters, because proper treatment of it required the empirical analysis and theory development undertaken in those chapters. But the time has come to tackle this third meaning. Thus, in the second half of this chapter I examine the work that a reduction in content diversity performs with respect to the culture and politics of contemporary social life. The analysis presented in previous chapters paints a worrisome picture based on the interactions of three potential trends. First is the growth in the proportion of generic news content shared across the mainstream media and the growth in the role of third-party providers, such as wire service agencies, that supply this content. This might drastically narrow the news agenda put forward by these media and concentrate a substantial portion of the power to set this agenda among a handful of players. Second is the reduction in the propensity of independent journalistic enterprises to perform their watchdog function in a vigorous fashion. This, in turn, could trigger shifts in the balance of power in favor of other actors that also wrestle to set the news agenda, such as government and resourceful private and nonprofit organizations. Third is the limited capacity of user-authored news initiatives to routinely offer diverse and comprehensive coverage of events. There have been some high-profile, positive experiences of peer-to-peer cultural production, ranging from open-source software such as Linux to reference sites such as Wikipedia. But the everyday character of online news consumption suggests that under normal circumstances the void in content diversity left by mainstream media is unlikely to be filled by a large cross section of the public.

A common thread connects these three issues. The reference in the title of this chapter to Benjamin's 1935 seminal essay "The Work of Art in the Age of Mechanical Reproduction" (2007) aims to capture this thread by evoking a sense of historical trajectory. Benjamin argues that the age of mechanical reproduction that was already in full force by the early twentieth century was marked by a concern with a loss of the authenticity and aura of the work of art. The shift from mechanical to digital reproduction in the news and other areas of symbolic work at the dawn of the twenty-first century introduced an age of information abundance that is characterized by a concern about growing trade-offs between the quantity and quality of this information.[1] The preoccupation with having more available information than resources to process it and the concern that this increase in quantity has caused deterioration in the quality of product outputs and consumer experiences are not new, but they have become greatly accentuated in recent years. The paradox of a loss of content diversity that is tied to a rise in the amount of online news is a critical expression of these larger trade-offs. I will end this chapter by arguing that imitation is essential to understanding not only the dynamics of this paradox but also its consequences for the emerging cultural and political landscape of an age of information abundance.

A Spiral of Sameness

The account presented in chapters 2–6 reveals a spiral of sameness (paraphrasing Noelle-Neumann [1993]) in the recent evolution of the Argentine news media. Online journalists reacted to their discovery of the news-at-work phenomenon by increasing the volume and frequency of publication of content, in particular hard-news stories. Aimed to satisfy perceived changes in consumption, this increase also had the unintended consequence of making the organizational field more visible to news workers. Journalists in charge of producing hard news took advantage of this greater visibility to intensify the monitoring of stories authored by their peers and to expand the imitation of these stories. They became progressively aware of this trend and disliked it but felt powerless to alter it. Over time, this led to a self-reinforcing process in which a growing portion of the work routine is spent monitoring and imitating an increasingly homogenized pool of hard-news stories. Online news consumers also show dislike and negative affect tied to the decrease in content diversity. Like journalists, they express a sense of powerlessness about their ability to alter this state of affairs. This invites a reaction of detachment and retreat rather than engagement and reform. Because, paraphrasing Thomas and Thomas (1970 [1917]), situations defined as real are real in their consequences, this symmetry of powerlessness between journalists and consumers contributes to the obduracy of this spiral of sameness.

The potential for this trend to continue raises the issue of novelty, because monitoring, imitation, and news homogeneity have long been staples of journalism. It is always hard to determine where the old ends and the new begins. However, the evidence presented in the previous chapters suggests a departure from the past. This evidence includes the expansion of monitoring and imitation practices of news production, the growth of homogeneity in the news, and the experience of many journalists and consumers of an increasingly similar editorial offering. But this departure has historical roots that have made it possible. For instance, without prior routines of monitoring and imitation, journalists who create hard news would not have realized the greater visibility of their organizational field that was linked to the rise in the volume and frequency of online news. The analysis also reveals novel features of consuming online news at the time and place of work that built on preexisting information acquisition habits. Thus, the discontinuity in the practices and products of imitation emerged from within patterns of continuity.

But to what extent might the findings presented in previous chapters travel across the borders of Argentina? The long-standing patterns of continuity and evidence of comparable recent discontinuous trends in other parts of the world suggest relatively common dynamics that might be enacted variously, depending on locally distinct circumstances.[2] This does not mean that the dynamics are applicable everywhere, but that they do not appear restricted to the Argentine context. Chapter 1 summarizes an array of articles and technical reports to show that the consumption of online news at the time and place of work, the accentuation of monitoring, the expansion of imitation practices, and the growing similarity in the resulting news products are present in the United States and Western Europe. Furthermore, chapter 2 argues that the relatively new logic of hard-news production at Clarín.com resonates with accounts of recent transformations in news work that are taking place in newsrooms across a broad spectrum of nations. In addition, chapter 5 presents evidence from studies of news consumption in countries as varied as the United States, Spain, and India that suggests a convergence in key aspects of how people get the news online. Finally, appendix B presents preliminary findings from a study about the news choices of journalists and consumers of leading online media in the United States during the 2008 election cycle. These findings resonate strongly with issues of news homogeneity and divergent story selection patterns of journalists and consumers addressed in chapters 4–6.

Understanding the empirical findings presented in this book highlights the value of its theoretical and methodological apparatus.

Making Sense of Imitation

In this book I develop a conceptual framework built on four premises: the heuristic benefits that might accrue from looking at production practices and product outcomes, the notion that variance in imitation emerges at the intersection of situational and structural factors, the need to examine the role of technology, and the importance of probing the consumption sphere. To this end, I adopted a mixed-methods research design that bridges the production-product divide while also integrating an examination of the consumption of homogenized news.

The account presented in chapters 2–4 demonstrates the value of an analysis that includes both production practices and product outcomes.

More precisely, this approach enables an account of how and why monitoring and imitation happen *and* a determination of their actual field-level effects for the selection, presentation, and narration of news. This allows the analyst to see more than she would have seen had she adopted the customary "either/or" stance. Had the inquiry looked solely inside the newsroom, it would have been able to only speculate about the field-level implications of the production processes for the news that circulates in society. Had the study concentrated exclusively on the homogenization of news products, it would have been more difficult to determine that homogenization resulted from an expansion of imitation in production (other processes could have generated greater similarity in the news) and to make sense of the timing and thematic composition of the trend.

A second set of analytical gains results from attention to the structural and situational factors that shape imitation. These gains became evident in the explanation of the intensification of monitoring and the expansion of imitation that prevailed among journalists who produced hard news. As shown in chapter 3, the changes in monitoring during news production would not have been possible without the increase in the volume and frequency of publication enabled by the Web. This increase triggered an alteration in the ability to observe the organizational field and the "publicness" of its knowledge. However, these structural transformations do not suffice to explain the observed variance between those who produce hard and soft news. This variance resulted from differences in editorial routines, intraorganizational relationships, representations of the public, and the management of reputation. Thus, only by looking at both structural and situational factors can one account for the mechanisms that shape the intensification of monitoring and its divergent enactment in relation to the labor involved in producing different kinds of news.

Imitation was also affected by structural alterations in the organizational field. These included the increase in the ease of information reproduction and distribution, the growth in competition, and a perception of change in consumer behavior. By themselves, these structural patterns cannot account for the major variance in the expansion of imitation between hard- and soft-news production, the comparatively minor variance by type of medium, and the effects of the differentiation efforts undertaken by online and print journalists. The major variance by type of content resulted from differences in sourcing practices, alignment processes between online and print newsrooms, representations of the public, ideational and affective experiences, and reputation management. The comparatively minor variance by type of medium and the efficacy of the differentiation efforts arose from divergent technological affordances, editorial routines, and levels of awareness about the growing homogenization of the news. A disregard for these situational factors would have made it impossible to explain why the rise in imitation predominantly affected the production of hard news. It would have also been impossible to shed light on why imitation affected story selection for print and online in a relatively similar fashion but affected presentation and narration of the content of these stories differently in each medium. Thus, because imitation emerges at the intersection of larger structural formations and situated patterns of practice, a focus on structural and situational factors helps to explain patterns of change in imitative activity.

Technological infrastructures, practices, and knowledge were central to the processes and consequences of increased imitation. Without the transformations of information creation and distribution brought about by the evolution of the Web, the intensification of monitoring and the expansion of imitation could not have occurred as they did, and perhaps not at all. However, this does not mean that technology determined these changes; if it had, the effects should have been felt shortly after its introduction and applied evenly, regardless of type of content and medium. On the contrary, it took more than five years after the launch of Clarín .com and Lanacion.com for the changes in imitation to be registered. Moreover, they varied depending on the type of content being produced and the medium in which production took place. Thus, the argument is not one of determination but of consequentiality. This is because technological transformations were coupled with variations in their uptake. It was only when online newsrooms took advantage of the Web's capabilities for information production and distribution that these artifacts became socially consequential. Furthermore, these consequences were realized differently, depending on whether and how actors relied on this information in their daily routines.

Related arguments shed light on the role of technology in consumption. The emergence of the workplace as a relatively new locus of online news consumption for large segments of the public would not have occurred without the growing reliance on digital networked infrastructures across many industries. The greater awareness of news homogenization among the public has been partly aided by how much easier online technologies afford comparison across sites than reliance on print and broadcast artifacts does. However, as shown in chapters 5 and 6, the potential of these technological capabilities was also realized differently among consumers, depending on factors that range from preexisting interest in the news to the situational configuration of the workplace. That the sheer availability of tools for peer-to-peer cultural production was not tied to a blossoming of user-authored news in a context marked by high dissatisfaction with homogenization in the content supplied by the media is a clear indicator that technology does not determine consumption dynamics either.

This examination of the role of technology reveals that, rather than a purely social matter, imitation should be conceptualized as a sociomaterial construction. An exclusive focus on the social dimension would have been unable to account for the expansion of imitation in editorial labor and the appropriation of the resulting news. A purely technological perspective would have been unable to understand the patterns of variance. Furthermore, taking technology into consideration also invites a revisit to a central factor in imitation scholarship: colocated social networks. Researchers argue that these networks often act as conduits for channeling information among the actors and therefore facilitate conformity processes. In contrast, the account offered in this book suggests that there might be a virtualization of the circuits that enable actors to know about the relevant others in their social world. Examples presented in chapters 1 and 3 indicate that these dynamics might apply to routines not only in the field of journalism but also in fields as disparate as finance and electoral politics.

The final set of theoretical contributions has consumption at its center. The analysis reveals a two-sided view of the role of consumption in imitation. On the one side, the practices and preferences of consumers did not play a major, direct role in determining the high rate of this similarity or challenge the status quo via consumer-driven reform. This reinforces the dominant production-centered perspective of imitation. On the other side, the consumption of online news at work was a critical trigger of the processes that eventually led to a growth of imitation in production and similarity in the resulting products. That is, an account that overlooked consumption would have been unable to understand how and why the changes in imitation processes began. Moreover, consumption forces might play an even greater role in other comparable cases whose understanding, in turn, could be improved by adopting a theoretical stance that does not take consumption for granted.

Making sense of how and why the expansion of imitation in production diverges from dominant patterns of consumer behavior, affect, and preferences leads to another theoretical benefit that arises from a focus on consumption. That benefit is the ability to assess the cultural and political consequences of imitation by embedding normative perspectives in the routines of news consumption. An examination of the consumption sphere fosters an appreciation of these consequences that includes a vision of what is normatively desirable within the boundaries of what is likely, given the contours of consumers' everyday practices. This allows the analysis to sidestep the common problems that emerge from assigning an unwarranted level of power to producers or overly idealistic potential to consumers.

The Cultural and Political Consequences of Imitation in the News

What do the empirical findings and theoretical analyses summarized in the two previous sections suggest about changes in the work that the news performs in social life? To answer this question, in this section I will focus on three issues at the heart of the cultural and political fabric of contemporary society: the evolution of the news, the balance of power in the polity, and the prospects for consumer-driven social reform.

The Evolution of the News

The interaction of trends in the production and consumption spheres points to two tensions for journalism and news organizations: the tension between the logic of the occupation of journalism and the logic of the market and the one between the elite and mass publics. The increase in news homogeneity is tied to an exacerbation of the tension between the logics of the occupation and the market described in chapter 6. Fifty years ago, news organizations could easily have ignored the gap between the more convergent and public affairs–oriented news choices of journalists and the more divergent and non–public affairs–oriented preferences of consumers. However, the contemporary scene has increased the ability to know these preferences and the cost of ignoring them. It is possible that news organizations might try to close this gap by reducing public affairs news and increasing the provision of a diverse menu of non–public affairs stories. Thus, if the logic of the market prevailed over that of the occupation, it might decrease news homogenization in a direction that would be pleasing to consumers and more competitive for organizations. However, this would have a detrimental effect on society in light of the function that robust public affairs reportage plays in the healthy functioning of the polity.

The tension between the elite and mass publics makes matters quite complicated for mainstream news organizations, such as those examined in this book. Journalists and media organizations try to set the news agenda by influencing their elite public, which is composed of key decision makers in government, business, and nonprofit organizations. Furthermore, this effort to shape the agenda is largely marked by public affairs stories, especially the top ones in a given news cycle. However, the news media's effectiveness in setting the agenda depends in part on the size and composition of their mass public. All else being equal, the elite public pays more attention to a news organization with a large mass public than to a news organization with a small one, and to one with a more resourceful and more influential public than to one with a less resourceful and less influential one. This interdependence between the elite and mass publics puts news organizations into a double bind when they are confronted with increased awareness of the mass public's preference for non–public affairs subjects and market pressures to cater to this preference. On the one hand, to disregard the mass public's interests could lead to the erosion of its size, loyalty, and overall affect. This could, in turn, weaken news organizations' ability to influence the news agenda and the elite public. On the other hand, to cater to the mass public's preference for non–public affairs stories could also diminish news organizations' ability to influence the agenda.

A different set of implications is based on the changing character of hard news as a cultural construction. Many observers predicted that the Web would shift journalistic practice toward a greater appreciation for depth of content than had been the case in traditional media. This prediction was accompanied by the hope that news organizations would deepen the amount, kind, and diversity of information tied to a particular story. This has happened in some cases, especially for the coverage of high-profile events. But the analysis presented in chapters 2 and 3 suggests that when it comes to the coverage of regular events, the routine practice of hard-news production in the online environment is one of breadth and volume rather than depth and diversity.

A parallel pattern dominates the experience of consumers, as shown in chapter 5. Much has been said about the almost-endless navigation possibilities of online news. Such navigation characterizes the behavior of the most devoted consumers and the consumption of high-profile events by average consumers. But the online consumer normally appropriates hard news about regular events more like the casual snorkeler than the avid scuba diver; that is, she focuses on the headline, sometimes also the lead, and far more sporadically on the rest of the content. This explains why the average time spent on a news site continues to be considerably shorter than the time spent reading its print counterpart. Furthermore, the growing consumption of news using mobile devices might intensify this trend. The news is not an immutable cultural construction but rather the outcome of what producers and consumers make of it. Together, these production and consumption patterns indicate that in an age of information plenty, hard news online might become a brief statement displayed on the surface of a single screen rather than a long narrative accessed on multiple pages and through several clicks.

These patterns also decrease the incentive for news organizations to devote considerable resources to traditional sourcing and authoring work. In addition, news organizations in many countries have substantively trimmed their personnel budgets in recent years, and some have even begun to outsource reporting to workers located in countries with lower labor costs (Poynter Online, 2008; Pritchard, 2007). Because most organizations need a steady and dependable news supply to satisfy their consumers' appetite for a broad spectrum of story headlines, the current context creates fertile ground for growth in the role played by wire service organizations. There has been a recent flurry of activity in the wire services sector, including the acquisition of Reuters by Thomson and of Dow Jones by News Corporation, CNN's plans to start its own wire service, and the efforts by the Associated Press to revamp its editorial offerings (Arango & Pérez-Peña, 2008; Austen, 2007; Pérez-Peña, 2007). This is probably a signal that, at the time of writing this book, wire service organizations perceive a growth opportunity and are moving to take advantage of it.

In sum, significant prospects emerge for the unfolding of three cross-cutting trends: (*a*) an intensification of tensions between the occupational and market logics and between the mass and elite publics, (*b*) the changing character of the production and consumption of hard news on the Web, and (*c*) an increase in the relative contribution and prominence of wire service agencies in the provision of such news. The combination of these trends, in turn, creates a fertile terrain for a media landscape marked by the dominance of generic content shared across many outlets, a narrowing of the resulting news agenda, and the concentration of power to set this agenda among a smaller number of players than before. Power dynamics also affect another matter touched on by the analysis offered in the previous chapters: the future of journalism's watchdog role.

The Balance of Power in the Polity

The news media have the ability to make an important contribution to the balance of power in democratic societies by virtue of their watchdog role. News organizations can help to control other powerful actors by gathering information about possible wrongdoing by these actors—information that by its very nature requires considerable effort to obtain—and communicating it to the general public. This control function is enacted in two ways. First, because the social costs of appearing to be involved in wrongful acts can be very high for some of these actors, the mere possibility that the media might exercise this function often serves as deterrence. Second, when wrongful acts are committed, the news media can bring these acts to light when the relevant public sector organizations are silent about their existence. If these organizations are not silent, the media can also make their work more visible and generate a sense of public outcry.

Although this function is valuable in more established democracies, it is particularly important in emerging democracies, such as the one studied for this book and many others around the globe. By regularly hosting free elections, democratic societies enable a "vertical accountability" that connects the demos to the elected officials. Emerging democracies often lack a robust "horizontal accountability" that arises from longstanding adherence to the liberal and republican values that inspire a separation and mutual oversight among the executive, legislative, and judicial branches and results in a well-functioning system of checks and balances (O'Donnell, 1998). The news media can partially offset a diminished horizontal accountability by facilitating the emergence of what Peruzzotti and Smulovitz have termed "social accountability": a combination of monitoring state actions by nongovernmental organizations and exposing cases of wrongdoing by journalists that "constitutes an alternative mechanism for the exercise of accountability regarding governmental actions" (2006, p. 4). It is then not surprising that the journalistic field has played such an important role in the transition to democracy and the subsequent strengthening of democratic reforms across Latin America (Benavides, 2000; Hallin & Papathanassopoulos, 2002; S. Hughes, 2006; Lawson, 2002; Levitsky & Murillo, 2005b; Waisbord, 2006). Skidmore asserts, "The media have had at least two essential functions in the democratization process: dissemination of information and political mobilization" (1993, p. 7). Waisbord argues, "Watchdog journalism, no matter its many imperfections, has contributed to the quality of South American democracies" (2000, p. 246).

If the evolving logic of hard-news production in online journalism, the overall expansion of imitation, and the resulting homogenization of news products deepen over time, they could have positive and negative consequences for the media's performance of their watchdog function. On the one hand, the intensification of monitoring and the growth of imitative activity could mean that if one news organization exposed a case of wrongdoing, many of the other organizations in the journalistic field could react by amplifying the information and creating a positive echo chamber effect. This, in turn, could increase deterrence effects due to the magnitude of the potential public reaction. On the other hand, the logic of hard-news production for online sites—less focused on original fact-finding than traditional news production—and the general expansion in imitation could hinder media's ability to play a watchdog role. The more that journalistic work is shaped by information that is already publicly available, the less effort will be spent on gathering data in a process that is often time-consuming, resource intensive, risky, and marred by all sorts of obstacles. In addition, the more the news is homogenized, the less will powerful actors fear the news media's watchdog function. This, in turn, could have a negative impact on the deterrence dimension of this function.

Overall, because actual wrongdoing by powerful actors is likely to be more widespread than the media's ability to contribute to its control, issues of accountability in the polity stand to lose more than they gain from the dynamics of imitation analyzed in this book. The negative political consequences documented in other forms of press failure further underscore the notion that an overly homogeneous news supply usually does not serve democracy well.[3]

The Prospects for Consumer-Driven Reform

The possible decline in the mainstream media's watchdog role, in particular, and the decrease in the content diversity of the overall news supply, in general, have led to discussions about how to compensate for these potential losses that affect society. One line of thought that has recently received considerable attention is the idea that consumer-driven social reform might be a feasible alternative. This idea is often discussed under rubrics such as the "Web 2.0" and "citizen journalism." The rationale behind this idea has technical and social components. The technical component is based on the premise that the low cost of information production and distribution on the Web has the potential to make every consumer a producer. According to Benkler, "It is the freedom to seek out whatever information we wish, to write about it, and to join and leave various projects and associations with others that underlies . . . the cooperative news and commentary production that form the basis of the networked public sphere" (2006, pp. 139–140). The social element relies on the assumption that consumers are generally willing to participate and engage in fact-finding and commentary on issues that matter to them.

Thus, lack of consumer participation is often taken as a problem that must be overcome. For instance, Jenkins proposes the notion of a "participation gap" to make sense of "the cultural factors that diminish the likelihood that different groups participate" (2006, p. 258) and constrain the realization of the full democratic potential of media convergence. Because consumers' interests and tastes are more diverse than those of the mainstream media, this engagement is supposed to yield a high level of content diversity and thus be beneficial to society.

However, the analysis presented in chapters 5 and 6 shows why this participation is *possible* but not *likely* in the case of online news. This is not to say that valuable consumer-authored news content does not exist or has made no difference in certain extraordinary or high-profile events. However, given the character of everyday online news consumption, it is unreasonable to believe that this mode of news production would compensate for a situation of press failure on a regular basis when it comes to the coverage of mundane events. Moreover, this relatively low likelihood of the routine participation that would be needed to sustain a consumer-driven reform movement results from the finding that consumers, at least those interviewed for this study, do not see their participation as an attractive way of engaging with news sites. That is, most of them choose not to overcome the "participation gap."

In addition to the likelihood of consumer-driven social reform is the desirability of an alternative agenda that might result from regular participation in online news production by a broad cross section of consumers. If the online news selection patterns of consumers provide any indication of the kind of stories they would be inclined to produce in a situation of sustained routine participation, it is unclear whether the balance of power in society and the diversity of ideas in the public sphere—networked or otherwise—would be well served by an emphasis on sports, crime, and entertainment stories. These consumer preferences are consistent with what has long been known about news consumption in traditional media. The analysis suggests that there is no reason to believe that news on the Web has altered these preferences.[4] Thus, although there is certainly nothing wrong at the individual level with news choices dominated by non–public affairs stories, it is hard to conceive a scenario in which an agenda marked by this type of content would replace the contributions that independent, robust news media have historically made to the quality of democratic life.

The prospect that regular online news production by consumers could fill the potential void left by the mainstream media might not be likely or inherently desirable. Yet there are two situations in which consumer-authored news has become common and made a positive contribution to the balance of power in the polity and the diversity of ideas in the public sphere. The first is when consumers report on a wide array of blogs about some specific issue that has been explicitly or by omission silenced by the mainstream media. In some of these cases, the blogosphere amplified a story in a way that grabbed the attention of mainstream outlets or made it impossible to sustain active efforts to avoid reporting on the story. Thus, this type of situation shows how consumers can harness the potential of the Web to become the watchdog of the watchdog and do so more effectively than was possible with the media artifacts widely available a couple of decades ago. The second alternative refers to the potential for consumers who are present during high-profile breaking and developing stories, such as the terrorist attacks in London, Mumbai, and Madrid, to provide timely coverage of these events before and after the media arrive on the scene. Because of the high-profile nature of these events, consumers are more motivated to contribute information and commentary about them than is normally the case with more mundane developments. These two situations suggest that consumer-authored news might become a complement to, rather than a replacement for, mainstream news.

In conclusion, the analysis presented in this book suggests that the prospects for consumer-driven alternatives to the homogenization of news in the mainstream media are not high. Although current technological and cultural conditions make these alternatives more possible than before, the character of everyday online news consumption indicates that they are still not very probable. The most likely scenario for consumer involvement with news production is supplementing the media rather than supplanting them. Furthermore, an analysis of the thematic preferences of online news consumers generates questions about the kind of agenda that might emerge if consumer-authored news routinely filled the void of content diversity left by the homogenization in the news of the mainstream media.

This analysis of the evolution of the news, the balance of power in the polity, and the prospects for consumer-driven reform points to a problematic cultural and political scenario if these trends deepen. Culturally, this scenario appears to be marked by a narrowing of the diversity of the agenda put forward by mainstream news organizations and the increased visibility of a gap between the thematic composition of this agenda and the preferences of online news consumers. Such a scenario is also signaled by the dislike of this agenda among these consumers and a retreat from peer-to-peer cultural production. Politically, it is characterized by the rise in the power of a handful of players to set this agenda and a diminished watchdog function with a concomitant drift of power toward resourceful actors in the public, nonprofit, and private sectors. It is also defined by the low likelihood of a consumer-driven reform movement whose membership comes from a large cross section of the public and that is able to provide a comprehensive news supply on a routine basis.

The analysis of this scenario overcomes two common limitations in accounts of these issues. On the one hand, political economy and institutional perspectives usually focus on the power of news organizations and elites. However, they often do not pay as much attention to how ordinary patterns of action among journalists contribute to imitation and homogenization dynamics. These patterns are critical to account for the emergence and, even more important, the endurance of these dynamics. Because social processes cannot remain forceful without being anchored in routines of actors at all relevant levels of organizational decision making, not just of those at the top, failure to understand the agency of the rank and file hinders the ability of these perspectives to grasp the obduracy of these dynamics and to devise realistic change strategies. On the other hand, normative analyses and cultural studies often assume that consumers want to participate in content creation. Thus, a lack of participation is normally seen as the result of external barriers imposed by regulatory policies, business strategies, and social inequality. The removal of these barriers should unleash a wave of public participation in cultural production. What these normative and cultural accounts neglect is the various modes of agency enacted in the consumption of online news and other cultural goods and the extent to which this agency is shaped by the situational and structural conditions of everyday life. Overlooking these agency dynamics frequently prevents these accounts from going beyond what is technically feasible and normatively desirable and into what is socially likely in light of the actual routines of a cross section of the public. By sidestepping these twin limitations, the analysis presented in this book depicts a dire but more realistic scenario of the consequences that an increase in imitation in the news might have and the likelihood of different avenues for social change.

Finally, this discussion of the cultural and political consequences of imitation brings us back to the larger concern regarding the trade-offs between quantity and quality in a situation of information plenty, as expressed in the loss of diversity in news content. The concern about this loss permeates several issues addressed above, including the changing character of the news, the role of wire services, and the control function of the news media. Even the possible solutions of potential problems are not without costs in terms of quality. The hypothetical scenarios of a stronger market orientation among news organizations than is currently the case or a robust tradition of consumer-authored news or both could increase diversity of content at the expense of public affairs reportage.

However, a loss in the diversity of content need not be an inevitable or durable trend. As the analysis has shown, this loss stems from a combination of social and technological factors that have shaped an expansion of imitation. But those factors do not have the power to determine action, as was demonstrated by the analysis of variance in this expansion. This supports the assertion that the paradox of more quantity and less quality of information is likely, given a certain set of conditions, but it is never inevitable. The blending of these conditions with a host of unpredictable developments in areas such as the economic foundations of the news industry and the innovation capacity of the information technology field indicates that this trend could cease or be reversed in the future.

Despite the uncertainty associated with the present and the unpredictability of the future, it is my hope that the account offered in this book shows that one thing is certain: imitation is the conceptual key to unlock the paradox of how more has become less in an evolving age of information abundance.

Appendix A:
Research Design

This appendix describes the four studies reported in chapters 2–6. Taken together, these studies constitute a research design developed to understand the dynamics of imitation in the news in a way that bridged production, product, and consumption. To this end, data collection combined ethnographic studies of content production and consumption with content analyses of the resulting news choices of journalists and consumers. The resulting data were analyzed using qualitative and quantitative methods.

An Examination of Imitation in the Production of News

This ethnography includes a field study of editorial work at Clarín .com and interviews with journalists at *Clarín*, *La Nación*, and Lanacion.com. The field study was undertaken as a team ethnography (Buford May & Patillo-McCoy, 2000; Erickson & Stull, 1998; Fujisaka & Grayzel, 1978; Perlman, 1970). The members of the team—all proficient in Spanish—were the author (the project director) and three or four research assistants, depending on the period of the project. The assistants were based in Buenos Aires, where Clarín.com's offices are located. The director traveled to Buenos Aires repeatedly during the project and supervised the team via biweekly conference calls, supplemented by electronic mail (email) communication. At the time the study took place, the director agreed with the director of Clarín.com that the site would be identified in the dissemination of research results. They also agreed that informants would be given a choice about whether they wanted to be identified. Hence, in the preceding chapters, some informants are identified by their real names, and others are not.

Data collection combined observations and interviews. Observations, undertaken by three research assistants, took place between April and June 2005. During this period each assistant spent two four-hour observation sessions per week, loosely following an observation guide developed before fieldwork began. This amounted to eighty-five four-hour sessions that yielded 200,000 words of field notes plus an array of sketches, photographs, and artifacts. In the initial sampling strategy, observations took place Monday through Friday between 9:00 AM and 6:00 PM and focused on one newsroom employee for the entire session. When most employees had been observed at least once and the team had reached a preliminary level of theoretical saturation (Strauss & Corbin, 1990), subsequent sampling strategies included observations during early mornings, evenings, and weekends. To examine the effects of the flow of information and the interaction dynamics on a single story, they also included simultaneous observations by the three assistants of various staffers undertaking different tasks in relation to a given story.

Forty semistructured interviews were conducted at Clarín.com between July and December 2005. The interviews addressed a list of topics developed at the end of the observation phase. The director conducted fifteen interviews, and two research assistants conducted the remaining twenty-five. Interviewees represented all hierarchical levels of newsroom full-time employees and all beats.

After the field study at Clarín.com had ended, the author conducted twenty-seven face-to-face interviews with journalists at *Clarín, La Nación,* and Lanacion.com during several trips to Buenos Aires that took place in 2006 and 2007. Interviewees represented hierarchical levels that ranged from deputy managing editor to reporter, and beats such as national, foreign, business, metro, sports, crime, technology, and culture.

The interviews at the two print and the two online newsrooms lasted an average of forty-five minutes each and were tape-recorded and transcribed in their entirety.

Data analysis mixed qualitative and quantitative methods. Qualitative analysis began after the first month of observation during the field study at Clarín.com. All researchers participated in this analysis, which unfolded in a grounded theory fashion (Strauss & Corbin, 1990). The validity of the analysis was ascertained in part through member checks and triangulations. Member checks included talks that featured preliminary findings given by the author to personnel at *Clarín* and Clarín.com and in public venues where journalists of Lanacion.com were also in attendance. These member checks helped to probe the main points of the analysis, generate alternative explanations, and identify factual errors. Triangulation was pursued by method and data source (Denzin, 1979). Methodological triangulation was possible by contrasting material gathered from observations and interviews. Triangulation by data source was achieved by having different people participate in data collection, observing tasks undertaken on different days and times, and interviewing actors from multiple units and hierarchical levels.

Quantitative analyses of the field notes were performed to more precisely determine the frequency and magnitude (Lofland & Lofland, 1984) of critical differences in four of the variables elicited through the qualitative analysis. These variables—

temporal patterns of content production, provenance of information, parts of the story, and newsroom communication tools—are defined in chapter 2. The team developed a coding instrument, and two of the research assistants undertook the analysis. Using a qualitative analysis software program, the assistants read the field notes and recorded every instance of a work practice that represented relevant options in one or more of the variables. Both assistants analyzed 10% of the data with levels of intercoder agreement that ranged from 84% to 100% and averaged 93%; then each assistant analyzed half of the remaining data. Doubts that emerged during the analysis were communicated to the author and were resolved consensually.

A Content Analysis of the Homogenization of News Products

As briefly introduced in chapter 1, this study examined the front pages of *Clarín* and *La Nación* and the most prominently displayed stories on the homepages of Clarín .com, Lanacion.com, and Infobae.com. Data from the front pages of *Clarín* and *La Nación* were gathered during four ten-week periods that yielded a total of 927 stories. Twenty days of front pages and associated stories, from Monday through Friday, with four instances of each day, were collected for each period. Data collection focused on Monday through Friday to assess possible changes in print tied to online papers during the online papers' days of peak activity. The first period was September to December 1995; the second was July to October 2000; the third was September to December 2004, and the fourth was September to December 2005. Data from Clarín.com, Lanacion.com, and Infobae.com were collected for ten weeks from September to December 2005, two days per week, from Monday through Friday (four instances of each day). The days of each Monday-to-Thursday period for the online data were the days before those of each Tuesday-to-Friday period included in the 2005 print sample. Data were gathered at three shifts: 11:00 AM, 3:00 PM, and 10:00 PM. For each shift, each online newspaper's homepage and its first nine stories (hereafter, the "homepage"), counting from left to right and from the top down in a gridlike manner, were collected. A total of 1,620 online stories were collected.

Stories were examined at three levels of analysis: selection, presentation, and narration. Each of these levels of analysis was succinctly introduced in chapter 4. The remainder of this section provides additional details.

Selection

The selection level examined what kinds of stories were selected for inclusion on a print paper's front page or an online newspaper's homepage. Each story was assessed using the following three variables.

1. CONTENT TYPE. This is the format of the story. The two main categories are hard and soft news. Building on the analysis presented in chapter 2, Tuchman's (1978) definition was utilized to distinguish between these types of news. For

Tuchman, two defining traits of hard news are that it deals with unscheduled or prescheduled events, and its publication is considered urgent. In contrast, soft news deals with nonscheduled events that need not be published urgently.[1] There were three additional categories. The first included editorials, opinion pieces, and columns. The second was a special type of soft news called "entertainment prescheduled news with no urgent dissemination." This kind of story covers content from the previous day's television programs. Because these stories deal with prescheduled events, they did not fit into the definition of soft news; and because their urgency of dissemination is lower than that specified for online hard news, they did not qualify as hard news. Third were stories about new products and services offered by each print and/or online newspaper.

2. CONTENT FOCUS. This is the subject matter of the story. Two broad categories were considered: public affairs (including politics, economics, and international news) and non–public affairs (addressing issues such as sports, crime, science, technology, and medicine, and natural disasters and accidents).

3. CONTENT OVERLAP. This variable is used to measure similarity in the selection of news products. Each story was coded for whether the event it addressed was the subject of a story in one or both print newspapers, or for a story published only online, whether the event it addressed was the subject of a story on one or more online news sites.

In addition, online stories with content overlap were assessed for their durability, that is, whether they had lasting power during the day or were transient. Specifically, the question was whether a story that had content overlap in one shift also had content overlap in at least one of the two other shifts that day. A story that had content overlap in only one shift was coded "No" (not durable). A story that had content overlap in more than one shift was coded "Yes" (durable). This latter coding category included cases in which a story had content overlap as part of a triad in one shift (i.e., all three outlets offered the same story content) but as part of a dyad in another shift (i.e., only two outlets offered the story content).

Initially, the author and a research assistant coded subsamples of print and online stories independently. Eighteen percent of the print data was coded for 1995 and 2005 and obtained intercoder agreement levels of 99% for content overlap, 87% for content focus, and 93% for content type. Seven percent of the online data was coded independently with intercoder agreement levels of 98% for content overlap, 91% for content focus, and 96% for content type. The research assistant then undertook the coding of the remaining stories and resolved doubts consensually with the author.

Presentation

This analysis was conducted on the subset of stories that displayed content overlap. The purpose was to analyze similarities and differences in story presentation on the front page or the homepage. A total of 318 print stories and 619 online stories were examined.

Each story was coded for its presentational similarity to the story or stories with which it overlapped. Because there were only two print outlets, any print story coded as having overlap formed a dyad with the similar story in its print competitor. But because there were three online outlets, an online story coded as having overlap might form either a dyad (if only one online competitor had a story with overlapping content) or a triad (if all three online outlets had overlapping content). Hence, in this analysis, triads of online stories with content overlap were decomposed into three pairs, and a given story's eventual coding reflected the average of its presentational similarity to the other two online stories with which its content overlapped.

Presentational similarity was assessed using the following six variables.

1. HEADLINE—SUBJECT. Stories were coded for similarity in the word or words used in the subject of the headline. Each story in the pair was assigned 0 if the main words used in the subject of the headline were different from the comparable ones in the other story; 1 if they were synonyms or had closely related meanings; and 2 if they were the same.

2. HEADLINE—VERB. Stories were coded for similarity in the main verb used in the headline. Each story in the pair was assigned 0 if the main verb was different from the comparable one in the other story; 1 if they were synonyms or had closely related meanings; and 2 if they were the same.

3. HEADLINE—REST OF THE SENTENCE. Stories were coded for similarity in the other words (besides subject and verb) used in the construction of the headline. Each story in the pair was assigned 0 if these other words were different from the comparable ones in the other story; 1 if they were synonyms or had closely related meanings; and 2 if they were the same.

4. ILLUSTRATIONS. Only print stories were coded for similarity in the uses of visual illustrations on the front pages. If one story had an illustration (photograph or infograph) and the other did not, each story in the pair was coded 0. If both stories had an illustration but the illustrations were different (e.g., if one story had a photograph and the other had an infograph, or if both stories had a photograph but different photographs were used), each story in the pair was coded 1. If neither story had an illustration, or if both stories had illustrations and the illustrations were very similar, each story in the pair was coded 2.

5. PLACEMENT. Only print stories were coded for similarity in placement on the front pages. Each front page was divided into a two-by-two grid of rows and columns, and each story in a pair was coded 0 if the other story did not spatially overlap in either rows or columns; 1 if the other story overlapped in either a row or a column; and 2 if the other story overlapped both horizontally and vertically.

The variables Illustrations and Placement were not analyzed for online stories because differences in design and use of visual resources would have introduced systematic biases into the comparison of Clarín.com, Lanacion.com, and Infobae .com homepages.

6. INTERPRETATION. Stories were coded for their overall degree of presentational similarity. Each story in a pair was assigned 0 if the coder judged that the other story had a low level of presentational similarity, 1 if this level was medium, and 2 if it was high.

These specific assessments were then added to yield a total presentational similarity score for each story. This score could range from 0 to 12 for print stories and from 0 to 8 for online stories. A presentational similarity metric was constructed for each time period (each year for print, each shift for online). The total presentational similarity scores for all the stories in a given time period were summed. A percentage-of-presentational-similarity metric was then computed for each time period by dividing that total by the number of possible points for that time period (given the number of stories it contained). So, for example, if a given time period contained 100 online stories with presentational similarity scores that totaled 650, the percentage-of-presentational-similarity metric would be 81.25% (650/800).

Data analysis proceeded in three steps. First, two coders analyzed each story in each pair independently. Then, they contrasted their individual coding results, discussed disagreements, and tried to come to a consensus on their own. Finally, when there was no consensus, the author was presented with the two alternatives and made a final decision.

Narration

The narration analysis was also conducted on the subset of stories that displayed content overlap. The purpose was to analyze similarities and differences in the narrative construction of the stories. As with the presentation level of analysis, each story was contrasted with the other one in its dyad or the other two in its triad and assessed using a second similarity index developed for the purposes of this study. A total of 318 print stories and 508 online stories were analyzed. The lower number of online stories, compared with the number examined for the presentation level of analysis, reflects a loss of data in the online stories due to technical problems. This loss affected some parts of the data set more than others. The technical problems were more severe in the case of non–public affairs stories of the morning shift. Approximately one in five of the pairs of stories of this kind were not fully saved. A decision was made to conduct the analysis based on the lowest common denominator of the properly saved pairs of stories regarding issues of shift and content focus. Thus, a "depurated" sample of the properly saved stories of completed pairs was built. This sample consisted of randomly selected pairs of the remaining stories composed of 82% of completed pairs about public affairs and non–public affairs in each shift. This depurated sample amounted to a total of 508 stories—down from the original 619 stories. However, the stories in completed pairs that were left out of this depurated sample were still analyzed. No significant differences were found in any of the major variables when they were compared with the stories in the depurated sample.

Narrative similarity was assessed using the following four variables.

1. WRITING. Stories were coded for similarity in the word or words used in the text, except for the use of sources, which were analyzed separately. Each story in the pair was assigned 0 if the text of the other story in its pair was completely different; 1 if it shared a few elements with the other story and was not fundamentally based on wire service copy; 2 if it was based on wire service copy but had additional information not included in the other story of its pair; 3 if it was based on the same wire service content as the other story in its pair but had some clear differences in the text due to copyediting; and 4 if it contained at least three paragraphs and two or more of its paragraphs were identical or almost identical with those in the other story, or if the story was no longer than two paragraphs, one paragraph was identical or almost identical.

2. SOURCES. Stories were coded for similarity in the use of sources. Each story in the pair was assigned 0 if it quoted sources and the other story in its pair did not; 1 if it quoted sources and the other story also did, but the sources were different; 2 if it quoted the same source used by the other story in its pair but resorted to different statements from this source; 3 if it shared one source and statement with the other story but at least one of the stories had two or more sources quoted; and 4 if it shared either at least two quotations with the same sources and statements with the other story in its pair or only one quotation but there were no more than two quotations in each story.

3. ILLUSTRATIONS. Print stories were coded for similarity in the uses of visual illustrations. Each story in the pair was assigned 0 if it had either a photograph or an infograph and the other did not; 1 if it had a photograph and the other an infograph, or if both had a photograph or an infograph but they were different; 2 if neither story had an illustration; 3 if it had a photograph or infograph similar to one utilized in the other story of its pair but at least one of these stories had one or more additional illustrations; and 4 if all of its illustrations were similar to those utilized in the other story.

The Illustrations variable was not analyzed for online stories because differences in design and use of visual resources would have introduced systematic biases into the comparison of Clarín.com, Lanacion.com, and Infobae.com.

4. INTERPRETATION. Stories were coded for their overall degree of narrative similarity. Each story in the pair was assigned 0 if the coder judged that it had a low level of narrative similarity with the other story in its pair; 2 if this level was medium; and 4 if it was high.

As with the calculation of presentational similarity, these assessments were added to yield a total narrative similarity score for each story. This score could range from 0 to 16 for print stories and from 0 to 12 for online stories. As in the calculation of results for the presentation level of analysis, a percentage-of-narrative-similarity metric was computed for each time period by dividing the total score for each period by the number of possible points for that period. Finally, data analysis proceeded in the same three steps used for issues of presentational similarity.

Accounting for the Consumption of an Increasingly Less Diverse News Supply

Two complementary studies were undertaken to understand the behaviors, interpretations, and experiences related to the consumption of homogeneous news. They were an ethnography of news consumption and a content analysis of the most-clicked stories on Clarín.com, Lanacion.com, and Infobae.com.

An Ethnography of Online News Consumption

This study is based on interviews with consumers of Argentine online news sites conducted by the author and two research assistants. All the interviews were conducted face-to-face and took place in Buenos Aires and its suburbs between November 2006 and April 2007. As with the ethnography of news production, the author traveled to Buenos Aires repeatedly during the interview process and supervised the research assistants via conference calls and email. The vast majority of the interviews were held in public places, such as cafés, restaurants, and bars near the workplace of the interviewee. In a few cases, interviews happened at the interviewee's place of work or her home. The interviews were loosely structured around a list of topics jointly elaborated by the author and the research assistants, who had also participated in the ethnography of news production and the two content analysis studies. The author conducted twenty-three of the interviews and the research assistants the remaining forty. Interviews lasted an average of forty-five minutes and were tape-recorded and transcribed in their entirety.

The author and the research assistants undertook the recruitment of interviewees by building a referral network of contacts that eventually yielded an interviewee pool that was socially distant from the research team. As stated in chapter 1, initially a few relatively distant acquaintances of the research assistants were invited to be interviewed. These acquaintances were chosen to constitute a diverse group of people in terms of gender, age group, and occupation (see additional details of the sampling rationale below). Each of these people was considered a "Level 1" interviewee (in terms of social distance) because each had one degree of separation from one of the researchers. At the end of the interview, each interviewee was asked to think of five of his or her acquaintances who fulfilled three criteria: used the Internet regularly, were diverse in terms of gender, age group, and occupation, and belonged to relatively different social networks. The interviewee was also asked to provide a very brief summary of each person, including age, occupation, and nature of their relationship. In addition, researchers requested permission to contact these acquaintances for the purposes of this study; interviewees were always copied in the first email message to each of their referrals. Approximately half of all the interviewees provided names of acquaintances to be contacted for additional interviews.

The research assistants randomly contacted some of these potential interviewees and placed the remainder on a waiting list. No more than three people referred by a single person were interviewed, and potential interviewees who were socially very close to the referrer (e.g., a family member or a person sharing the same living quarters) were discarded from the study. An interviewee who was referred by a Level 1 person was considered a Level 2 person. At the end of the interview with a Level 2 person, interviewees were invited to refer people from their social network to be included in this study; these referrals were considered Level 3 interviewees. This recruitment process continued for several iterations (eventually reaching some Level 7 interviewees) until the interview pool exhibited, in the aggregate, a sufficient degree of social distance from the research team. A total of 129 people were contacted and 63 were interviewed.

Of the 63 interviewees, 50 were included in the final sample. The 13 people who were excluded consisted of all Level 1 interviewees and those who were subsequently discovered either to be socially very close to their respective referrers or to be in an age group or occupation that was already overrepresented in the interview pool by the time the interview took place. However, analyses of these 13 interviews revealed no major difference in any of the relevant variables with the findings that emerged from the main interview sample. The final sample's social distance ("Level") scores ranged from 2 to 7, with a mean of 3.26 and a standard deviation of 1.45. The median degree of social distance was 3, or a Level 3 person—that is, someone separated by two unknown social contacts from the research team.

Together, these 50 people formed an interview pool that loosely mirrored the adult population who accessed the Internet in Argentina at the time of the study in terms of gender and age. The gender distribution (24 women and 26 men; thus, 48% female and 52% male) represents quite adequately the adult population who accessed the Internet in Argentina at the time of the study. According to a survey by D'Alessio—IROL (2006), 47% of the consumers were female and 53% were male. For assessing age distribution, interviewees were divided into three age groups: 18 to 29 ($n = 23$, 46%), 30 to 49 ($n = 23$, 46%), and 50 and older ($n = 4$, 8%); each group was quite evenly divided in terms of gender. According to the survey by D'Alessio—IROL (2006), the general population who accessed the Internet in Argentina in 2006 was younger than the sample used for this study: 55% were between 18 and 29, 35% were between 30 and 49, and 10% were 50 or older. However, the more specific population of those who routinely accessed the Internet at the time and place of work was older: 30% were between 18 and 29, 55% were between 30 and 49, and 15% were 50 or older. Thus, the sampling decisions followed in this study yielded an interview pool with an age distribution midway between that of the general population who accessed the Internet and the specific population who did so primarily at work.

The interviewees in the final sample represented a broad spectrum of occupations. Nine people had various managerial roles, six occupied clerical or administrative positions, and four were in college. Several were liberal professionals, such as lawyers, physicians, and teachers; others were in a technical field, such as engineering or computer analysis; still others had jobs in the cultural sphere, such as screenwriter and graphic designer; three were unemployed, and two were retired. All the interviewees had finished high school, and most had at least started college studies. Although no specific questions were asked about their household income, from this information about occupational affiliation and level of educational attainment it is reasonable to infer that the main interview sample had a relatively high socioeconomic level. It is likely that the majority of these people belonged to the top levels of the socioeconomic pyramid. In a country with high levels of income inequality, the interviewees' socioeconomic status mirrored that of approximately eight out of ten Internet users but reflected far less than half of the country's adult population (D'Alessio—IROL, 2006; Internet Advertising Bureau—Argentina, 2007). Thus, although it captured the majority of the population who accessed the Internet in Argentina at the time of the study, this main sample still underrepresented those at the bottom of the socioeconomic pyramid. This is related to the fact that a large fraction of those in a situation of socioeconomic disadvantage did not own a computer and did not have jobs with computer access, but they went online in call centers—*locutorios* in Spanish. Despite several attempts to recruit call center users for this study, it was not possible for the research team to do so. Employees who worked at call centers were uneasy about identifying their regular customers for the researchers and were uncomfortable about having a researcher approach customers without their consent.

Qualitative analysis of the data began after the first few interviews. It continued during the data collection process and ended a few months after the last interview was conducted. The author and the two research assistants participated in the analysis. Like the ethnography of production analysis, the consumption data were also examined in a grounded theory fashion. The validity of the analysis was ascertained by sharing preliminary findings with interviewees during interviews—especially in the interviews conducted during the second half of the data collection effort. The validity was also established by data source triangulation that was achieved by interviewing a relatively broad spectrum of online news consumers.

Analysis of the Most-Clicked Stories of the Day

This study examined the top ten most-clicked stories on Clarín.com, Lanacion .com, and Infobae.com. It also looked at a control group of each site—two randomly selected stories from the top one-third of the homepage, two from the middle section, and two from the bottom third. Data were collected for fourteen weeks from July to November 2006, five days per week, from Monday through Sunday, for a total of seventy days (ten instances of each day of the week). As stated in chapter 1, although most technical details about the measurement procedures at these three online newspapers could not be obtained, consultations with their respective managers revealed that their procedures recorded site traffic as it accumulated during the day and reset the counter at midnight of each day. Furthermore, data about Lanacion.com and Infobae.com were publicly available. Data about Clarín .com, which were not published on its site during the period of data collection, were gathered through a special arrangement that allowed research assistants for this project to visit the newsroom a few times a week and record this information. For twenty-eight of the seventy days, data about Lanacion.com and Infobae .com were gathered five times a day—at 7:00 AM, 11:00 AM, 3:00 PM, 7:00 PM, and 11:00 PM—to assess the unfolding of possible patterns of news consumption as the day evolved. For the remaining forty-two days, data from both sites were collected solely at 11:00 PM. In the case of Clarín.com, for all seventy days data were captured only once a day at midnight, due to these conditions of data access. When the data from the three online sites were compared, only the 11:00 PM figures from Lanacion.com and Infobae.com were used. The data yielded 1,820 most-clicked stories and 1,092 control group stories each for Lanacion.com and Infobae.com, and 700 most-clicked stories and 420 control group stories for Clarín.com.

Stories were examined only for the selection level of analysis described above. Each story was also analyzed on the same three variables—content overlap, content focus, and content type—that were utilized to examine the top stories of the day. Initially, two research assistants coded 6% of the data independently and obtained intercoder agreement levels of 100% for content overlap, 100% for content focus, and 93% for content type. Then, each research assistant undertook the coding of half of the remaining stories and resolved doubts consensually with the other research assistant and the author.

Appendix B:
Supplementary Studies

This appendix summarizes two studies that were undertaken after fieldwork for this book had concluded. It focuses on the main findings that directly relate to issues explored in this book. The first study looks at whether structural and leadership changes in the organizations studied for the ethnography of news production challenge the dynamics of monitoring, imitation, and editorial criteria presented in chapters 2, 3, and 6. The second study examines the top news choices of journalists and consumers of leading online media in the United States during the 2008 election cycle. It addresses issues pertaining to homogeneity in the news and the gap between journalists' and consumers' choices that relate to findings presented in chapters 4–6. Together, these studies suggest substantive temporal and spatial continuities with the arguments put forward in previous chapters of this book.

On the Timing of Research

Online news is a fast-changing research object. Therefore, is it possible that the timing of fieldwork affected the essence of the account presented in previous chapters? A study undertaken in the summer of 2008, nearly one and a half years after fieldwork for this book had ended, provides new data to answer this question. It featured interviews with editors at six news sites in Argentina, including Clarín.com and Lanacion.com.[1] Some notable changes took place at these two newspapers during this intervening period. Among the changes were the departure of Clarín.com's founding director and longtime leader, Guillermo Culell, and his replacement by Darío D'Atri, who had joined the *Clarín* newsroom relatively recently to revamp its weekly business print supplement and related daily site. They also included the integration of the respective print and online newsrooms at both *Clarín* and *La Nación,* following a recent trend that has become increasingly common in Europe and the United States.

The analysis of the 2008 interviews suggests that the fundamental contours of the dynamics of monitoring and imitation at these two news sites reported in chapter 3 have remained largely unaffected by these organizational changes. For instance, Clarín.com's Darío D'Atri, confesses:

All the time [monitoring takes place]. As a matter of fact, we have screens in the [news-room] that show us the competitors' sites. Of course, one single person can't look at all these screens twenty-four hours per day. So there are lots of people looking at the same time. Many of them approach the [new newsroom space] where we coordinate the print and online newspapers in an integrated fashion [and tell us,] "Take a look at this medium which publishes that story" [or] "Let's check if we have this story in this particular way." . . . And . . . we have a person per shift who is devoted to surveying . . . what's going on in the main Spanish-speaking and American sites. So if we get a piece of news from the wires, we [first] review these sites to see how they treated it. And all media are doing the same. **(PERSONAL COMMUNICATION, JULY 22, 2008)**

Daniel Vittar, one of two editors at Clarín.com with primary responsibility for the site's homepage, monitors the competition "permanently. . . . We look at them to see if they publish a piece of news before we do it, or if we do it first. Because copying is ultrafast on the Internet: you publish something and five minutes later the others publish it too" (personal communication, July 29, 2008). Similar prac-tices are also prevalent at Lanacion.com. One of its editors mentions looking at competitors' sites "all the time. . . . Because it's the best tool to know if I'm missing a story. So it's a task you have to do every day. . . . You cannot not do it. And I guess that at other sites it is the same" (personal communication, August 4, 2008).

Editors are as aware of the existence of a gap between the most-clicked stories and those that they consider to be the most newsworthy as they were at the time of fieldwork for this book. Lanacion.com's content manager Gastón Roitberg com-ments, "Most of the time entertainment and sports [stories are] first in the ranking of the most-clicked stories" (personal communication, August 8, 2008). Journalists take the existence of this gap largely for granted. When asked what he thought about this gap, Clarín.com's other homepage editor Federico Kotlar answered, "Well, it's the reality. [Silence] It's like discussing what I think about the fact that the Great Wall of China has the shape it has" (personal communication, July 24, 2008).

Echoing the comments included in chapter 6, journalists interviewed for the 2008 study say that although this gap makes the public's preferences very visible to them, they normally choose stories according to traditional editorial criteria that often diverge from these preferences. Lanacion.com's Roitberg says, "I don't have any doubt that if you let a user be editor and put together the homepage for a day, they would probably [select] other topics. But the reality is that the editors are here [in the newsroom], not outside it" (personal communication, August 15, 2008). In a related vein, Clarín.com's Darío D'Atri states, "We cannot ignore what people are interested in, but we cannot make the news as a function of those interests either. . . . I believe that journalism has a role that is different from following those [demand] trends" (personal communication, July 22, 2008).

In sum, the evidence collected during the 2008 study indicates that key production and consumption dynamics analyzed in previous chapters remain mostly unaffected by recent organizational changes in online news.

On the Location of Research

Preliminary analyses from a study about online news in the United States conducted while writing this book yield additional findings that resonate with dynamics analyzed in chapters 4–6. The U.S. study examined the top ten stories that journalists chose to display most prominently on each of six leading online news sites and contrasted these stories with the top ten most read stories by consumers of each of these sites. The data were gathered during the final stages of America's 2008 electoral campaign cycle, or from August 1 to December 1. This was a period marked by events of major historical significance in which the relaxation of normal resource constraints for the coverage of these events and the perception of heightened public interest in them created a fertile ground for news organizations to compete by differentiating their editorial offerings. The sites are all affiliated with cable, television, and print media of national reach. They are ABCnews.com, CBSnews.com, CNN.com, Foxnews.com, USAToday.com, and Washingtonpost .com.[2] These sites were among the top ten of either the most visited news sites or the most visited newspaper sites in the United States in 2008 (Nielsen, 2008; Journalism.org, 2009). They had a combined monthly average of more than 65 million unique users during the data collection period. Their combined size and the status of these sites endow them with strong agenda-setting power at the national level.

The analysis shows that 51% of the top ten public affairs stories chosen by journalists on one of these sites were about an event that was displayed prominently by at least one of the other sites.[3] That public affairs stories with overlap constituted the majority (although only by one percentage point) of the top ten stories is a telling metaphor of the low level of diversity in the coverage of political, business, and international news. In contrast, only 38% of non–public affairs news had overlap among two or more sites.[4] Thus, the much higher diversity of non–public affairs news indicates that the homogenization of public affairs news is not inevitable.

Like the data from Argentine news sites reported in chapter 6, there was substantively less homogenization in the top choices of consumers of these sites: 37%

of the public affairs stories and 25% of their non–public affairs counterparts were about events featured in stories included in more than one of the top ten most read lists.[5] These gaps between the convergent public and non–public affairs news choices of journalists and consumers give added credence to the notion elaborated in chapter 6 that the homogenization of the news cannot be attributed to consumption patterns. This notion is further reinforced by looking at the stories that captured the greatest attention of journalists and consumers. These are the stories that overlapped among the six sites in either the journalists' or consumers' lists. A simple quantitative comparison reveals stark differences between journalists and consumers in the number of their respective convergent choices and in the thematic distribution of these choices. There were 390 stories that overlapped in the journalists' lists of the six sites. In contrast, there were only sixty-six stories that overlapped among the most read news of all sites. In addition, the thematic distribution of these stories differs markedly between journalists and consumers. For journalists, 77% were about public affairs subjects and 23% about non–public affairs news. For consumers, 35% were about the first category and 65% about the second one.

A qualitative analysis of the eleven events reported in these sixty-six stories that made it to the top ten most read stories of all six sites (of more than 4,500 top ten, consumer-chosen stories that were analyzed) offers a unique window into the public's interest.[6] This window, in turns, provides a sobering look at the kind of alternative agenda that could emerge if the void in content diversity left by the homogenization in the news of the mainstream media were filled by consumer-authored content.[7] The largest topical category was natural disasters. The disasters were the subject of stories that reported on five of the eleven events. Two of the events had to do with different moments in the evolution of Hurricane Gustav and three with Hurricane Ike. Furthermore, the first wave of news about Hurricane Gustav published on August 31, 2008, received the highest average ranking of the most read stories that converged among all sites: it occupied the first place on ABCnews.com, CNN.com, and Foxnews.com, the second on CBSnews.com and USAToday.com, and the third on Washingtonpost.com. The remaining six events were the death of actor Bernie Mac, the killing of an American athlete's relative during the Beijing Olympics, the disappearance of the nephew of actress Jennifer Hudson, a sighting of the legendary monster Bigfoot, the terrorist attacks in Mumbai, and the admission by former presidential candidate John Edwards of a sexual affair.

It is quite ironic that the only event in this list that was related to the presidential election concerned a personal, rather than a policy, matter. More generally, it appears that the average top news preferences of Argentines and Americans who consume large, mainstream media are not similar. The majority of the former privilege sports news, and most of the latter are strongly drawn to bad weather. But beneath this pattern of local variation is a fundamental common ground: on average, neither of these two publics is as intensely interested in political, economic, and foreign news. While the United States was gearing up to elect the first African

American president in its history and the markets were pulverizing the assets and dreams of thousands of businesses and millions of households, the convergent news choices of consumers of the country's leading online media were not about the actions of Barack Obama or Ben Bernanke but about rain, death, monsters, and sex.

Thus, the findings from this study resonate strongly with the dynamics of news homogeneity and the story selection patterns of journalists and consumers presented in previous chapters of this book.

Notes

1. Here, and in the rest of this book, the affiliation of each actor is the one she or he held at the time the reported event
   or the interview took place.
2. An examination of site usage data of Lanacion.com (Clarín
   .com's main competitor), available on its site on a monthly
   basis from mid-2004 to 2006, reveals a comparable temporal
   patterning of online news consumption. For instance, on
   average, daily visits to the site in September 2006 were approximately two-thirds higher from Monday to Friday than
   on weekends (Lanacion.com, 2006). Moreover, during the
   workweek, the peak of site access was from 8:00 AM to 6:00 PM.
   Figures from the Internet Advertising Bureau—Argentina
   about hourly patterns of site usage of the country's main
   newspaper-based sites, including Clarín.com and Lanacion
   .com, also show that the peak time of access was from 8:00 AM
   to 6:00 PM (Internet Advertising Bureau—Argentina, 2006b).
   Chapter 1 summarizes studies that show that this temporal and spatial pattern of online news consumption is also
   prevalent in North America and Europe.
3. Some specialized publics, such as journalists, public relations
   workers, and taxi drivers have long accessed the news at the
   time and place of work.
4. They include Cockburn and Ormond (1993), Gamson
   (1994), Grindstaff (2002), and Pinch and Trocco (2002).

1. This research builds on the notion of a general tendency to
   homogenize media products that has been well established,

at least since analysts began to adapt Hotelling's (1929) insights on the spatial dynamics of market competition to the economics of production and distribution of news and entertainment. See Neuman (1991) for an overview of this research.

2. This dearth of systematic empirical evidence of homogenization is even more pronounced in studies that take the story as the unit of analysis (Napoli, 1999; Voakes, Kapfer, Kurpious, & Shano-Yeon, 1995).

3. The relatively few existing empirical studies are of two kinds. The first undertakes cross-sectional analyses of television newscasts and newspaper stories (Atwater, 1986; Bigman, 1948; Davie & Lee, 1993; Dean & Pertilla, 2007; Donohue & Glasser, 1978; Fowler & Showalter, 1974; Lemert, 1974; Mazharul Haque, 1986). The second research is animated by the concern that growing ownership concentration might stifle diversity of news content (Busterna, 1988; Hicks & Featherstone, 1978; Lacy, 1987, 1991).

4. Specific financial information was not disclosed to me and could not be obtained through public records because both sites were part of privately owned companies during the period of this study.

5. For multiple perspectives on the character of each newspaper and various aspects of the differences between them in several historical periods, see Blaustein and Zubieta (2006), Luchessi (2008), Miceli and Belinche (2002), Sidicaro (1993), Ulanovsky (2005a, 2005b), and Zukernik (2005).

6. Top stories are also important foci of competition across news organizations in a given market. Whether this competition invites imitation or differentiation should not be taken as a given but should be determined after the inquiry process.

7. For instance, the 2001 national census revealed that 32% of the population lived in Buenos Aires and neighboring towns (Instituto Nacional de Estadísticas y Censos, 2008).

8. For instance, the Gini Index for 2005 was 0.524 (Economic Commission for Latin America and the Caribbean, 2008).

9. Historically, Argentina has also had one of the most developed media systems in Latin America (Buckman, 1996; Ferreira, 2006; Fox, 1988a; Fox & Waisbord, 2002a; Schwoch, 1993).

10. Not surprisingly, access to the Internet is highly stratified by income: as of 2005, the top 20% of the income distribution represented 80% of those who had access (D'Alessio—IROL, 2006).

11. Article 43 of Law 12,908 (the "Journalist's Statute") establishes that in case of unjustified dismissal, a full-time journalist is entitled to (*a*) one or two months of notice beforehand, depending on tenure; (*b*) one month of compensation for every year worked; and (*c*) an additional six-month compensation regardless of tenure. Thus, for instance, if a journalist with ten years of tenure in a newspaper is fired without justified reason, she is entitled to receive notification of this action two months prior to the date of employ-

ment termination—a period during which she can start looking for another job—and sixteen months of salary. This statute does not apply to personnel not hired in a full-time capacity, such as independent contractors, freelancers, and interns. These other types of employment relationships were more common in online than in print media during the period of study, which might account for the greater fluctuations in personnel among the former than the latter.

12. This is not to say that there were no attempts by the government to influence the press during the presidential administrations since the return to democracy in 1983, especially that of Carlos Menem. However, analysts and practitioners agree that the magnitude and efficacy of these attempts increased substantially during the administration of Néstor Kirchner.

CHAPTER TWO

1. García (2008) provides an account of some aspects of the evolution of Clarín.com relevant to this and the next chapter.

2. Studies of technology and media show that the ways producers conceive of their intended public are consequential for the resulting product and its subsequent uptake and circulation in society (Akrich, 1992, 1995; Ang, 1991; Bardini, 2000; Boczkowski, 2004; Ettema & Whitney, 1994; Mackay, Carne, Beynon-Davies, & Tudhope, 2000; Woolgar, 1991).

3. This division was terminated in autumn 2008.

4. Here and in other comparable analyses throughout this book, the tests of statistical significance of the differences between proportions were based on the effect size index h—the difference between the arcsine-transformed proportions—and, as appropriate, the harmonic mean of the n's, following J. Cohen's (1988) procedures and tabled critical values.

5. Ethnographies that examine distinctive modes of information gathering and story authoring related to the context of journalistic work (Bishara, 2006; Clausen, 2004; Hasty, 2006; S. Hughes, 2006; Stahlberg, 2006) suggest some distinctive traits of Clarín.com at the time of this study that might restrict the broader heuristic value of these conclusions about the divergent logics of hard- and soft-news production. First, Clarín.com had a higher level of resources than other online news sites, which might have contributed to developing a robust soft-news production unit and multiple kinds of journalism. Second, it operated in a more competitive environment than other news organizations, which might have intensified the hard-news production patterns observed. Third, because the kind of hard-news production described here conflicts with traditional journalism's organizational routines and professional values, sites that are more integrated with traditional counterparts might enact less differentiated hard- and soft-news practices. Fourth, Clarín.com conceived a significant portion of its public as being highly interested in up-to-the-minute and comprehensive

hard-news coverage; media that represent their publics differently might engage in less divergent hard- and soft-news practices.

CHAPTER THREE

1. These names are pseudonyms.
2. The stories published in *Clarín* that morning were available on Clarín.com.
3. This was also the lead story of *La Nación* that day. Displayed with a placement and size on its front page that were strikingly similar to those on *Clarín*'s front page, *La Nación*'s headline read: "[then Buenos Aires mayor Jorge] Telerman surprised by scheduling the elections on June 3rd" (*Sorprendió Telerman al fijar los comicios para el 3 de junio*). Some of the words are different from those used on *Clarín*'s front page (most notably, the treatment given to the subject of the sentence), but the majority of both headlines expresses convergent interpretive strategies and editorial emphases.
4. This kind of differentiation attempt is the opposite of making decisions about the treatment of a given story to conform to knowledge about competitors' coverage. It resonates with attempts by print journalists to differentiate by way of what they call "*la mirada.*"
5. For various uses of the notion of affordance in studies of media and information technologies, see Boczkowski (2001), Gibson (1977, 1986), Norman (1988, 1993), Pea (1993), and Wellman et al. (2003).
6. For general discussions on technological determinism, see Bijker (1995) and Brey (2003), MacKenzie (1984), Staudenmaier (1989), Williams and Edge (1996), and S. Wyatt (2007). For discussions focused on media and information technologies, see Dutton (2005), Edwards (1995), Kling (1994), Pfaffenberger (1989), Slack and Wise (2002), and Winner (1986).
7. This attempt to highlight how technology matters is inspired by recent calls, such as from Bijker (2001) and Bowker and Star (1999), to inquire into the consequences of material configurations in a way that avoids the pitfalls of technological determinism.

CHAPTER FOUR

1. The basic ideas behind the notions of hard and soft news used for the coding of the stories included in the content analysis correspond to those laid out in chapter 2. For more details on these notions and issues of operationalization, see appendix A.
2. Because the study did not systematically collect data in consecutive days, it is not possible to examine the proportion of stories that appeared for the first time in the evening shift of one day and also in the morning or afternoon shifts of the following day. However, because the proportion of public affairs news in these two latter shifts is so much higher than in the evening shift, it is very unlikely that most of the dyads and triads of

non–public affairs stories with overlap would continue to have overlap or even be featured by just one of these online news sites on the following day.

3. As mentioned in chapter 1, *Infobae* is a small financial daily. Thus, its content and format differ markedly from those of large generalist newspapers such as *Clarín* and *La Nación*. I did not collect data from the print *Infobae* because these differences would have made it very difficult to undertake meaningful comparisons with *Clarín* and *La Nación* on the issues that are relevant for this book.

4. This sample is different from the main 2005 print sample utilized in this study and was collected and analyzed solely for the purpose of examining the ties between the print front pages and the online morning homepages.

5. Because the data concentrated on publication during the workweek, a subsample of online evening editions from Monday through Thursday and the following day's print editions were analyzed. Thus, the online data collected on Friday were not included because it would have meant including print data from Saturday.

6. Detailed information about measurement criteria and coding procedures for the analyses reported in this and the next section is provided in appendix A.

7. The English translation overlooks a slight difference between these two headlines in Spanish: whereas *Clarín* put the subject before the verb (*"Bush destacó el liderazgo de Brasil en Latinoamérica"*), *La Nación* reversed the order of these two syntactic elements (*"Destacó Bush el liderazgo de Brasil en la región"*).

8. There was a loss of data regarding online stories due to technical problems (see appendix A for a detailed description of the nature of the lost data and measures undertaken to alleviate this problem). Thus, only 508 of the 619 online stories are examined in the narration level of analysis.

9. The English translation obscures a slight difference between these two headlines regarding the order of the words: "Lavagna dijo que un acuerdo con el FMI 'no es imprescindible'" (Clarín.com) and "Lavagna dice que no es imprescindible un acuerdo con el FMI" (Lanacion.com).

10. NA is the acronym of Noticias Argentinas, a local news agency.

11. Diego Maradona began his soccer career playing for Argentinos Juniors.

12. It is possible that most of these differentiation attempts were directed at other types of content, such as soft news and commentary pieces. This type of content is far less prone to register overlap in story selection. An analysis of the data presented in table 4.1 shows that the proportion of hard-news stories on front pages decreased from 89% in the *Before* period to 82% in the *After* period. Furthermore, the proportion of hard-news stories on homepages was 73%, which is also lower than in the print *Before* period. Although these data suggest that some differentiation efforts might have been allocated to types of content other than hard news, it is important to

keep in mind that hard news still represents the majority of front-page and homepage content. Thus, the failure of product differentiation efforts to counter imitation dynamics in hard news has major consequences for the totality of the news product. This is so even after taking into account the potential existence of differentiation strategies that focus on soft news and commentary.

13. The Kirchner administration was well known for its lack of interest in international affairs.

14. In the *Before* period, of the 140 stories with overlap, 68 were in the national news subsample and 72 in the other news subsample. In the *After* period, 92 stories were in the national news subsample and 86 in the other news subsample.

15. The rate of increase for all stories is not the average between national and the rest because the gap between these two categories grew from 6% in the *Before* period to 10% in the *After* period, in the direction of less national news.

CHAPTER FIVE

1. For studies of whether the use of online sites displaces or complements consumption of news in print and broadcast media, see, e.g., Ahlers (2006), Chyi and Lasorsa (2002), Dimmick, Chen, and Li (2004), Dutta-Bergman (2004), and Lin, Salwen, Garrison, and Driscoll (2005). More specifically, for present purposes, a recent survey conducted in six European countries found that 27% of the respondents who accessed online news at work read print newspapers less often (Online Publishers Association—Europe, 2007).

2. Socialization in the household and the school during childhood and adolescence (Mindich, 2005) and in the transition to independence during early adulthood (Bogart, 1989) has often been considered crucial to the formation of news consumption habits. The workplace becomes a key socialization locus for online news consumption in a country such as Argentina where the office is the first environment in which many young people enjoy widespread broadband access to the Internet on a regular basis. This is also consistent with recent studies undertaken in industrialized nations about the relatively high prevalence of displacement effects from traditional to online media among young consumers (Coleman & McCombs, 2007; Diddi & LaRose, 2006; Hasebrink & Paus-Hasebrink, 2007; Ogan, Ozakca, & Groshek, 2008).

3. A similar analysis was not undertaken for Clarín.com because data were collected only at the end of the day or for Infobae.com because of the negligible role played by its print counterpart.

4. This is an expression of the common yet often ignored spaces of moral ambiguity in organizational life that Anteby has aptly called "grey zones"—

"areas at work in which workers and their supervisors together engage in practices that are officially forbidden, yet tolerated by the organization" (2008, p. 10).

5. A survey of Internet users in six European countries finds that whereas 16% download music at work, 55% do it at home; 16% watch video at work, but 41% do it at home; and 8% play online games at work, but 28% do it at home (Online Publishers Association—Europe, 2007).

6. As Nippert-Eng finds, people differ in their stance regarding the boundaries between the spaces of work and home. These differences can be conceptualized in a continuum that "range[s] from 'integration' to 'segmentation'" (1995, p. 5). It is reasonable to expect that people who undertake paid labor in the home space lean toward the integration stance, and those who work in an office setting lean toward the segmentation approach.

7. For an array of perspectives on the prevalence and implications of political content in workplace interactions, see, e.g., Beck (1991), Conover, Searing, and Crewe (2002), Finifter (1974), Mutz (2006), Mutz and Mondak (2006), Putnam (2000), Rosenberg (1955), and R. Wyatt, Katz, and Kim (2000).

8. To borrow from Eliasoph's analysis of political apathy in everyday life, it "takes work to produce" (1998, p. 6) the avoidance of politics in workplace conversations.

9. The important presence of sports stories in workplace conversations, which is in part related to the popularity of these stories among online news consumers, resonates with B. Erickson's findings about the interclass coordination effect of sports in her study of interaction patterns in Canadian firms: "Sports is so much a cross-class widespread interest that it is very useful in tending work relationships between or within classes" (1996, p. 235).

10. This was part of an environmental protest over the building of paper-processing plants in Fray Bentos, a city across the river in Uruguay.

11. This separation echoes Stark's (2009) notion of a division between the study of economic action and accounts of the social relations that shape this action, a division that has long marked the respective jurisdictional spaces of economics and sociology.

CHAPTER SIX

1. A memorable dialogue between Natalio Botana, the legendary publisher of the turn-of-the-century Argentine newspaper *Crítica,* and one of his editors vividly illustrates this stance of disregard. When the editor noted that the public was not going to like a forthcoming article, Botana replied, "We have to teach the public what it has to like" (Ulanovsky, 2005a, p. 97).

2. This use of the notion of "decoding" centers on consumers' story selection practices, not on the interpretive practices of the selected stories. That is, it focuses on the work that goes into decoding the overall editorial offer to decide which stories are worth reading and which ones are not.

3. The choices of consumers are not independent from those of journalists. Consumers can click only on the stories that journalists choose to publish. In light of the quantitative and qualitative evidence presented in chapter 5 about the kinds of stories that consumers find most appealing, this dependency introduces the possibility of a conservative bias in this comparison of consumers' and journalists' choices. It is reasonable to expect that if consumers could choose from the full set of potentially newsworthy stories available to journalists (rather than from the stories journalists deem newsworthy enough to be published), their choices would be even more divergent from those of journalists than in the analysis that follows.

4. Because the data from Clarín.com were collected only in the evening, this section relies only on data collected at 11:00 PM from Lanacion.com and Infobae.com.

5. There was a small minority of soft-news stories with content overlap in the data set of consumers' choices. Of 540 soft-news stories, 27 (5%) had content overlap. Moreover, aggregating all the stories with content overlap yields a total of 343 stories, and soft-news stories with overlap amount to 8% of this figure. Whether understood as a proportion of the total number of soft-news stories or of the total number of stories with overlap, soft-news stories with content overlap constitute a small minority of consumers' choices. Thus, to enable the contrast of comparable kinds of content, the analysis presented in this chapter focuses only on hard-news stories. Moreover, if all the stories were used as the denominator in both sets, the proportion of content overlap would be 38% for the journalists and 21% for the consumers. This would amount to a significant ($p < .01$) difference of seventeen percentage points.

6. Because the consumers' data were collected at the end of the day, a second analysis compared these issues of content overlap considering only the evening shift of the journalists' data. The results exhibited no major variation. The respective differences—all of which were significant ($p < .01$)—increased to 17% in content overlap, decreased to 18% in content focus, and remained at 22% in level of concentration.

7. For different accounts of the effects of agenda-setting processes on online news, see Althaus and Tewksbury (2002), Coleman and McCombs (2007), Lee (2007), Schiffer (2006), Schoenbach, de Waal, and Lauf (2005), and Zhou and Moy (2007).

8. For an illuminating analysis of cynicism and the news, see Cappella and Jamieson (1997).

9. The peak of the crisis and the periods immediately before and after it were marked by intense social mobilization, but this faded once everyday life had acquired a sense of normalcy (Grimson and Kessler, 2005; Peruzzotti, 2005).

10. For different perspectives on "political efficacy," or the belief that an actor has about her or his ability to alter the balance of power in society, see Campbell, Gurin, and Miller (1954), Clarke and Acock (1989), Easton and Dennis (1967),

and Niemi, Craig, and Mattei (1991). For recent studies that examine the dynamics of political efficacy in relation to digital media, see Kaid, McKinney, and Tedesco (2007), Kenski and Stroud (2006), Livingstone and Markham (2008), Scheufele and Nisbet (2002), and Tolbert and McNeal (2003).

11. The results presented in chapter 5 about the substantive presence of print newspaper content in online news consumption suggest that it is likely that these patterns also spill over to the practices and experiences of appropriating homogenized news originally created for traditional media.

CHAPTER SEVEN

1. For an analysis of the rise of information available to the average American household in recent decades, see Neuman (2009).

2. It is worth considering at least three distinct elements of the Argentine setting. First, the high level of ownership concentration and the national character of the newspaper industry in Argentina might have exacerbated the trends toward increased monitoring and imitation in editorial work and homogeneity in the news. There are grounds to believe that a comparatively lower level of ownership concentration and a more geographically dispersed composition might moderate the trend toward greater similarity. Second, there was a relatively higher level of stability among full-time print newsroom personnel during the period when news homogenization increased. This might have uniquely affected issues of imitation when compared with recent labor trends to downsize newsrooms in other countries. This stability and the fact that Clarín.com and Lanacion.com increased their newsroom personnel while news homogenization was on the rise diminish the pertinence of explanations based on resource allocation patterns. This means, not that these explanations are inadequate, but that they are not necessary to account for the observed patterns. Because overdetermination adds strength and stability to social processes, the patterns analyzed in this book might deepen in countries where journalists labor under different conditions than their Argentine peers. The third distinct feature of the Argentine context shifts the register from production to consumption. Chapter 6 argues that the stance of retreat that dominated consumer sentiment was related to coping with a condition of institutional weakness. In this condition, consumers became savvy readers of news texts in an effort to anticipate future institutional transformations, while reducing their expectations of contributing toward positive social change. These contextual factors might have affected the stance of consumers in a way that does not apply to democratic regimes in which greater institutional strength fosters a heightened sense of political efficacy among the population.

3. See, for instance, the brilliant analysis of the journalistic establishment's silence during the invasion and occupation of Iraq by U.S. military forces (Bennett, Lawrence, & Livingston, 2007).

4. This is consistent with the main results of a recent study about a thematic gap in the story selection patterns of journalists and consumers in an array of online news media in the United States (Boczkowski & Peer, in press) and also with findings presented in appendix B.

APPENDIX A

1. According to Tuchman, "A *non*scheduled event-as-news is an occurrence whose date of dissemination as news is determined by the newsworkers. A *pre*scheduled event-as-news is an occurrence announced for a future date by its convenors; news of it is to be disseminated the day it occurs or the day after. An *un*scheduled event-as-news is one that occurs unexpectedly; news of it is to be disseminated the day or the day after" (1978, pp. 51–52, emphasis in original). Urgent dissemination was operationalized differently for print and online. For print, it meant publication of a story within twenty-four hours or less once the major events had taken place, and for online within two hours or less. The two-hour window was chosen because it better captures the pattern of temporal rotation of most top news stories in the online newspapers that were studied.

APPENDIX B

1. The interviews were conducted face-to-face by a research assistant in Buenos Aires between June and August 2008. Twelve editors and editorial directors from six top-ranked Argentine online newspapers were recruited. The news sites (Clarín.com, Lanacion.com, Infobae.com, Criticadigital .com, Perfil.com, and Página12.com) were selected according to their online readership as measured by Alexa Rankings and Google Web Trends. They also provide a wide spectrum of ideological orientation and type of audience. Five interviewees were editorially in charge of their respective sites, and seven were editors directly involved with management of the homepage. The interviews lasted an average of forty minutes and were recorded and transcribed in their entirety. For more information, see Boczkowski and Mitchelstein (in press).
2. Data were collected on seventy-nine days during nineteen weeks—approximately four days from Monday to Sunday for each of the weeks. Because one objective of this study was to examine the difference between journalists' and consumers' online news choices during a period marked by events of heightened political importance, the selection of data collection days was conducted randomly during most of the weeks and purposively during periods of prescheduled major political events, such as the conventions, presidential debates, and election day. On each data collection day, a research assistant retrieved data from all six sites at 10:00 AM U.S. central time. For each data collection day, the research assistant identified

the top stories selected by journalists and consumers, respectively. The former consisted of each homepage's first ten stories (hereafter, "journalists' list") counting from left to right and from the top down in a gridlike manner. The latter were the top five to ten stories in the "most read list" (hereafter, "consumers' list") made publicly available by each of these sites. Five of the sites made ten stories from the consumers' list available every day, but CBSnews.com made between five and ten, depending on the day—or an average of 7.6 stories per day. A total of 4,730 stories from the journalists' lists and 4,537 from the consumers' lists from all the sites were analyzed. The difference from the expected number of stories (n = 4,740 for the journalists' lists and 4,550.4 [(5 × 10 × 79) + (1 × 7.6 × 79)] for the consumers' lists, considering that CBSnews.com made, on average, 7.6 stories available in the consumers' list) results from the retrieval of repeated stories that were later excluded from analysis (journalists' list) and the fact that these sites posted fewer than ten stories in their "most read" rankings (consumers' list) during a few days. The difference between the expected and actual number of stories is 0.21% for the journalists' list and 0.29% for the consumers' list. The unit of analysis was the story. Two main variables were coded—content focus and content overlap—using the same definitions provided in appendix A. Three trained research assistants coded the stories. Intercoder agreement was assessed on a subset of 11% of the data. Regular intercoder agreement levels averaged 87% for content focus and 90% for content overlap. Doubts about the coding were discussed among the members of the research team and resolved consensually.

3. This figure reflects the proportion of stories with content overlap divided by the *total of all stories* in the sample. This is different from the procedure used in the book, which focused on hard news only. This divergence in the metrics is due to the adoption of a coding scheme that did not examine stories in terms of hard and soft news. As demonstrated in previous chapters, hard-news stories tend to have a disproportionate share of similarity in story selection in comparison to other formats, so the findings of content overlap for this study would have been substantively higher had the calculation looked at hard news only.

4. Thirty-seven percent of the public affairs stories and 25% of the non–public affairs stories overlapped among three or more sites.

5. Twenty-one percent of the public affairs stories and 14% of the non–public affairs stories overlapped among the top ten most read lists of three or more sites.

6. Further evidence of the extent to which these stories strongly captured the attention of consumers is that their average ranking was 2.71 out of 10.

7. There is little reason to assume that what people want to read differs from what they might like to write about.

Bibliography

Abrahamson, E. (1991). Managerial fads and fashions: The diffusion and rejection of innovations. *Academy of Management Review, 16,* 586–612.

Ahlers, D. (2006). News consumption and the new electronic media. *Harvard International Journal of Press-Politics, 11*(1), 29–52.

Akrich, M. (1992). The de-scription of technical objects. In W. Bijker & J. Law (Eds.), *Shaping technology/building society* (pp. 205–224). Cambridge, MA: MIT Press.

Akrich, M. (1995). User representations: Practices, methods and sociology. In A. Rip, T. Misa, & J. Schot (Eds.), *Managing technology in society* (pp. 167–184). London: Pinter Publishers.

Albornoz, L. (2007). *Periodismo digital: Los grandes diarios en la red.* Buenos Aires, Argentina: La Crujía.

Albornoz, L., & Hernández, P. (2005). La radiodifusión en Argentina entre 1995 y 1999: Concentración, desnacionalización y ausencia del control público. In G. Mastrini (Ed.), *Mucho ruido, pocas leyes: Economía y políticas de comunicación en la Argentina (1920–2004)* (pp. 257–286). Buenos Aires, Argentina: La Crujía.

Allan, S. (2006). *Online news.* Maidenhead, UK: Open University Press.

Althaus, S., & Tewksbury, D. (2002). Agenda setting and the "new" news: Patterns of issue importance among readers of the paper and online version of the *New York Times. Communication Research, 29,* 180–206.

Alves, R. C. (2005). From lapdog to watchdog: The role of the press in Latin America's democratization. In H. De Burgh (Ed.), *Making journalists* (pp. 181–202). New York: Routledge.

Anand, B., Di Tella, R., & Galetovic, A. (2007). Information or opinion? Media bias as product differentiation. *Journal of Economics and Management Strategy, 16,* 635–682.

Anand, N., & Peterson, R. (2000). When market information constitutes fields: Sensemaking of markets in the commercial music industry. *Organization Science, 11,* 270–284.

Ang, I. (1989). *Watching "Dallas": Soap opera and the melodramatic imagination.* New York: Routledge.

Ang, I. (1991). *Desperately seeking the audience.* London: Routledge.

Anteby, M. (2008). *Moral gray zones: Side productions, identity, and regulation in an aeronautic plant.* Princeton, NJ: Princeton University Press.

Arango, T., & Pérez-Peña, R. (2008, December 1). CNN pitches a cheaper wire service to newspapers. *New York Times.* Retrieved December 1, 2008, from http://www.nytimes.com/2008/12/01/business/media/01cnn.html?_r=1&ref=media&pagewented=print.

Armony, A., & Armony, V. (2005). Indictments, myths, and citizen mobilization in Argentina: A discourse analysis. *Latin American Politics and Society, 47,* 27–54.

Associated Press. (2008). *A new model for news: Studying the deep structure of young-adult news consumption.* New York: Author.

Atwater, T. (1986). Consonance in local television news. *Journal of Broadcasting and Electronic Media, 30*(4), 467–472.

Auerbach, E. (2003 [1953]). *Mimesis: The representation of reality in Western literature* (W. Trask, Trans.; 2nd ed.). Princeton, NJ: Princeton University Press.

Austen, I. (2007, May 16). Thomson adds Reuters in $17 billion bid to be giant. *New York Times.* Retrieved December, 29, 2008, from http://www.nytimes.com/2007/05/16/business/media/16thomson.html.

Auyero, J. (2007). *Routine politics and violence in Argentina: The gray zone of state power.* New York: Cambridge University Press.

Avery, C., & Zemsky, P. (1998). Multidimensional uncertainty and herd behavior in financial markets. *American Economic Review, 88,* 724–748.

Bagdikian, B. (2004). *The new media monopoly.* Boston: Beacon.

Baisnee, O., & Marchetti, D. (2006). The economy of just-in-time television newscasting: Journalistic production and professional excellence at Euronews. *Ethnography, 7,* 99–123.

Baker, C. E. (1994). *Advertising and a democratic press.* Princeton, NJ: Princeton University Press.

Baker, C. E. (2002). *Media, markets and democracy.* New York: Cambridge University Press.

Baller, R., & Richardson, K. (2002). Social integration, imitation, and the geographic patterning of suicide. *American Sociological Review, 67,* 837–888.

Bandura, A., Ross, D., & Ross, S. (1963). Imitation of film-mediated aggressive models. *Journal of Abnormal and Social Psychology, 66,* 3–11.

Banerjee, A. (1992). A simple model of herd behavior. *Quarterly Journal of Economics, 107,* 797–817.

Baranchuk, M. (2005). Canales 11 y 13: La primera privatización de la década menemista. In G. Mastrini (Ed.), *Mucho ruido, pocas leyes: Economía y políticas de comunicación en la Argentina (1920–2004)* (pp. 211–234). Buenos Aires, Argentina: La Crujía.

Bardini, T. (2000). *Bootstrapping: Douglas Engelbart, coevolution, and the origins of personal computing.* Stanford, CA: Stanford University Press.

Barley, S. (1986). Technology as an occasion for structuring: Evidence from observations of CT scanners and the social order of radiology departments. *Administrative Science Quarterly, 31,* 78–108.

Barley, S. (1990). The alignment of technology and structure through roles and networks. *Administrative Science Quarterly, 35,* 61–103.

Barley, S., & Kunda, G. (2004). *Gurus, hired guns, and warm bodies: Itinerant experts in a knowledge economy.* Princeton, NJ: Princeton University Press.

Barreto, I., & Baden-Fuller, C. (2006). To conform or to perform? Mimetic behaviour, legitimacy-based groups and performance consequences. *Journal of Management Studies, 43,* 1559–1581.

Barry, A., & Thrift, N. (2007). Gabriel Tarde: Imitation, invention and the economy. *Economy and Society, 36,* 509–525.

Baum, M. (2002). Sex, lies, and war: How soft news brings foreign policy to the inattentive public. *American Political Science Review, 96*(1), 91–109.

Baum, M. (2003). *Soft news goes to war.* Princeton, NJ: Princeton University Press.

Baum, M. (2007). Hard and soft news. In T. Schaefer & T. Birkland (Eds.), *Encyclopedia of media and politics* (pp. 106–107). Washington, DC: CQ Press.

Bausinger, H. (1984). Media, technology and daily life. *Media, Culture and Society, 6,* 343–351.

Baym, N., Zhang, Y. B., & Lin, M.-C. (2004). Social interactions across media: Interpersonal communication on the Internet, telephone and face-to-face. *New Media and Society, 6,* 299–318.

Beck, P. (1991). Intermediation environments in the 1986 presidential contest. *Public Opinion Quarterly, 55,* 371–394.

Bellando, O. (1995, October 18). Cumbre: Menem admitió cambios en Castro. *La Nación,* p. 8.

Benavides, J. L. (2000). Gacetilla: A keyword for a revisionist approach to the political economy of Mexico's print news media. *Media, Culture and Society, 22,* 85–104.

Benjamin, W. (2007). *Illuminations: Essays and reflections* (H. Zohn, Trans.). New York: Schocken.

Benkler, Y. (2006). *The wealth of networks: How social production transforms markets and freedom.* New Haven, CT: Yale University Press.

Bennett, W. L. (2003). *News: The politics of illusion* (5th ed.). New York: Longman.

Bennett, W. L., Lawrence, R., & Livingston, S. (2007). *When the press fails: Political power and the news media from Iraq to Katrina.* Chicago: University of Chicago Press.

Berger, P., & Luckmann, T. (1966). *The social construction of reality: A treatise in the sociology of knowledge.* Garden City, NY: Doubleday.

Bernhardt, D., Hughson, E., & Kutsoati, E. (2006). The evolution of managerial expertise: How corporate culture can run amok. *American Economic Review, 96,* 195–221.

Bigman, S. K. (1948). Rivals in conformity: A study of two competing dailies. *Journalism Quarterly, 25*(June), 127–131.

Bijker, W. (1995). *Of bicycles, Bakelites, and bulbs: Toward a theory of sociotechnical change.* Cambridge, MA: MIT Press.

Bijker, W. (2001). Social construction of technology. In N. J. Smelser & P. B. Baltes (Eds.), *International encyclopedia of the social and behavioral sciences* (Vol. 23, pp. 15522–15527). Oxford: Elsevier.

Bikhchandani, S., Hirshleifer, D., & Welch, I. (1992). A theory of fads, fashion, custom, and cultural change as informational cascades. *Journal of Political Economy, 100,* 992–1026.

Bikhchandani, S., Hirshleifer, D., & Welch, I. (1998). Learning from the behavior of others: Conformity, fads, and informational cascades. *Journal of Economic Perspectives, 12,* 151–170.

Bikhchandani, S., & Sharma, S. (2001). Herd behavior in financial markets. *IMF Staff Papers, 47,* 279–310.

Bird, S. E. (1992). *For enquiring minds.* Knoxville: University of Tennessee Press.

Bird, S. E. (2003). *The audience in everyday life: Living in a media world.* New York: Routledge.

Bird, S. E., & Dardenne, R. (1988). Myth, chronicle, and story: Exploring the narrative qualities of news. In J. Carey (Ed.), *Media, myths, and narratives* (pp. 67–86). Newbury Park, CA: Sage.

Bishara, A. (2006). Local hands, international news: Palestinian journalists and the international media. *Ethnography, 7,* 19–46.

Blanck, J. (2007, December 1). Cristina Kirchner renueva la batalla por la "construcción" de la realidad. *Clarín,* p. 10.

Blanco, D., & Germano, C. (2005). *20 años de medios y democracia en la Argentina.* Buenos Aires, Argentina: La Crujía.

Blaustein, E., & Zubieta, M. (2006). *Decíamos ayer: La prensa argentina bajo el Proceso.* Buenos Aires, Argentina: Colihue.

Blustein, P. (2005). *And the money kept rolling in (and out): Wall Street, the IMF, and the bankrupting of Argentina.* New York: Public Affairs.

Boczkowski, P. (2001). *Affording flexibility: Transforming information practices in online newspapers.* Unpublished doctoral dissertation, Cornell University, Ithaca, NY.

Boczkowski, P. (2002). The development and use of online newspapers: What research tells us and what we might want to know. In L. Lievrouw & S. Livingstone (Eds.), *The handbook of new media* (pp. 270–286). London: Sage.

Boczkowski, P. (2004). *Digitizing the news: Innovation in online newspapers.* Cambridge, MA: MIT Press.

Boczkowski, P., & de Santos, M. (2007). When more media equals less news: Patterns of content homogenization in Argentina's leading print and online newspapers. *Political Communication, 24,* 167–190.

Boczkowski, P., & Mitchelstein, E. (in press). Is there a gap between the news choices of journalists and consumers? A relational and dynamic approach. *International Journal of Press/Politics.*

Boczkowski, P., & Peer, L. (in press). The choice gap: The divergent online news preferences of journalists and consumers. *Journal of Communication.*

Bogart, L. (1955). Adult conversation about newspaper comics. *American Journal of Sociology, 61,* 26–30.

Bogart, L. (1989). *Press and public: Who reads what, when, where, and why in American newspapers* (2nd ed.). Hillsdale, NJ: Lawrence Erlbaum.

Borland, E., & Sutton, B. (2007). Quotidian disruption and women's activism in times of crisis, Argentina, 2002–2003. *Gender and Society, 21,* 700–722.

Bourdieu, P. (1984). *Distinction: A social critique of the judgment of taste* (R. Nice, Trans.). Cambridge, MA: Harvard University Press.

Bourdieu, P. (1998). *On television.* New York: The New Press.

Bowker, G., & Star, S. (1999). *Sorting things out: Classification and its consequences.* Cambridge, MA: MIT Press.

Braslavsky, G. (2005, September 27). Represión ilegal: Kirchner relevó al jefe de Gendarmería. *Clarín,* p. 3.

Braverman, H. (1974). *Labor and monopoly capital: The degradation of work in the twentieth century.* New York: Monthly Review Press.

Breed, W. (1955). Newspaper "opinion leaders" and the processes of standardization. *Journalism Quarterly, 32*(Summer), 277–284.

Brewer, P., & Cao, X. (2006). Candidate appearances on soft news shows and public knowledge about primary campaigns. *Journal of Broadcasting and Electronic Media, 50*(1), 18–35.

Brey, P. (2003). Theorizing modernity and technology. In T. Misa, P. Brey, & A. Feenberg (Eds.), *Modernity and technology* (pp. 33–71). Cambridge, MA: MIT Press.

Buckman, R. (1996). Current status of the mass media in Latin America. In R. Cole (Ed.), *Communication in Latin America: Journalism, mass media, and society* (pp. 3–35). Wilmington, DE: Scholarly Resources.

Buford May, R., & Patillo-McCoy, M. (2000). Do you see what I see? Examining a collaborative ethnography. *Qualitative Inquiry, 6,* 65–87.

Bull, M. (2007). *Sound moves: iPod culture and urban experience.* New York: Routledge.

Busterna, J. C. (1988). Television station ownership effects on programming and idea diversity. *Journal of Media Economics, 1*(2), 63–74.

Campbell, A., Gurin, G., & Miller, W. (1954). *The voter decides.* Evanston, IL: Row Peterson.

Cappella, J., & Jamieson, K. H. (1997). *Spiral of cynicism: The press and the public good.* New York: Oxford University Press.

Carroll, R. (1985). Content values in TV news programs in small and large markets. *Journalism Quarterly, 62,* 877–882, 938.

Centro de Estudios Legales y Sociales. (2007). *Derechos humanos en Argentina: Informe 2007.* Buenos Aires, Argentina: Author.

Chamley, C. (2004). *Rational herds: Economic models of social learning*. Cambridge: Cambridge University Press.

Chan, T. W., & Goldthorpe, J. H. (2007). Social status and newspaper readership. *American Journal of Sociology, 112*, 1095–1134.

Choi, J. (1997). Herd behavior, the "penguin effect," and the suppression of informational diffusion: An analysis of information externalities and payoff interdependency. *Rand Journal of Economics, 28*, 407–425.

Chyi, H. I., & Lasorsa, D. L. (2002). An explorative study on the market relation between online and print newspapers. *Journal of Media Economics, 15*(2), 91–106.

Cipriani, M., & Guarino, A. (2005). Herd behavior in a laboratory financial market. *American Economic Review, 95*, 1427–1443.

Clarke, H., & Acock, A. (1989). National elections and political attitudes: The case of political efficacy. *British Journal of Political Science, 19*, 551–562.

Clausen, L. (2004). Localizing the global: "Domestication" processes in international news production. *Media, Culture and Society, 26*, 25–44.

Cockburn, C., & Ormond, S. (1993). *Gender and technology in the making*. London: Sage.

Cohen, E. (2002). Online journalism as market-driven journalism. *Journal of Broadcasting and Electronic Media, 46*, 532–548.

Cohen, J. (1988). *Statistical power analysis for the behavioral sciences* (2nd ed.). Hillsdale, NJ: Lawrence Erlbaum.

Cohen, W., Nelson, R., & Walsh, J. (2000). Protecting their intellectual assets: Appropriability conditions and why U.S. manufacturing firms patent (or not). *NBER Working Paper Series, Working Paper 7552*.

Coleman, R., & McCombs, M. (2007). The young and the agenda-less? Exploring age-related differences in agenda setting on the youngest generation, baby boomers and the civic generation. *Journalism and Mass Communication Quarterly, 84*(3), 495–508.

Colonna, L. (2005, September 27). Relevaron al jefe de la Gendarmería. *La Nación*, p. 6.

Com, S. (2005). Alfonsinismo, contexto sociopolítico y medios de comunicación. In G. Mastrini (Ed.), *Mucho ruido, pocas leyes: Economía y políticas de comunicación en la Argentina (1920–2004)* (pp. 185–210). Buenos Aires, Argentina: La Crujía.

Comisión Nacional sobre la Desaparición de Personas. (1984). *Nunca más*. Buenos Aires, Argentina: Eudeba.

Conell, C., & Cohn, S. (1995). Learning from other people's actions: Environmental variation and diffusion in French coal mining strikes, 1890–1935. *American Journal of Sociology, 101*, 366–403.

Conover, P., Searing, D., & Crewe, I. (2002). The deliberative potential of political discussion. *British Journal of Political Science, 32*, 21–62.

Cook, T. (1998). *Governing with the news*. Chicago: University of Chicago Press.

Cook, T. (2006). The news media as a political institution: Looking backward and looking forward. *Political Communication, 23,* 159–171.

Corporación Latinobarómetro. (2008). *Informe 2008.* Santiago de Chile: Author.

Cottle, S. (2003). Media organisation and production: Mapping the field. In S. Cottle (Ed.), *Media organization and production* (pp. 3–24). Thousand Oaks, CA: Sage.

Couldry, N., Livingstone, S., & Markham, T. (2006). *Media consumption and the future of public connection.* Report. London: London School of Economics and Political Science.

Couldry, N., & Markham, T. (2008). Troubled closeness or satisfied distance? Researching media consumption and public orientation. *Media, Culture and Society, 30,* 5–21.

Cowan, R. S. (1983). *More work for mother: The ironies of household technology from the open hearth to the microwave.* New York: Basic Books.

Crouse, T. (2003 [1972]). *The boys on the bus.* New York: Random House.

Curran, J., Douglas, A., & Whannel, G. (1980). The political economy of the human-interest story. In A. Smith (Ed.), *Newspapers and democracy* (pp. 288–316). Cambridge, MA: MIT Press.

D'Alessio—IROL. (2006). *Internet en la Argentina: 2005–2006.* Buenos Aires, Argentina: Eduardo D'Alessio y Asociados.

Daniels, A. (1981). Introduction to the Transaction edition. In H. Hughes (Ed.), *News and the human interest story* (pp. v–xxvi). New Brunswick, NJ: Transaction Books.

Daniels, G. L. (2006). The role of Native American print and online media in the "era of big stories": A comparative case study of Native American outlets' coverage of the Red Lake shootings. *Journalism, 7,* 321–342.

Darnton, R. (1975). Writing news and telling stories. *Daedalus, 104*(Spring), 175–194.

Davie, W. R., & Lee, J. S. (1993). Television news technology: Do more sources mean less diversity? *Journal of Broadcasting and Electronic Media, 37,* 453–464.

Davis, G., & Greve, H. (1997). Corporate elite networks and governance changes in the 1980s. *American Journal of Sociology, 103,* 1–37.

Dayan, D., & Katz, E. (1992). *Media events: The live broadcasting of history.* Cambridge, MA: Harvard University Press.

Dean, W., & Pertilla, A. (2007). "I-Teams" and "Eye Candy": The reality of local TV news. In T. Rosenstiel, M. Just, T. Belt, A. Pertilla, W. Dean, & D. Chinni (Eds.), *We interrupt this newscast: How to improve local news and win ratings, too* (pp. 30–50). New York: Cambridge University Press.

Delli Carpini, M. X., & Williams, B. (2001). Let us infotain you: Politics in the new media environment. In W. L. Bennett & R. Entman (Eds.), *Mediated politics: Communication in the future of democracy* (pp. 160–181). New York: Cambridge University Press.

Delli Carpini, M. X., & Williams, B. (2008). *And the walls came tumbling down: The eroding boundaries between news and entertainment and what it means for mediated politics in the 21st century.* Unpublished manuscript.

Denzin, N. (1979). *The research act.* New York: McGraw-Hill.

Deuze, M. (2003). The Web and its journalisms: Considering the consequences of different types of news media online. *New Media and Society, 5,* 203–230.

Deuze, M. (2005). Popular journalism and professional ideology: Tabloid reporters and editors speak out. *Media, Culture and Society, 27*(6), 861–882.

Deuze, M., Bruns, A., & Neuberger, C. (2007). Preparing for an age of participatory news. *Journalism Practice, 1,* 322–338.

Devenow, A., & Welch, I. (1996). Rational herding in financial economics. *European Economic Review, 40,* 603–615.

Diddi, A., & LaRose, R. (2006). Getting hooked on news: Uses and gratifications and the formation of news habits among college students in an Internet environment. *Journal of Broadcasting and Electronic Media, 50*(2), 193–210.

Diego se aleja de los colores de Boca por 90 minutos. (2005, November 22). *Infobae.com.* Retrieved from http://www.infobae.com/notas/nota.php?Idx= 224073&IdxSeccion=1 (now listed under the title Diego no para de sorprender: Se hará hincha de River).

DiMaggio, P., & Powell, W. (1983). The iron cage revisited: Institutional isomorphism and collective rationality in organizational fields. *American Sociological Review, 97,* 147–160.

Dimmick, J., Chen, Y., & Li, Z. (2004). Competition between the Internet and traditional news media: The gratification-opportunities niche dimension. *Journal of Media Economics, 17*(1), 19–33.

Dobrev, S. (2007). Competing in the looking-glass market: Imitation, resources, and crowding. *Strategic Management Journal, 13,* 1267–1289.

Domingo, D. (2008a). Inventing online journalism: A constructivist approach to the development of online news. In C. A. Paterson & D. Domingo (Eds.), *Making online news: The ethnography of new media production* (pp. 15–28). New York: Peter Lang.

Domingo, D. (2008b). When immediacy rules: Online journalism models in four Catalan online newsrooms. In C. A. Paterson & D. Domingo (Eds.), *Making online news: The ethnography of new media production* (pp. 113–126). New York: Peter Lang.

Donohue, T., & Glasser, T. (1978). Homogeneity in coverage of Connecticut newspapers. *Journalism Quarterly, 55*(Autumn), 592–596.

Donsbach, W. (1999). Journalism research. In H.-B. Brosius & C. Holtz-Bacha (Eds.), *German communication yearbook* (pp. 159–180). Cresskill, NJ: Hampton Press.

Douglas, M., & Isherwood, B. (1979). *The world of goods: Towards an anthropology of consumption.* New York: Routledge.

Douglas, S. (1988). *Inventing American Broadcasting, 1899–1922.* Baltimore, MD: Johns Hopkins University Press.

Drehmann, M., Oechssler, J., & Roider, A. (2005). Herding and contrarian behavior in financial markets: An Internet experiment. *American Economic Review, 95,* 1403–1426.

Dunwoody, S. (1980). The science writing inner club: A communication link between science and lay people. *Science, Technology, and Human Values, 5,* 14–22.

Dutta-Bergman, M. J. (2004). Complementarity in consumption of news types across traditional and new media. *Journal of Broadcasting and Electronic Media, 48*(1), 41–60.

Dutton, W. (2005). Continuity or transformation? Social and technical perspectives on information and communication technologies. In W. Dutton, B. Kahin, R. O'Callaghan, & A. Wyckoff (Eds.), *Transforming enterprise: The economic and social implications of information technology* (pp. 12–24). Cambridge, MA: MIT Press.

Easton, D., & Dennis, J. (1967). The child's acquisition of regime norms: Political efficacy. *American Political Science Review, 61,* 25–38.

Economic Commission for Latin America and the Caribbean. (2008). Cepalstat. Retrieved November 28, 2008, from http://www.eclac.org/estadisticas/ bases/.

Edwards, P. (1995). From "impact" to social process: Computers in society and culture. In S. Jasanoff, G. Markle, J. Petersen, & T. Pinch (Eds.), *Handbook of science and technology studies* (pp. 257–285). Thousand Oaks, CA: Sage.

Edwards, P. (2003). Infrastructure and modernity: Force, time, and social organization in the history of sociotechnical systems. In T. Misa, P. Brey, & A. Feenberg (Eds.), *Modernity and technology* (pp. 185–225). Cambridge, MA: MIT Press.

Ehrlich, M. (1996). The journalism of outrageousness: Tabloid television news vs. investigative news. *Journalism and Mass Communication Monographs, 155,* 1–24.

Eliasoph, N. (1998). *Avoiding politics: How Americans produce apathy in everyday life.* New York: Cambridge University Press.

Elsbach, K., & Kramer, R. (1996). Members' responses to organizational identity threats: Encountering and countering the *Business Weeks* rankings. *Administrative Science Quarterly, 41,* 442–476.

Erickson, B. (1996). Culture, class, and connections. *American Journal of Sociology, 102,* 217–251.

Erickson, K., & Stull, D. (1998). *Doing team ethnography.* Thousand Oaks, CA: Sage.

Espeland, W., & Sauder, M. (2007). Rankings and reactivity: How public measures recreate social worlds. *American Journal of Sociology, 113,* 1–40.

Ettema, J., & Whitney, D. C. (Eds.). (1994). *Audiencemaking: How the media create the audience.* Thousand Oaks, CA: Sage.

Feenberg, A. (1992). From information to communication: The French experience with videotex. In M. Lea (Ed.), *Contexts of computer-mediated communication* (pp. 168–187). London: Harvester-Wheatsheaf.

Ferreira, L. (2006). *Centuries of silence: The story of Latin American journalism.* Westport, CT: Praeger.

Finifter, A. (1974). The friendship group as a protective environment for political deviants. *American Political Science Review, 68,* 607–625.

Fischer, C. (1988). "Touch someone": The telephone industry discovers sociability. *Technology and Culture, 29,* 32–61.

Fischer, C. (1992). *America calling: A social history of the telephone to 1940.* Berkeley and Los Angeles, CA: University of California Press.

Fishman, M. (1980). *Manufacturing the news.* Austin: University of Texas Press.

Fligstein, N., & Dauter, L. (2007). The sociology of markets. *Annual Review of Sociology, 33,* 105–128.

Foot, K., & Schneider, S. (2006). *Web campaigning.* Cambridge, MA: MIT Press.

Fowler, J. S., & Showalter, S. W. (1974). Evening network news selection: A confirmation of news judgment. *Journalism Quarterly, 51,* 712–715.

Fox, E. (1988a). Media policies in Latin America: An overview. In E. Fox (Ed.), *Media and politics in Latin America: The struggle for democracy* (pp. 6–35). Newbury Park, CA: Sage.

Fox, E. (1988b). Nationalism, censorship, and transnational control. In E. Fox (Ed.), *Media and politics in Latin America: The struggle for democracy* (pp. 36–44). Newbury Park, CA: Sage.

Fox, E., & Waisbord, S. (2002a). Introduction. In E. Fox & S. Waisbord (Eds.), *Latin politics, global media* (pp. ix–xxii). Austin: University of Texas Press.

Fox, E., & Waisbord, S. (2002b). Latin politics, global media. In E. Fox & S. Waisbord (Eds.), *Latin politics, global media* (pp. 1–21). Austin: University of Texas Press.

Fujisaka, S., & Grayzel, J. (1978). Partnership research: A case of divergent ethnographic styles in prison fieldwork. *Human Organization, 37,* 172–179.

Galaskiewicz, J., & Wasserman, S. (1989). Mimetic processes within an inter-organizational field: An empirical test. *Administrative Science Quarterly, 34,* 454–479.

Gal-Or, E., & Dukes, A. (2003). Minimum differentiation in commercial media markets. *Journal of Economics and Management Strategy, 12,* 291–325.

Gamson, J. (1994). *Claims to fame: Celebrity in contemporary America.* Berkeley and Los Angeles: University of California Press.

Gamson, J. (2001). Normal sins: Sex scandal narratives as institutional morality tales. *Social Problems, 48,* 185–205.

Gandy, O. (2001). Dividing practices: Segmentation and targeting in the emerging public sphere. In W. L. Bennett & R. Entman (Eds.), *Mediated politics: Communication in the future of democracy* (pp. 141–159). New York: Cambridge University Press.

Gans, H. (1980). *Deciding what's news: A study of "CBS Evening News," "NBC Nightly News," "Newsweek," and "Time."* New York: Vintage.

Gans, H. (2003). *Democracy and the news.* New York: Oxford University Press.

Garay, C. (2007). Social policy and collective action: Unemployed workers, community associations, and protest in Argentina. *Politics and Society, 35,* 301–328.

García, E. (2008). Print and online newsrooms in Argentinean media: Autonomy and professional identity. In C. Paterson & D. Domingo (Eds.), *Making online news: The ethnography of new media production* (pp. 61–75). New York: Peter Lang.

García Aviles, J., & León, B. (2004). Journalists at digital television newsrooms in Britain and Spain: Workflow and multi-skilling in a competitive environment. *Journalism Studies, 5,* 87–100.

Gauntlett, D., & Hill, A. (1999). *TV living: Television, culture, and everyday life.* New York: Routledge.

Gebauer, G., & Wulf, C. (1995). *Mimesis: Culture, art, society* (D. Reneau, Trans.). Berkeley and Los Angeles: University of California Press.

Gemser, G., & Wijnberg, N. (2001). Effects of reputational sanctions on the competitive imitation of design innovations. *Organization Studies, 22,* 563–591.

Gentzkow, M., & Shapiro, J. (2006). Media bias and reputation. *Journal of Political Economy, 114,* 280–316.

Gentzkow, M., & Shapiro, J. (2007). *What drives media slant? Evidence from U.S. daily newspapers.* Cambridge, MA: National Bureau of Economic Research.

George, L., & Waldfogel, G. (2003). Who affects whom in daily newspaper markets. *Journal of Political Economy, 111,* 765–784.

Gerbner, G., Gross, G., Morgan, M., & Signorielli, N. (1994). Growing up with television: The cultivation perspective. In J. Bryant & D. Zillman (Eds.), *Media effects: Advances in theory and research* (pp. 17–42). Hillsdale, NJ: Lawrence Erlbaum.

Gibson, J. (1977). The theory of affordances. In R. Shaw & J. Bransford (Eds.), *Perceiving, acting, and knowing: Towards an ecological psychology* (pp. 67–83). Hillsdale, NJ: Lawrence Erlbaum.

Gibson, J. (1986). *The ecological approach to visual perception.* Hillsdale, NJ: Lawrence Erlbaum.

Gillmor, D. (2004). *We the media: Grassroots journalism by the people, for the people.* Sebastopol, CA: O'Reilly.

Girard, R. (1966). *Deceit, desire, and the novel* (Y. Freccero, Trans.). Baltimore, MD: Johns Hopkins University Press.

Glasser, T. (1992). Professionalism and the derision of diversity: The case of the education of journalists. *Journal of Communication, 42,* 131–140.

Goldsmith, B. (2005). *Imitation in international relations: Observational learning, analogies, and foreign policy in Russia and Ukraine.* New York: Palgrave.

Graber, D. (1971). The press as public opinion resource during the 1968 presidential campaign. *Public Opinion Quarterly, 35,* 162–182.

Graber, D. (1984). *Processing the news: How people tame the information tide* (2nd ed.). White Plains, NY: Longman.

Greve, H. (1996). Patterns of competition: The diffusion of a market position in radio broadcasting. *Administrative Science Quarterly, 41,* 29–60.

Greve, H. (1998). Managerial cognition and the mimetic adoption of market positions: What you see is what you do. *Strategic Management Journal, 19,* 967–988.

Grimson, A., & Kessler, G. (2005). *On Argentina and the Southern Cone: Neoliberalism and national imaginations.* New York: Routledge.

Grindstaff, L. (2002). *The money shot: Trash, class, and the making of TV talk shows.* Chicago: University of Chicago Press.

Guillen, M. (2002). Structural inertia, imitation, and foreign expansion: South Korean firms and business groups in China, 1987–95. *Academy of Management Journal, 3,* 509–525.

Haas, T. (2005). From "public journalism" to the "public's journalism"? Rhetoric and reality in the discourse on weblogs. *Journalism Studies, 6*(3), 387–396.

Hagen, I. (1994). The ambivalence of TV news viewing: Between ideals and everyday practices. *European Journal of Communication, 9,* 193–220.

Hall, S. (1980). Encoding/decoding. In S. Hall & D. Hobson (Eds.), *Culture, media and language* (pp. 128–138). London: Hutchinson.

Hallin, D., & Mancini, P. (2004). *Comparing media systems.* New York: Cambridge University Press.

Hallin, D., & Papathanassopoulos, S. (2002). Political clientelism and the media: Southern Europe and Latin America in comparative perspective. *Media, Culture and Society, 24,* 175–195.

Halliwell, S. (2002). *The aesthetics of mimesis.* Princeton, NJ: Princeton University Press.

Halloran, J., Elliot, P., & Murdock, G. (1970). *Demonstrations and communication: A case study.* Harmondsworth, UK: Penguin Books.

Halperín, J. (2007). *Noticias del poder: Buenas y malas artes del periodismo político.* Buenos Aires, Argentina: Aguilar.

Hamilton, J. (2004). *All the news that's fit to sell.* Princeton, NJ: Princeton University Press.

Hampton, K. (2007). Neighborhoods in the network society: The e-neighbors study. *Information, Communication and Society, 10,* 714–748.

Hampton, K., & Wellman, B. (2003). Neighboring in Netville: How the Internet supports community and social capital in a wired suburb. *City and Community, 2*(4), 277–311.

Hasebrink, U., & Paus-Hasebrink, I. (2007). Young people's identity construction and patterns of media use and participation in Germany and Austria. In P. Dahlgren (Ed.), *Young citizens and new media: Learning for democratic participation* (pp. 81–101). New York: Routledge.

Hasty, J. (2006). Performing power, composing culture: The state press in Ghana. *Ethnography, 7,* 69–98.

Haunschild, P. (1993). Interorganizational imitation: The impact of interlocks on corporate acquisition activity. *Administrative Science Quarterly, 38,* 564–592.

Haunschild, P., & Beckman, C. (1998). When do interlocks matter? Alternate sources of information and interlock influence. *Administrative Science Quarterly, 43,* 815–844.

Haunschild, P., & Miner, A. (1997). Modes of interorganizational imitation: The effects of outcome salience and uncertainty. *Administrative Science Quarterly, 42,* 472–500.

Haveman, H. (1993). Follow the leader: Mimetic isomorphism and entry into new markets. *Administrative Science Quarterly, 38,* 593–627.

Heath, C., & Luff, P. (2000). *Technology in action.* Cambridge: Cambridge University Press.

Herring, S. C., Scheidt, L. A., Bonus, S., & Wright, E. (2005). Weblogs as a bridging genre. *Information, Technology, and People, 18*(2), 142–171.

Hicks, R., & Featherstone, J. (1978). Duplication of newspaper content in contrasting ownership situations. *Journalism Quarterly, 55,* 549–569.

Hindman, M. (2009). *The myth of digital democracy.* Princeton, NJ: Princeton University Press.

Hotelling, H. (1929). Stability in competition. *Economic Journal, 34,* 41–57.

Huesmann, L. R., Moise-Titus, J., Podolski, C.-L., & Eron, L. (2003). Longitudinal relations between children's exposure to TV violence and their aggressive and violent behavior in young adulthood: 1977–1992. *Developmental Psychology, 39,* 201–221.

Hughes, H. (1981). *News and the human interest story.* New Brunswick, NJ: Transaction.

Hughes, S. (2006). *Newsrooms in conflict.* Pittsburgh, PA: University of Pittsburgh Press.

Hujanen, J., & Pietikainen, S. (2004). Interactive uses of journalism: Crossing between technological potential and young people's news-using practices. *New Media and Society, 6*(3), 383–401.

Hurley, S., & Chater, N. (Eds.). (2005a). *Perspectives on imitation from neuroscience to social science: Vol. 2. Imitation, human development, and culture.* Cambridge, MA: MIT Press.

Hurley, S., & Chater, N. (Eds.). (2005b). *Perspectives on imitation from neuroscience to social science: Vol. 1. Mechanisms of imitation and imitation in animals.* Cambridge, MA: MIT Press.

Instituto Nacional de Estadísticas y Censos. (2008). *Población—composición y distribución: Censo 2001.* Retrieved November 28, 2008, from http://www.indec.mecon.ar/default.htm.

Instituto Verificador de Circulaciones. (2006). *IVC online datos gratuitos.* Retrieved June 8, 2006, from http://www.ivc.com.ar/consulta.

Internet Advertising Bureau—Argentina. (2006a). *El IAB publica ranking de audience de sitios de Internet de Agosto.* Retrieved March 22, 2008, from http://www.iabargentina.com.ar/metricas_agosto_06.php.

Internet Advertising Bureau—Argentina. (2006b). *El IAB publica ranking de audience de sitios de Internet de Septiembre.* Retrieved March 22, 2008, from http://www.iabargentina.com.ar/metricas_septiembre_06.php.

Internet Advertising Bureau—Argentina. (2007). *Métricas: Usuarios de Internet.* Retrieved March 22, 2008, from http://www.iabargentina.com.ar/metricas-usua.php.

Jackson, S., Edwards, P., Bowker, G., & Knobel, C. (2007). Understanding infrastructure: History, heuristics, and cyberinfrastructure policy. *First Monday, 12*(6). Retrieved October 24, 2007, from http://firstmonday.org/issues/issue12_6/jackson/index.html.

Jamieson, K. H., & Campbell, K. K. (1983). *The interplay of influence: Mass media and their publics in news, advertising, politics.* Belmont, CA: Wadsworth.

Jamieson, K. H., & Cappella, J. (2008). *Echo chamber: Rush Limbaugh and the conservative media establishment.* New York: Oxford University Press.

Jamieson, P., Jamieson, K., & Romer, D. (2003). The responsible reporting of suicide in print journalism. *American Behavioral Scientist, 46,* 1643–1660.

Jenkins, H. (1992). *Textual poachers: Television fans and participatory culture.* New York: Routledge.

Jenkins, H. (2006). *Convergence culture: Where old and new media collide.* New York: New York University Press.

Jensen, K. B. (1990). The politics of polysemy: Television news, everyday consciousness and political action. *Media, Culture and Society, 12,* 57–77.

Jenson, D. (2001). *Trauma and its representations: The social life of mimesis in postrevolutionary France.* Baltimore, MD: Johns Hopkins University Press.

Journalism.org. (2006). *The state of the news media.* Project for Excellence in Journalism. Retrieved June 9, 2006, from http://www.stateofthemedia.org/2006/.

Journalism.org. (2007). *The state of the news media.* Project for Excellence in Journalism. Retrieved November 27, 2007, from http://www.stateofthemedia.org/2007/.

Journalism.org. (2008). *The state of the news media.* Project for Excellence in Journalism. Retrieved May 5, 2008, from http://www.stateofthemedia.org/2008/.

Journalism.org. (2009). *The state of the news media.* Project for Excellence in Journalism. Retrieved June 1, 2009, from http://www.stateofthemedia.org/2009/.

Journalism.org. (2010). *How news happens: A study of the news ecosystem of one American city.* Project for the Excellence in Journalism. Retrieve January 28, 2010, from http://www.journalism.org/sites/journalism.org/files/Baltimore%20Study_Jan2010_0.pdf.

Kaid, L. L., McKinney, M. S., & Tedesco, J. C. (2007). Political information efficacy and young voters. *American Behavioral Scientist, 50*(9), 1093–1111.

Katz, E. (1996). And deliver us from segmentation. *Annals of the American Academy of Political and Social Science, 546,* 22–33.

Katz, E. (2006). Rediscovering Gabriel Tarde. *Political Communication, 23,* 263–270.

Katz, E., Blumler, J., & Gurevitch, M. (1974). Utilization of mass communication by the individual. In J. Blumler & E. Katz (Eds.), *The uses of mass communications: Current perspectives on gratifications research* (pp. 19–32). Beverly Hills, CA: Sage.

Kenski, K., & Stroud, N. J. (2006). Connections between Internet use and political efficacy, knowledge, and participation. *Journal of Broadcasting and Electronic Media, 50*(2), 173–192.

Keynes, J. (1964). *The general theory of employment, interest, and money.* New York: Harcourt, Brace & World.

Kiernan, V. (2003). Embargoes and science news. *Journalism and Mass Communication Quarterly, 80,* 903–920.

Kline, R. (2000). *Consumers in the country: Technology and social change in rural America.* Baltimore, MD: Johns Hopkins University Press.

Klinenberg, E. (2002). *Heat wave.* Chicago: University of Chicago Press.

Klinenberg, E. (2005). Convergence: News production in a digital age. *Annals of the American Academy of Political and Social Science, 597,* 48–64.

Klinenberg, E. (2007). *Fighting for air: The battle to control America's media.* New York: Metropolitan Books.

Kling, R. (1994). Reading "all about" computerization: How genre conventions shape nonfiction social analysis. *Information Society, 10,* 147–172.

Knorr Cetina, K. (2003). From pipes to scopes: The flow architecture of financial markets. *Distinktion, 7,* 7–23.

Knorr Cetina, K. (2005). Complex global microstructures. *Theory, Culture and Society, 22,* 213–234.

Knorr Cetina, K., & Bruegger, U. (2002). Global microstructures: The virtual societies of financial markets. *American Journal of Sociology, 107,* 905–950.

Knorr Cetina, K., & Grimpe, B. (2008). Global financial technologies: Scoping systems that raise the world. In T. Pinch & R. Swedberg (Eds.), *Technology and economic sociology* (pp. 161–190). Cambridge, MA: MIT Press.

Knorr Cetina, K., & Preda, A. (2007). The temporalization of financial markets: From network to flow. *Annual Review of Theory, Culture, and Society, 24,* 116–138.

Korczynski, M. (2003). Music at work: Towards a historical overview. *Folk Music Journal, 8,* 314–334.

Korczynski, M. (2007). Music and meaning on the factory floor. *Work and Occupations, 34,* 253–289.

Labianca, G., & Fairbank, J. (2005). Interorganizational monitoring: Processes, choices, and outcomes. *Advances in Strategic Management, 22,* 117–150.

Lacoue-Labarthe, P. (1989). *Typography: Mimesis, philosophy, politics.* Cambridge, MA: Harvard University Press.

Lacy, S. (1987). The effect of intracity competition on daily newspaper content. *Journalism Quarterly, 64,* 281–301.

Lacy, S. (1991). Effects of group ownership on daily newspaper content. *Journal of Media Economics, 4,* 35–47.

Lakoff, A. (2005). *Pharmaceutical reason: Knowledge and value in global psychiatry.* New York: Cambridge University Press.

Lanacion.com. (2006). *Novedades: Les detallamos los números de Septiembre.* Retrieved October 20, 2006, from www.lanacion.com.ar.

Landi, O. (1988). Media, cultural processes, and political systems. In E. Fox (Ed.), *Media and politics in Latin America: The struggle for democracy* (pp. 138–147). Newbury Park, CA: Sage.

Latour, B. (2002). Gabriel Tarde and the end of the social. In P. Joyce (Ed.), *The social in question: New bearings in history and the social sciences* (pp. 117–132). London: Routledge.

Latour, B. (2005). *Reassembling the social: An introduction to actor-network theory.* New York: Oxford University Press.

Lavagna dice que no es imprescindible un acuerdo con el FMI. (2005, November 9). *Lanacion.com.* Retrieved November 9, 2005, from http://www.lanacion .com.ar/nota.asp?nota_id=754940&high=Lavagna.

Lavagna dijo que un acuerdo con el FMI "no es imprescindible." (2005, November 9). *Clarín.com.* Retrieved November 9, 2005, from http://www.clarín .com/diario/2005/11/09/um/m-01086694.htm.

Lavieri, O. (1996). The media in Argentina: Struggling with the absence of a democratic tradition. In R. Cole (Ed.), *Communication in Latin America: Journalism, mass media, and society* (pp. 183–198). Wilmington, DE: Scholarly Resources.

Lawrence, R. (2006). Seeing the whole board: New institutional analysis of news content. *Political Communication, 23,* 225–230.

Lawson, C. (2002). *Building the fourth estate: Democratization and the rise of a free press in Mexico.* Berkeley and Los Angeles: University of California Press.

Lawson-Borders, G. (2006). *Media organizations and convergence: Case studies of media convergence pioneers.* Mahwah, NJ: Lawrence Erlbaum.

Lazarsfeld, P., & Merton, R. (1948). Mass communication, popular taste, and organized social action. In L. Bryson (Ed.), *The communication of ideas* (pp. 95–118). New York: Harper.

Lee, J. K. (2007). The effect of the Internet on homogeneity of the media agenda: A test of the fragmentation thesis. *Journalism and Mass Communication Quarterly, 84,* 745–760.

Lemert, J. B. (1974). Content duplication by the networks in competing evening newscasts. *Journalism Quarterly, 51,* 238–244.

Levin, R., Klevorick, A., Nelson, R., & Winter, S. (1987). Appropriating the returns from industrial research. *Brooking Papers on Economic Activity, 3,* 783–820.

Levitsky, S. (2005). Argentina: Democratic survival amidst economic failure. In F. Hagopian & S. Mainwaring (Eds.), *The third wave of democratization in Latin America: Advances and setbacks* (pp. 63–89). New York: Cambridge University Press.

Levitsky, S., & Murillo, M. V. (2005a). Building castles in the sand? The politics of institutional weakness in Argentina. In S. Levitsky & M. V. Murillo (Eds.), *Argentine democracy: The politics of institutional weakness* (pp. 21–44). University Park: Pennsylvania State University Press.

Levitsky, S., & Murillo, M. V. (2005b). Introduction. In S. Levitsky & M. V. Murillo (Eds.), *Argentine democracy: The politics of institutional weakness* (pp. 1–17). University Park: Pennsylvania State University Press.

Levitsky, S., & Murillo, M. V. (2005c). Theorizing about weak institutions: Lessons from the Argentine case. In S. Levitsky & M. V. Murillo (Eds.), *Argentine democracy: The politics of institutional weakness* (pp. 268–289). University Park: Pennsylvania State University Press.

Levitsky, S., & Murillo, M. V. (2009). Variations in institutional strength. *Annual Review of Political Science, 12,* 115–133.

Lieberman, M., & Asaba, S. (2006). Why do firms imitate each other? *Academy of Management Review, 31,* 366–385.

Liebes, T., & Katz, E. (1990). *The export of meaning: Cross-cultural readings of Dallas.* New York: Oxford University Press.

Lin, C., Salwen, M. B., Garrison, B., & Driscoll, P. D. (2005). Online news as a functional substitute for offline news. In M. B. Salwen, B. Garrison, & P. D. Driscoll (Eds.), *Online news and the public* (pp. 237–255). Mahwah, NJ: Lawrence Erlbaum.

Ling, R. (2008). *New tech, new ties: How mobile communication is reshaping social cohesion.* Cambridge, MA: MIT Press.

Livingstone, S., & Markham, T. (2008). The contribution of media consumption to civic participation. *British Journal of Sociology, 59*(2), 351–371.

Lofland, J., & Lofland, H. (1984). *Analyzing social settings* (2nd ed.). Belmont, CA: Wadsworth.

Lowrey, W. (2006). Mapping the journalism-blogging relationship. *Journalism, 7*(4), 477–500.

Lowrey, W., & Latta, J. (2008). The routines of blogging. In C. A. Paterson and D. Domingo (Eds.), *Making online news: The ethnography of online news production.* New York: Peter Lang.

Luchessi, L. (2008). Politics and media in the 2007 Argentine presidential election. *Press/Politics, 13,* 345–351.

Lull, J. (1980). The social uses of television. *Human Communication Research, 6,* 197–209.

Lull, J. (1982). How families select television programs: A mass-observational study. *Journal of Broadcasting and Electronic Media, 26,* 801–811.

MacGregor, P. (2007). Tracking the online audience. *Journalism Studies, 8*(2), 280–298.

Mackay, H., Carne, C., Beynon-Davies, P., & Tudhope, D. (2000). Reconfiguring the user: Using rapid application development. *Social Studies of Science, 30,* 737–757.

MacKenzie, D. (1984). Marx and the machine. *Technology and Culture, 25,* 473–502.

MacKenzie, D. (2006). *An engine, not a camera: How financial models shape markets.* Cambridge, MA: MIT Press.

Malharro, M., & D. López-Gijsberts (2003). *La tipografía de plomo: Los grandes medios gráficos en la Argentina y su political editorial durante 1976–1983.* La Plata, Argentina: EPC Medios.

Manski, C. (2000). Economic analysis of social interactions. *Journal of Economic Perspectives, 14*(3), 115–136.

Maradona: "El domingo voy a hinchar por River." (2005, November 22). *Clarín. com.* Retrieved November 22, 2005, from http://www.clarín.com/diario/2005/11/22/um/m-01094457.htm.

Marley, C. (2007). Metaphors of identity in dating ads and newspaper articles. *Text and Talk, 27,* 55–78.

Martin, M. (1991). *"Hello Central?" Gender, technology and culture in the formation of telephone systems.* Montreal: McGill-Queen's University Press.

Martin, V. B. (2008). Attending the news: A grounded theory about a daily regimen. *Journalism, 9,* 76–94.

Martini, S., & Luchessi, L. (2004). *Los que hacen la noticia: Periodismo, información y poder.* Buenos Aires, Argentina: Biblos.

Marvin, C. (1988). *When old technologies were new: Thinking about electric communication in the late nineteenth century.* New York: Oxford University Press.

Mastrini, G., & Becerra, M. (2006). Periodistas y magnates: Estructura y concentración de las industrias culturales en América Latina. Buenos Aires, Argentina: Prometeo.

Mazharul Haque, S. M. (1986). News content homogeneity in elite Indian dailies. *Journalism Quarterly, 63*(4), 827–833.

McManus, J. (1994). *Market-driven journalism: Let the citizen beware?* Thousand Oaks, CA: Sage.

Miceli, W., & Belinche, M. (2002). *Los procesos de edición periodística en los medios gráficos: El caso Clarín.* La Plata, Argentina: Ediciones de Periodismo y Comunicación.

Mills, C. W. (1951). *White collar: The American middle classes.* New York: Oxford University Press.

Mindich, D. (2005). *Tuned out: Why Americans under 40 don't follow the news.* New York: Oxford University Press.

Mitchelstein, E., & Boczkowski, P. (2009). Between tradition and change: A review of recent research on online news production. *Journalism: Theory, Practice, and Criticism, 10,* 562–568.

Morley, D. (1992). *Television, audiences and cultural studies.* London: Routledge.

Mullainathan, S., & Shleifer, A. (2005). The market for news. *American Economic Review, 95,* 1031–1053.

Muraro, H. (1988). Dictatorship and transition to democracy: Argentina, 1973–86. In E. Fox (Ed.), *Media and politics in Latin America: The struggle for democracy* (pp. 116–124). Newbury Park, CA: Sage.

Mustapic, A. (2005). Inestabilidad sin colapso. La renuncia de los presidentes: Argentina en el año 2001. *Desarrollo económico, 45,* 263–280.

Mutz, D. (2006). *Hearing the other side: Deliberative versus participatory democracy.* New York: Cambridge University Press.

Mutz, D., & Mondak, J. (2006). The workplace as a context for cross-cutting political discourse. *Journal of Politics, 68*(1), 140–155.

Napoli, P. (1999). Deconstructing the diversity principle. *Journal of Communication, 49,* 7–34.

Natarajan, K., & Xiaoming, H. (2003). An Asian voice? A comparative study of Channel News Asia and CNN. *Journal of Communication, 53,* 300–314.

Neuman, W. R. (1991). *The future of the mass audience.* Cambridge: Cambridge University Press.

Neuman, W. R. (2001). The impact of the new media. In W. L. Bennett & R. Entman (Eds.), *Mediated politics: Communication and the future of democracy* (pp. 299–320). New York: Cambridge University Press.

Neuman, W. R. (2009, August 7–11). The flow of mediated culture: Trends in supply and demand, 1960–2005. Paper presented at the annual meeting of the American Sociological Association, San Francisco, CA.

Nielsen (2008). Nov. 2008: U.S. news sites see post-election growth. Retrieved April 30, 2009, from http://blog.nielsen.com/nielsenwire/online_mobile/nov-2008-us-news-sites-see-post-election-growth/#more-6425.

Niemi, R., Craig, S., & Mattei, F. (1991). Measuring internal political efficacy in the 1988 National Election Study. *American Political Science Review, 85,* 1407–1413.

Nippert-Eng, C. (1995). *Home and work.* Chicago: University of Chicago Press.

Noelle-Neumann, E. (1973). Return to the concept of powerful mass media. *Studies of Broadcasting, 9*(Spring), 67–112.

Noelle-Neumann, E. (1993). *The spiral of silence: Public opinion—our social skin* (2nd ed.). Chicago: University of Chicago Press.

Noelle-Neumann, E., & Mathes, R. (1987). The "event as event" and the "event as news": The significance of consonance for media effects research. *European Journal of Communication, 2,* 392–414.

Norman, D. (1988). *The psychology of everyday things.* New York: Basic Books.

Norman, D. (1993). *Things that make us smart: Defending human attributes in the age of the machine.* Reading, MA: Addison-Wesley.

Norris, P. (2000). *A virtuous circle.* Cambridge: Cambridge University Press.

O'Donnell, M. (1998). Horizontal accountability in new democracies. *Journal of Democracy, 9,* 112–126.

O'Donnell, M. (2007). *Propaganda K: Una maquinaria de promoción con el dinero del estado.* Buenos Aires, Argentina: Planeta.

Ogan, C. L., Ozakca, M., & Groshek, J. (2008). Embedding the Internet in the lives of college students: Online and offline behavior. *Social Science Computer Review, 26*(2), 170–177.

Online Publishers Association—Europe. (2007). *OPA Europe Internet use at work media consumption study 2007.* Paris: Author.

Open Society Institute. (2005). *Buying the news: A report on financial and indirect censorship in Argentina.* New York: Author.

Orlikowski, W. (1992). The duality of technology: Rethinking the concept of technology in organizations. *Organization Science, 3,* 397–427.

Orlikowski, W. (2000). Using technology and constituting structures: A practice lens for studying technology in organizations. *Organization Science, 11,* 404–428.

Ornebring, H. (2008). The consumer as a producer of what? *Journalism Studies, 9,* 771–785.

Orvell, M. (1989). *The real thing: Imitation and authenticity in American culture, 1880–1940.* Chapel Hill: University of North Carolina Press.

Ottaviani, M., & Sorensen, P. (2000). Herd behavior and investment: Comment. *American Economic Review, 90,* 695–704.

Oudshoorn, N., & Pinch, T. (2003). Introduction: How users and non-users matter. In N. Ousdhoorn & T. Pinch (Eds.), *How users matter: The co-construction of users and technologies* (pp. 1–25). Cambridge, MA: MIT Press.

Paik, H., & Comstock, G. (1994). The effects of television violence on antisocial behavior: A meta-analysis. *Communication Research, 21,* 516–546.

Palmgreen, P., Wenner, L., & Rayburn II, J. D. (1980). Relations between gratifications sought and obtained: A study of television news. *Communication Research, 7,* 161–192.

Papacharissi, Z. (2007). The blogger revolution? Audiences as media producers: Content analysis of 260 blogs. In M. Tremayne (Ed.), *Blogging, citizenship, and the future of media* (pp. 21–38). New York: Routledge.

Park, R. (1981 [1940]). Introduction. In H. Hughes, *News and the human interest story.* New Brunswick, NJ: Transaction.

Patterson, T. (2000). Doing well and doing good: How soft news and critical journalism are shrinking the news audience and weakening democracy—and what news outlets can do about it. Unpublished manuscript, Cambridge, MA.

Pavlik, J. (2000). The impact of technology on journalism. *Journalism Studies, 1,* 229–237.

Pavlik, J. (2001). *Journalism and new media.* New York: Columbia University Press.

Pazos, N., Santoro, D., & Viceconte, A. (1995, October 18). Piden que finalice el embargo commercial de EE.UU. a Cuba. *Clarín,* pp. 2–3.

Pea, R. (1993). Practices of distributed intelligence and designs for education. In G. Salomon (Ed.), *Distributed cognitions: Psychological and educational considerations* (pp. 47–87). Cambridge: Cambridge University Press.

Pérez-Peña, R. (2007, December 14). News Corp. completes takeover of Dow Jones. *New York Times.* Retrieved December 29, 2008, from http://www.nytimes.com/2007/12/14/business/media/14dow.html?scp=1&sq=news+corp+%2B+dow+jones&st=nyt.

Perlman, M. (1970). The comparative method: The single investigator and the team approach. In R. Narroll & R. Cohen (Eds.), *A handbook of method in cultural anthropology* (pp. 353–365). New York: Columbia University Press.

Peruzzotti, E. (2005). Demanding accountable government: Citizens, politicians, and the perils of representative democracy in Argentina. In S. Levitsky & M. V. Murillo (Eds.), *Argentine democracy: The politics of institutional weakness* (pp. 229–249). University Park: Pennsylvania State University Press.

Peruzzotti, E., & Smulovitz, C. (2006). Social accountability: An introduction. In E. Peruzzotti & C. Smulovitz (Eds.), *Enforcing the rule of law: Social accountability in the new Latin American democracies* (pp. 3–33). Pittsburgh, PA: University of Pittsburgh Press.

Pew. (2008a). *Networked workers*. Washington, DC: Pew Internet and American Life Project.

Pew. (2008b). *Pew Research Center Biennial News Consumption Survey*. Washington, DC: Pew Research Center for the People and the Press.

Pfaffenberger, B. (1989). The social meaning of the personal computer: Or, why the personal computer revolution was no revolution. *Anthropological Quarterly, 61*, 39–47.

Pinch, T., & Swedberg, R. (2008). Introduction. In T. Pinch & R. Swedberg (Eds.), *Living in a material world: Economic sociology meets science and technology studies* (pp. 1–26). Cambridge, MA: MIT Press.

Pinch, T., & Trocco, F. (2002). *Analog days: The invention and impact of the Moog synthesizer*. Cambridge, MA: Harvard University Press.

Pirkis, J., Burgess, P., Francis, C., Blood, R., & Jolley, D. (2006). The relationship between media reporting of suicide and actual suicide in Australia. *Social Science and Medicine, 62*, 2874–2886.

Plasser, F. (2005). From hard to soft news standards? How political journalists in different media systems evaluate the shifting quality of news. *Press/Politics, 10*(2), 47–68.

Ponce de Leon, C. (2002). *Self-exposure: Human-interest journalism and the emergence of celebrity in America, 1890–1940*. Chapel Hill: University of North Carolina Press.

Postolski, G., & Marino, S. (2005). Relaciones peligrosas: Los medios y la dictadura entre el control, la censura y los negocios. In G. Mastrini (Ed.), *Mucho ruido, pocas leyes: Economía y políticas de comunicación en la Argentina (1920–2004)* (pp. 155–184). Buenos Aires, Argentina: La Crujía.

Poynter Online. (2008). Tag search results for layoffs/buyouts/staff+cuts. *Poynter .org*. Retrieved December 29, 2008, from http://www.poynter.org/search/category.asp?k=Layoffs%2Fbuyouts%2Fstaff+cuts.

Prior, M. (2002). Any good news in soft news? The impact of soft news preference on political knowledge. *Political Communication, 20*, 149–171.

Prior, M. (2007). *Post-broadcast democracy*. Cambridge: Cambridge University Press.

Pritchard, J. (2007, May 10). Calif. Web site outsources reporting. *SFGate.com*. Retrieved May 14, 2007, from http://sfgate.com/cgi-bin/article.cgi?f=/n/a/2007/05/10/financial/f113814D68.DTL.

Putnam, R. (2000). *Bowling alone: The collapse and revival of American community*. New York: Simon & Schuster.

Quandt, T. (2008). News tuning and content management: An observation study of old and new routines in German online newsrooms In C. A. Paterson & D. Domingo (Eds.), *Making online news: The ethnography of new media production* (pp. 77–97). New York: Peter Lang.

Radway, J. (1991). *Reading the romance: Women, patriarchy, and popular literature* (2nd ed.). Chapel Hill: University of North Carolina Press.

Rao, H., Greve, H., & Davis, G. (2001). Fool's gold: Social proof in the initiation and abandonment of coverage by Wall Street analysts. *Administrative Science Quarterly, 46*, 502–526.

Reese, S. D., Rutigliano, L., Hyun, K., & Jeong, J. (2007). Mapping the blogosphere: Professional and citizen-based media in the global news arena. *Journalism, 8*(3), 235–261.

Reinemann, C. (2004). Routine reliance revisited: Exploring media importance for German political journalists. *Journalism and Mass Communication Quarterly, 81*, 857–876.

Reinoso, S. (2007, February 4). Los periodistas ya no son intermediarios necesarios. *La Nación*, Enfoques Section, p. 1.

Rhee, M., Kim, Y.-C., & Han, J. (2006). Confidence in imitation: Niche-width strategy in the UK automobile industry. *Management Science, 52*, 501–513.

Rice, R., & Gattiker, U. (2001). New media and organizational structuring. In F. Jablin & L. Putnam (Eds.), *The new handbook of organizational communication: Advances in theory, research, and methods* (pp. 544–581). Thousand Oaks, CA: Sage.

Rivkin, J. (2000). Imitation of complex strategies. *Management Science, 46*, 824–844.

Roa, R. (2007, December 4). La redacción definida por el contenido. Paper presented at the seminar "Convergence: The new multimedia newsroom," Inter-American Press Association, Miami, FL.

Robinson, J. P., & Levy, M. (1986). Interpersonal communication and news comprehension. *Public Opinion Quarterly, 50*, 160–175.

Romero, L. A. (2002). *A history of Argentina in the twentieth century* (J. Brennan, Trans.). University Park: Pennsylvania State University Press.

Rosenberg, M. (1955). Determinants of political apathy. *Public Opinion Quarterly, 18*, 349–366.

Rosenkopf, L., & Tushman, M. (1994). The coevolution of technology and organization. In J. Baum & J. Singh (Eds.), *Evolutionary dynamics of organizations* (pp. 403–424). New York: Oxford University Press.

Rosenstiel, T. (2005). Political polling and the new media culture: A case of more being less. *Public Opinion Quarterly, 69*, 698–715.

Rossi, D. (2005). La radiodifusión entre 1990–1995: Exacerbación del modelo privado-comercial. In G. Mastrini (Ed.), *Mucho ruido, pocas leyes: Economía y políticas de comunicación en la Argentina (1920–2004)* (pp. 235–255). Buenos Aires, Argentina: La Crujía.

Sahlins, M. (1976). *Culture and practical reason.* Chicago: University of Chicago Press.

Sauder, M., & Lancaster, R. (2006). Do rankings matter? The effects of *U.S. News & World Report* rankings on the admissions process of law schools. *Law and Society Review, 40,* 105–134.

Scharfstein, D., & Stein, J. (1990). Herd behavior and investment. *American Economic Review, 80,* 465–479.

Scharfstein, D., & Stein, J. (2000). Herd behavior and investment: Reply. *American Economic Review, 90,* 705–706.

Scheufele, D. A., & Nisbet, M. C. (2002). Being a citizen online: New opportunities and dead ends. *Harvard International Journal of Press-Politics, 7*(3), 55–75.

Schiffer, A. J. (2006). Blogswarms and press norms: News coverage of the Downing Street Memo controversy. *Journalism and Mass Communication Quarterly, 83*(3), 494–510.

Schifferes, S., Ward, S., & Lusoli, W. (2007). What's the story . . . ? Online news consumption in the 2005 UK election. Unpublished manuscript.

Schiller, D. (1981). *Objectivity and the news.* Philadelphia: University of Pennsylvania Press.

Schiller, H. (1973). *The mind managers.* Boston: Beacon Press.

Schoenbach, K., de Waal, E., & Lauf, E. (2005). Research note: Online and print newspapers—their impact on the extent of the perceived public agenda. *European Journal of Communication, 20*(2), 245–258.

Schudson, M. (1978). *Discovering the news.* New York: Basic Books.

Schudson, M. (1986). Deadlines, datelines, and history. In R. Manoff & M. Schudson (Eds.), *Reading the news* (pp. 79–108). New York: Pantheon.

Schudson, M. (2003). *The sociology of news.* New York: W. W. Norton.

Schwoch, J. (1993). Broadcast media and Latin American politics: The historical context. In T. Skidmore (Ed.), *Television, politics, and the transition to democracy in Latin America* (pp. 38–54). Baltimore, MD: Johns Hopkins University Press.

Scott, D., & Gobetz, R. (1992). Hard news/soft news content of the national broadcast networks, 1972–1987. *Journalism Quarterly, 69*(2), 406–412.

Scott, W. R. (2001). *Institutions and organizations* (2nd ed.). Thousand Oaks, CA: Sage.

Shoemaker, P., & Cohen, A. (Eds.). (2006). *News around the world.* New York: Routledge.

Shoemaker, P., & Reese, S. (1996). *Mediating the message: Theories of influences on mass media content.* New York: Longman.

Sidicaro, R. (1993). *La política mirada desde arriba: Las ideas del diario "La nación," 1909–1989.* Buenos Aires, Argentina: Sudamericana.

Silverstone, R. (1994). *Television and everyday life.* London: Routledge.

Silverstone, R., & Haddon, L. (1996). Design and domestication of information and communication technologies: Technical change and everyday life. In R. Mansell & R. Silverstone (Eds.), *Communication by design: The politics of information and communication technologies* (pp. 44–74). New York: Oxford University Press.

Skidmore, T. (1993). Politics and the media in a democratizing Latin America. In T. Skidmore (Ed.), *Television, politics, and the transition to democracy in Latin America* (pp. 1–22). Baltimore, MD: Johns Hopkins University Press.

Slack, J. D., & Wise, J. M. (2002) Cultural studies and technology. In L. A. Lievrouw & S. Livingstone (Eds.). *The handbook of new media: Social shaping and consequences of ICTs* (pp. 485–501). London: Sage.

Smith, F. L. (1990). *Perspectives on radio and television* (3rd ed.). New York: Harper & Row.

Sousa, H. (2006). Information technologies, social change and the future: The case of online journalism in Portugal. *European Journal of Communication, 21,* 373–387.

Sparks, C. (2000). The panic over tabloid news. In C. Sparks & J. Tulloch (Eds.), *Tabloid tales: Global debates over media standards* (pp. 1–40). Lanham, MD: Rowman & Littlefield.

Spence, M. (1976). Product differentiation and welfare. *American Economic Review, 66,* 407–414.

Spence, M., & Owen, B. (1977). Television programming, monopolistic competition, and welfare. *Quarterly Journal of Economics, 91,* 103–126.

Spigel, L. (1992). *Make room for TV: Television and the family ideal in postwar America.* Chicago: University of Chicago Press.

Spragens, W. (1995). *Electronic magazines.* Westport, CT: Praeger.

Sproull, L., & Kiesler, S. (1991). *Connections: New ways of working in the networked organization.* Cambridge, MA: MIT Press.

Stack, S. (2000). Media impacts on suicide: A quantitative review of 293 findings. *Social Science Quarterly, 81,* 957–971.

Stahlberg, P. (2006). On the journalist beat in India: Encounters with the near familiar. *Ethnography, 7,* 47–67.

Standard and Poor's. (2005). *Arte Grafico Editorial Argentino S.A.: Rating report.* Buenos Aires, Argentina: Author.

Star, S. L., & Bowker, G. (2002). How to infrastructure. In L. Lievrouw & S. Livingstone (Eds.), *Handbook of new media* (pp. 151–162). London: Sage.

Star, S. L., & Ruhleder, K. (1996). Steps toward an ecology of infrastructure: Design and access for large information spaces. *Information Systems Research, 7,* 111–134.

Stark, D. (2009). *The sense of dissonance: Accounts of worth in economic life.* Princeton, NJ: Princeton University Press.

Staudenmaier, J. (1989). *Technology's storytellers: Reweaving the human fabric.* Cambridge, MA: MIT Press.

Steiner, P. (1952). Program patterns and preferences, and the workability of competition in radio broadcasting. *Quarterly Journal of Economics, 66,* 194–223.

Strang, D., & Macy, M. (2001). In search of excellence: Fads, success stories, and adaptive emulation. *American Journal of Sociology, 107,* 147–182.

Strauss, A., & Corbin, J. (1990). *Basics of qualitative research.* Newbury Park, CA: Sage.

Suchman, L. (2000, February 28). Working relations of technology production and use. Paper presented at the Heterarchies Seminar, Columbia University, NY.

Sumpter, R. (2000). Daily newspaper editors' audience construction routines: A case study. *Critical Studies in Media Communication, 17,* 334–346.

Sunstein, C. (2001). *Republic.com.* Princeton, NJ: Princeton University Press.

Sunstein, C. (2006). *Infotopia: How many minds produce knowledge.* New York: Oxford University Press.

Sutton, B. (2007). *Poner el cuerpo:* Women's embodiment and political resistance in Argentina. *Latin American Politics and Society, 49,* 129–162.

Svampa, M. (2005). *La sociedad excluyente: La Argentina bajo el signo del neoliberalismo.* Buenos Aires, Argentina: Taurus.

Tarde, G. (1903 [1890]). *The laws of imitation* (E. C. Parsons, Trans.). New York: Henry Holt.

Taussig, M. (1993). *Mimesis and alterity: A particular history of the senses.* New York: Routledge.

Tewksbury, D., Hals, M., & Bibart, A. (2008). The efficacy of news browsing: The relationship of news consumption style to social and political efficacy. *Journalism and Mass Communication Quarterly, 85,* 257–272.

Thomas, W., & Thomas, D. (1970 [1917]). Situations defined as real are real in their consequences. In G. Stone & H. Farberman (Eds.), *Social psychology through symbolic interaction* (pp. 54–155). Waltham, MA: Xerox Publishers.

Thorson, E. (2007). Changing patterns of news consumption and participation: News recommendation engines. *Information, Communication, and Society, 4,* 473–489.

Thurman, N. (2008). Forums for citizen journalists? Adoption of user generated content initiatives by online news media. *New Media and Society, 10*(1), 139–157.

Tolbert, C. J., & McNeal, R. S. (2003). Unraveling the effects of the Internet on political participation? *Political Research Quarterly, 56*(2), 175–185.

Trammell, K. D., Tarkowski, A., & Sapp, A. M. (2006). Rzeczpospolita blogow [republic of blog]: Examining Polish bloggers through content analysis. *Journal of Computer-Mediated Communication, 11*(3). Retrieved June 9, 2008, from http://jcmc.indiana.edu/v0111/issue3/trammell.html.

Trueman, B. (1994). Analyst forecasts and herding behavior. *Review of Financial Studies, 7,* 97–124.

Tuchman, G. (1978). *Making news.* New York: Free Press.

Turow, J. (1983). Local television: Producing soft news. *Journal of Communication, 33,* 111–123.

Turow, J. (1997). *Breaking up America: Advertisers and the new media world.* Chicago: University of Chicago Press.

Turow, J. (2005). Audience construction and culture production: Marketing surveillance in the digital age. *Annals of the American Academy of Political and Social Science, 597,* 103–121.

Turow, J. (2006). *Niche envy: Marketing discrimination in the digital age.* Cambridge, MA: MIT Press.

Ulanovsky, C. (2005a). *Paren las rotativas: Diarios, revistas y periodistas (1920–1969).* Buenos Aires, Argentina: Emece.

Ulanovsky, C. (2005b). *Paren las rotativas: Diarios, revistas y periodistas, 1970–2000* (2nd ed.). Buenos Aires, Argentina: Emece.

Ulanovsky, C., Merkin, M., Panno, J. J., & Tijman, G. (2005a). *Días de radio, 1920–1959* (2nd ed.). Buenos Aires, Argentina: Emece.

Ulanovsky, C., Merkin, M., Panno, J. J., & Tijman, G. (2005b). *Días de radio, 1960–1995* (2nd ed.). Buenos Aires, Argentina: Emece.

Underwood, D. (1993). *When MBAs rule the newsroom: How marketers and managers are reshaping today's media.* New York: Columbia University Press.

Velthuis, O. (2006). Inside a world of spin: Four days at the World Trade Organization. *Ethnography, 7,* 125–150.

Voakes, P. S., Kapfer, J., Kurpious, D., & Shano-Yeon, D. C. (1995). Diversity in the news: A conceptual and methodological framework. *Journalism and Mass Communication Quarterly, 73,* 582–593.

Waisbord, S. (2000). *Watchdog journalism in South America: News, accountability, and democracy.* New York: Columbia University Press.

Waisbord, S. (2006). Reading scandals: Scandals, media, and citizenship in contemporary Argentina. In E. Peruzzotti & C. Smulovitz (Eds.), *Enforcing the rule of law: Social accountability in the new Latin American democracies* (pp. 272–303). Pittsburgh, PA: University of Pittsburgh Press.

Webster, J. (1998). The audience. *Journal of Broadcasting and Electronic Media, 42,* 190–207.

Webster, J., & Phalen, P. (1997). *The mass audience: Rediscovering the dominant model.* Mahwah, NJ: Lawrence Erlbaum.

Weimann, G., & Fishman, G. (1995). Reconstructing suicide: Reporting suicide in the Israeli press. *Journalism and Mass Communication Quarterly, 72,* 551–558.

Welch, I. (1992). Sequential sales, learning, and cascades. *Journal of Finance, 47,* 695–732.

Wellman, B., Quan-Haase, A., Boase, J., Chen, W., Hampton, K., Isla de Diaz, I., et al. (2003). The social affordances of the Internet for networked individualism. *Journal of Computer-Mediated Communication, 8*(3). http://www3 .interscience.wiley.com/cgi-bin/fulltext/120837880/HTMLSTART.

Wermers, R. (1999). Mutual fund herding and the impact on stock prices. *Journal of Finance, 54,* 581–622.

Westney, D. E. (1987). *Imitation and innovation: The transfer of Western organizational patterns to Meiji Japan.* Cambridge, MA: Harvard University Press.

White, H. (1981). Where do markets come from? *American Journal of Sociology, 87,* 514–547.

White, P. (1997). Death, disruption and the moral order: The narrative impulse in mass-media "hard news" reporting. In F. Christie & J. Martin (Eds.), *Genres and institutions: Social processes in the workplace and school* (pp. 101–133). London: Cassell.

Whitson, R. (2007). Hidden struggles: Spaces of power and resistance in informal work in urban Argentina. *Environment and Planning A, 39,* 2916–2934.

Williams, B. A., & Delli Carpini, M. X. (2000). Unchained reaction: The collapse of media gatekeeping and the Clinton-Lewinsky scandal. *Journalism, 1*(1), 61–85.

Williams, R., & Edge, D. (1996). The social shaping of technology. *Research Policy, 25,* 865–899.

Winner, L. (1986). Mythinformation. In L. Winner (Ed.), *The whale and the reactor: A search for limits in an age of high technology* (pp. 98–117). Chicago: University of Chicago Press.

Woolgar, S. (1991). Configuring the user: The case of usability trials. In J. Law (Ed.), *A sociology of monsters* (pp. 57–99). London: Routledge.

World Bank. (2008). *Data and research.* Retrieved November 28, 2008,from //web.worldbank.org/WBSITE/EXTERNAL/DATASTATISTICS/0,,contentMDK:205 35285~menuPK:1192694~pagePK:64133150~piPK:64133175~theSitePK: 239419,00.html.

Wyatt, R., Katz, E., & Kim, J. (2000). Bridging the spheres: Political and personal conversation in public and private places. *Journal of Communication, 50,* 71–92.

Wyatt, S. (2007). Technological determinism is dead; long live technological determinism. In E. Hackett, O. Amsterdamska, M. Lynch, & J. Wajcman (Eds.), *The handbook of science and technology studies* (3rd ed., pp. 165–180). Cambridge, MA: MIT Press.

Yates, J. (1989). *Control through communication: The rise of system in American management.* Baltimore, MD: Johns Hopkins University Press.

Yates, J. (2005). *Structuring the information age: Life insurance and technology in the twentieth century.* Baltimore, MD: Johns Hopkins University Press.

Ye, X., & Li, X. (2006). Internet newspapers' public forum and user involvement. In X. Li (Ed.), *Internet newspapers: The making of a mainstream medium* (pp. 243–259). Mahwah, NJ: Lawrence Erlbaum.

Young, D., & Tisinger, R. (2006). Dispelling late-night myths: News consumption among late-night comedy viewers and the predictors of exposure to various late-night shows. *Harvard International Journal of Press/Politics, 11,* 113–134.

Zaller, J. (2003). A new standard of news quality: Burglar alarms for the monitorial citizen. *Political Communication, 20,* 109–130.

Zelizer, B. (1993). Journalists as interpretive communities. *Critical Studies in Mass Communication, 10,* 219–237.

Zelizer, B. (2004). *Taking journalism seriously.* Thousand Oaks, CA: Sage.

Zelizer, V. (2005a). Culture and consumption. In N. Smelser & R. Swedberg (Eds.), *The handbook of economic sociology* (2nd ed., pp. 331–354). Princeton, NJ: Princeton University Press.

Zelizer, V. (2005b). *The purchase of intimacy*. Princeton, NJ: Princeton University Press.

Zelizer, V. (2009). Intimacy in economic organizations. *Research in the Sociology of Work, 19*, 23–55.

Zhou, Y. Q., & Moy, P. (2007). Parsing framing processes: The interplay between online public opinion and media coverage. *Journal of Communication, 57*(1), 79–98.

Zuboff, S. (1988). *In the age of the smart machine: The future of work and power*. New York: Basic Books.

Zuckerman, E., & Sgourev, S. (2006). Peer capitalism: Parallel relationships in the U.S. economy. *American Journal of Sociology, 111*, 1327–1366.

Zukernik, E. (2005). *Hechos y noticias: Claroscuros de la prensa gráfica en la Argentina*. Buenos Aires, Argentina: La Crujía.

Zukin, S., & Smith Maguire, J. (2004). Consumers and consumption. *Annual Review of Sociology, 30*, 173–197.

Zuleta-Puciero, E. (1993). The Argentine case: Television in the 1989 presidential campaign. In T. Skidmore (Ed.), *Television, politics, and the transition to democracy in Latin America* (pp. 55–81). Baltimore, MD: Johns Hopkins University Press.

Zwiebel, J. (1995). Corporate conservatism and relative compensation. *Journal of Political Economy, 103*, 1–25.

Index